ACKNOWLEDGEMENTS

I AM glad to have this opportunity to express my gratitude to the following scholars: to the late A. W. Gomme for his kind encouragement and unfailing advice; to my colleagues K. J. Hancock and E. A. Russell who helped me to comprehend some of the problems associated with peasant farming in economically underdeveloped countries; and above all to historians E. Badian, G. T. Griffith, A. H. M. Jones, and A. H. McDonald, who were kind enough to read the typescript at various stages of composition. I have learned much from their illuminating comments, and their wisdom has saved me from many errors. For the deficiencies which will still be found in this work the responsibility, of course, rests on me alone.

A. F.

THE GROWTH OF THE
ATHENIAN ECONOMY

THE GROWTH OF THE
ATHENIAN ECONOMY

by

A. FRENCH

GREENWOOD PRESS, PUBLISHERS
WESTPORT, CONNECTICUT

Library of Congress Cataloging in Publication Data

French, Alfred.
  The growth of the Athenian economy.

    Reprint of the ed. published by Routledge &
Paul, London.
    Bibliography: p.
    Includes index.
    1. Athens--Economic conditions. I. Title.
HC37.F7 1975   330.9'385   75-31363
ISBN 0-8371-8506-8

Originally published in 1964 by Routledge & Kegan Paul,
London

Reprinted with the permission of Routledge & Kegan Paul Ltd.

Reprinted in 1975 by Greenwood Press,
a division of Williamhouse-Regency Inc.

Library of Congress Catalog Card Number 75-31363

ISBN 0-8371-8506-8

Printed in the United States of America

CONTENTS

INTRODUCTION

BETWEEN the early sixth and the late fifth century a transformation took place in the fortunes of Athens. Unimportant in the affairs of Greece at the beginning of the sixth century she drew her livelihood from a peasant economy which had become depressed and chaotic. A century later she was leading the Greek confederate states against the forces of Persia itself. By the middle of the fifth century she was the richest, the most powerful, and the most feared state in Europe: visible signs of her wealth and power were the structures, then beginning to rise, which were to make her the wonder of her own age and of millennia to come.

It is the aim of this study briefly to document, and if possible to explain this transformation, as far as the surviving data permit. The wealth of Athens in the Periclean period is often attributed to her leadership of the Confederacy of Delos: this assumption can be validated only by showing precisely how the leadership made Athens richer, bearing in mind the fact that the tribute did not begin to be fed directly into the Athenian economy before 450 B.C. Moreover, the transformation of Athens from an economically backward to a comparatively developed state can obviously not be explained merely by her exploitation of the allies, for at the inception of the League she was already a powerful maritime nation, nor would she otherwise have been able to assume its leadership in 477 B.C. The power and wealth of fifth-century Athens were made possible only by that measure of economic development which she was able to achieve in the preceding century.

This study falls naturally into three main parts. First, it is necessary to trace the growth of the Athenian economy from the time of Solon to the period of the Persian wars. For the development of Attica during this time much of the credit must be attributed to the Tyrants, for it was they who not only made effective the administrative unification of the country, thereby creating conditions favourable for economic progress, but also actively pushed her in that direction by their commercial enterprise. Perhaps the success of their ventures across the sea was due in no small measure to the changing conditions in the north-east Aegean in consequence of the collapse of the Lydian, and the advance of Persian power. But the assertion of Phoenician naval supremacy in this area, and the revolution at Athens, brought this period of commercial expansion temporarily to an end. Yet the problem of feeding an urban population swollen by the expansion which had occurred drove the Athenians into adventurous policies by land and sea: an ultimate result was the naval rearmament programme financed by the silver strike at Laureion.

Secondly, in describing how Athenian wealth increased during the imperial period, it will be necessary to determine how far the increase was due merely to predatory action on her part, and how far it can be attributed to genuine economic growth: that is, whether Athens became richer only by making others poorer, or whether she increased the pool of goods and services of the whole area by improved use of its human and material resources. The conclusion which will be offered is that, while there was a shift in distribution to the advantage of Athens and the disadvantage of the subject states, the Athenian economy itself went through a period of rapid economic growth in at least two directions. In the first place the organisation of the carrying trade of the Aegean by the Athenians turned their city into an entrepot from which radiated a network of distribution to states even outside the League: this network of trade utilised the skills and resources of the Attic population and made profitable the exploitation of her mineral resources: at the same time it also served and simplified the supply problems of other members of the trading area. In the second place, the collection of a great urban population in Athens, and the securing of a large share in the Aegean trade, caused a steep demand for the products of the Attic countryside. This growth of demand released the farmers from the tyranny of subsistence farming and enabled them to grow the crops for which their land was best suited; in other words, the growth of a market economy made possible an increased degree of specialised production on the land.

Lastly, it is necessary to ask what were the effects of economic development on Attica. The most spectacular visible effect was certainly the growth of a great cosmopolitan city which was quickly to become the cultural centre of Greece and of Europe. But within this city the material living standards of the average dweller, as far as it is possible to estimate them, seem to have risen very little; and this disparity between the rate of economic growth and that of material betterment it is natural to connect with the increase of population, which absorbed, and at times outstripped, the increase in real wealth. An attempt will be made to show that this growth in population was not due to natural increase but rather to immigration, and that since the immigrants were debarred from attaining citizen status, the rise in total population was accompanied by a fall in the proportion of citizens. This trend was the result of deliberate choice by the citizens themselves, on the grounds that as their privileges in the community mounted, so it was in their interest to limit the circle of the privileged.

Thus the economic development of Athens, which was accelerated by her imperial position, resulted in changes in the pattern of her cultural, social, and political life; and among the more interesting results was the growth of a new class system in which a minority of the community, now organised as a citizen democracy, took the place, and to some extent inherited the privileges, of the old oligarchy of nobles.

The scope of this study is from the late seventh century to the beginning of the Peloponnesian war: it is then that the period of rapid economic development can be said to have come to an end; and the adjustment of the Athenian economy to the long war is a separate topic, beyond the scope of this book. But from one point of view the break at 431 can be regarded as artificial, if only because some of the data for conditions in the fifth century are found in references in later literature, especially in the work of the fourth-century orators. The various changes brought about by economic development took some time, as we might expect, to find expression in the literary record. Yet although we may accept the truth of this, we cannot but acknowledge the dangers involved in using such evidence as a guide to earlier conditions, for rarely can we be sure for what period of preceding time the evidence is valid. In fact the student of ancient history is forced to work with a body of evidence which would be considered by students of modern economic history as meagre, unreliable, and deficient in helpful statistics. For this reason classicists often prefer to reserve judgement on economic matters. Unfortunately, those who wish to write about the ancient world are forced to make judgements of an economic character about it, since economic problems continually impinge upon the political, social, and cultural questions with which they wish to deal. At such times agnosticism is perforce abandoned, and writers on Greek history or literature sometimes offer economic judgements whose full implications have rarely been considered, and which could be scarcely substantiated in any plausible economic model. In presenting the present work the writer is aware of the limitations both of its scope and method. Its merit, if any, must be found in the attempt to provide a consequential account of a process of development which is of exceptional historical interest, and whose main lines are clear, even though many of its details remain obscure.

I

THE NATURAL BACKGROUND

THE lands which fringe the Mediterranean sea share a climate so individual as to be considered a type, and from it has been coined a term applied to similar climatic conditions wherever they occur in the world. The Mediterranean climate is characterised by the concentration of an adequate annual rainfall into the autumn, winter, and spring; and by the limited range of the temperatures produced. These conditions occur within the temperature zones around a certain latitude (35°–40°) in lands which receive rain-laden westerly winds in winter, and north-east winds in summer. Whereas elsewhere (*e.g.* in California or South Australia) these conditions are fulfilled only over a comparatively small area of land facing a western sea, they extend over a very large area around the inland sea of the Mediterranean. The development of early civilisations in this area has sometimes been attributed to the existence of this wide belt of temperate and homogeneous climate: it was not suited to large-scale cereal production, consequently it could not be expected to carry an enormous population; it did however allow an adequate production of food to small communities, and when population outran supply, it encouraged the free movement of migrants to more distant areas offering similar geographical conditions, combined with the stimulus of social change.

Greece is in many ways the most typical of the Mediterranean lands. Here, amid dried-up water-courses, the summer drought withers the pastures, severely limiting the cattle population and, in consequence, the output of dairy products: their place in man's diet[1] is taken by oil from the olives, whose roots run deeply into the subsoil and between the rocks. As familiar a sight as the olive trees are the vines, which in late summer funnel to man the sweetened moisture of the subsoil; for it is deep in the earth that they find the water to swell their fruit. Where rain is heavier on the upper slopes, the pine, the oak, and sometimes the chestnut and the beech are to be found: but, generally speaking, great stands of trees are scarce, for rarely is there sufficient water available to feed their spreading roots, and the hot breezes of summer draw heavily on moisture from their leaves. On the lower slopes a familiar covering is the scrubby undergrowth, the maquis, tangled with creeper, and gay with flowers in spring. Seeds and roots form the staple diet of man, but flowers and fruits are the typical products of the Mediterranean earth.

Since Greece can from its own resources feed only a limited population, for long periods in its history it has been an area from which people have migrated, and into which food has been transported, almost invariably by sea. For if Greece is poorly endowed with material resources, the geographical situation which she occupies in the eastern Mediterranean marks her out as a natural centre of trade and communications. Her ports are calling-places for ships sailing from Egypt to the Black Sea, and from Italy to Asia Minor: in early times the difficulties of land transport across the Balkans ensured that the Mediterranean should carry all but a fraction of what commerce passed between Europe and Asia. But the Aegean sea provided more than a convenient highway: the dotted headlands which rise from its waters gave landmarks by which to steer, the winds which in summer blow steadily from the north-east provided the motive power for the ships, and the innumerable bays and inlets of the archipelago gave the terminals and resting-places which sea-going transport demands. Thus the ports and coastal areas of Greece were marked out to become a meeting-place for three continents, and a bridge across which their products could be exchanged.

The geographical pattern of Greece is not so homogeneous as to exclude a wide range of local variations. Although it includes some impressive rolling country, much of its land surface is covered by mountains thrown up by the natural convulsions to which the area is subject. The moist winds of winter, sweeping in from the west, strike upon the ranges and drop much of their rain upon the western areas of the country, less on the eastern: then, passing over the Aegean, they replenish their supply of moisture, and heavily water the western coastal plains of Asia Minor. Higher rainfall usually means greater fertility: we might therefore expect to find in history examples of the Greeks who lived on the eastern side of the mainland crossing the ranges westwards, or the sea eastwards, as migrants or as would-be conquerors. Among the most fertile areas of Greece is the great plain of Messenia in the south-west of the Peloponnese. This is one of the few areas capable of feeding a larger population than that which actually worked it, and for much of the classical period its resources were tapped by foreign masters whose homes lay east of the ranges in Laconia. One other area of great food potential deserves mention: this is the large plain of Thessaly in the north-easterly part of the mainland. Boxed in on all sides by mountains, and heavily watered by their streams, the land was a heat-trap in summer, and in winter suffered extremes of cold unusual in these latitudes. These two great plains were potentially the richest areas in Greece in terms of food production, and it is interesting to note that they produced none of those city communities which were to play a dominant role in Greek history. Messenia suffered the perils of its wealth and open position: Thessaly was safe in its mountain fastness, yet its very safety ensured that for long it was to remain, by the standards of Athens or Corinth, a backward area.

The rolling plain is an unusual sight in Greece: more familiar is the magnificent but stark scenery formed by craggy mountain ranges, amid which the eye can follow the naked contours of rock from peak to stony valley. Out to sea the peaks rise sheer out of the water, forming little islands which tower above the drowned valleys below. But inland too there are buried valleys where the seeming wilderness suddenly reveals oases of plenty. For at times the downward curve of the rock is horizontally intersected by strips of level plainland; here the detritus of centuries, drawn from near or distant slopes, has concealed the lower contours, filling the valleys with many feet of earth and forming deep-soiled plains. The winter rains which fall on the surrounding high ground make their way through streams and springs to water these precious acres, which for long have

3

supplied the livelihood of the dwellers around them. Such are the plains of Argos, Corinth, Mycenae, and Athens. In the level land between the slopes lay the concentrated wealth of the surrounding countryside. From the grain crops which the plain produced, were fed not only the farmers who tended them, but also a scattered population of goatherds and shepherds living on the neighbouring hills: such communities comprised an inner and an outer zone of production complementary to each other. In the case of all these settlements a peak, dominating the plain and within sight of the sea, formed a centre of defence and of social contact. It was here, not in the rolling plains, that were to be found the centres of early Greek civilisation.

Attica lies across the peninsula of central Greece, naturally divided from her northern neighbour Boeotia by the ranges of Cithaeron and Parnes; these provided protection not only against the winter gales but also against the invasion of man. Amid the competitive atmosphere of early Greece it was important that a state's frontiers should be naturally defensible; and although this condition was fulfilled on Attica's northern side, her western side, where the plain runs into Megarian territory, was the route of many invasions. A natural prize for contention between Athens and Megara was the rocky island of Salamis, which ran within tantalising distance of both their shores. Unfortunately for Attica its long coastline was almost indefensible against a sea-power, and the coastal plains were a ready target. It was the danger of raids from the sea which drove the people of central Attica to build their settlement around the Acropolis of Athens, a sheer rock overlooking the plain and within five miles of the sea at its nearest point.

But though Attica's location held disadvantages from the point of view of defence, it had many advantages from the point of view of sea-borne inter-state commerce. Not only was the coastline extensive and well endowed with natural harbours, but it faced in two directions. On the eastern side it was sheltered by, and within easy reach of Euboea; on the western side its proximity to the Corinthian isthmus allowed it to share in the trade which passed that way between the cities of Asia Minor and those of Italy and Sicily. As a potential trading community Athens was handicapped by a shortage of timber for shipbuilding; on the other hand she was rich in some of the minerals which figured largely in early trade. In south-east Attica were to be found good deposits of silver, lead, and zinc, the last-named being unused in classical times. Lead was of great value as an alloy in the manufacture of bronze, but it was primarily for her silver that Athens was to become famous. The clay deposits around the bed of the river Cephesus provided the material for a brilliant ceramic industry whose products figured in Aegean trade from the ninth century B.C.

Although Athens played some part in the early trade of the Aegean, it was not until the sixth century that she began seriously to exploit the commercial advantages of her geographical position. Until that time at least, her economy centred on food production: this meant that apart from the minor, though important role played by fishing, overwhelmingly her greatest economic concern was farming, and it was with the operation of this industry that many of her social, as well as economic problems were to be concerned. In considering her agricultural potential we may take account both of the climate which she enjoyed, and the extent and quality of the land surface of which she disposed.

Extremes of temperature all the year round were reduced in Attica by the proximity of the sea; and the shielding of the countryside from the cold gales of winter meant that the temperature rarely fell below freezing point. The mildness of the climate was of great value to Athens in allowing the olive tree to flourish, for without its oil the deficiency of fats would have kept the human population down to a fraction of the size it reached. Apart from the olive, the vine and the fig throve on the plains or the lower slopes. But the sheltered position of Attica also meant that she received less than her fair share of rain. The average annual precipitation in modern times is about sixteen inches; but this figure covers a range of variations from year to year, and the general unreliability of the rainfall pattern can increase the problems of farming. In classical times the plains of Attica were not well watered by mountain streams: the only river of any consequence was the Cephesus, running through the central plain and issuing on the south-west coast near Phaleron: other streams flowed from Parnes to Marathon and to Eleusis. The towns of Athens, Marathon, and Eleusis owed no small part of their importance to the presence of flowing water nearby, and the river banks were the richest potential source of fodder. But the quantity of water was insufficient for large-scale irrigation, and Athens was forced to base her agriculture throughout the classical period on dry farming methods. None of the rivers was navigable, and this, allied to the difficulty of land transport, meant that the natural lines of communication lay not inland but round the coast. The distribution of water was a factor rigidly restricting the collection of population in community settlements, and a town could arise only where, as at Athens, springs were fairly numerous and flowed strongly all the year.

The land of Attica is divided by the hills of Pentelicus and Hymettus, which separate the central plain from the eastern farmland and from the rough country of the south-east, where the metallic deposits are found. To the north-west the arable land extended over the so-called Thriasian plain, with its capital city of Eleusis; east of the central plain, and between Mount Hymettus and the east coast, lay the plain of the Mesogeia: north of this, beyond Mount Pentelicus, was the small alluvial plain of Marathon. The total area of arable land covered by these plains was in classical times in the vicinity of 85,000 acres, more than a third of which lay in the central plain on which stood the city of Athens. In addition to the major plains there were smaller stretches of arable ground scattered over the rough land and the lower slopes.

The growing season in Attica was from the commencement of the autumn rains in October to the setting in of the dry summer: ploughing had to wait for the rains to soften the ground; the seed could be sown as soon as the soil had been properly broken, and before it became too cold for the seed to commence its period of growth. This meant furious activity from the onset of the rains until the seed was in, and follow-up rains had allowed it to germinate. If wheat was sown, a false start to the season and a cessation of rain for a few days might possibly ruin the crop. Harvest was during May or June, and there was little danger of summer rain which would have spoiled the standing grain. With the full blast of summer heat and the virtual end of the rains, pasture began to wither in the plains, and arable land stood idle. There were thus in effect two dormant periods, a short mid-winter pause during January and February, when

6

winter grain was already rooted, and the summer pause from about July to September, when the lower land was bared of annuals, except for the pockets where irrigation was practicable. The extent of the dormant periods meant that for almost half the year there was little to do on the farms, and the under-employment of the human population was to have serious social consequences. Because of the harsh summer conditions only deep-rooted trees and shrubs could survive on the plains: on the slopes, where topsoil was scarce, the best suited to survive were those whose narrow leaves reduced evaporation and whose roots were able to penetrate the ground deeply in search of moisture and food: here the wild olive held its place among the maquis. The extent of the rainfall on the hills was not sufficient to promote a large crop of timber, and Athens suffered from a chronic shortage of wood for building and fuel. This shortage was aggravated by the bushfires which could sweep through the scrub in the dry summer without a check; destruction was not confined to the standing timber, for not only was the soil structure damaged, but the burning of protective vegetation could cause the thin topsoil to slide away to the valley below, uncovering the rock.

The withering of the grass on the plains in summer meant that animals were driven to the hills to graze on the scrub and the young shoots. This had a double effect: it stunted the vegetation of the hills and prevented its rehabilitation, thus contributing to the shortage of wood: secondly, it robbed the plains of the manure that they so badly needed for the grain crops to be sown in the coming autumn. During the winter the animals grazed on the fallow or were stall-fed on the fodder grown on river loam. Amid such stringent conditions the number of animals on the farm had to be kept to a minimum. Horses were a luxury out of the reach of any but the landed gentry with plain land to waste. Oxen were kept for draught purposes and young cattle were slaughtered only on festive occasions, which served to keep the cattle population down to the carrying capacity of the farm, and also to enrich the diet with some meat: the latter end was also served by the keeping of poultry and some pigs, which could be fed from waste.

The basis of the subsistence farm is the arable land on which breadcrops are produced. Unless there is suitable land lying to waste, this capital cannot be extended as population increases; unfortunately its extent can easily be diminished by natural catastrophe or unskilful husbandry. If population rises to a level above the carrying capacity of the ploughland, either the excess mouths must be fed by the importing of corn grown on foreign topsoil; or else the excess population must move to where extra food is available: if neither of these alternatives is practicable, a situation of acute social tension is likely to arise, in which men will resort to violent ends to avoid starvation falling on themselves or their families. In the case of Attica the extent of the ploughland was not inconsiderable by Greek standards, and promised a reasonable degree of social stability provided that population did not expand too rapidly, and the produce was fairly evenly distributed through the population. Wheat was, as might be expected, the grain most in demand for breadmaking: unfortunately wheat is somewhat exacting not only in the quality of the soil but also in its demands for an even supply of moisture during the germination period, so that it can be ruined by a few days' dry spell after sowing. Barley seed is much hardier, and was accordingly better suited to the climatic conditions of central Greece; barley continued to be the staple grain product of Attica, but it is not suitable for breadmaking, hence porridge and mash had to play a large part in Athenian diet.

We can assume that most of Attica's good arable land was used for food production, and since flax competes with grain for such land, it perforce occupied only a minor place in the scheme of Attic production: linen was a luxury item throughout, and Thucydides mentions it, together with gold ornaments, as a sign of gracious living among Athenian upper classes of the older generation. The fibres available for standard textiles were wool and goats' hair (mohair), which formed part of the subsistence farmer's production, together with the skins and hides of the grazing animals.

If Athens is compared to other Greek states in terms of natural resources, clearly she had no special advantages in the quality of her soil or the extent of her rainfall. But her seaboard was by Greek standards unusually long, her farming area unusually extensive, and this area contained the necessary complementary zones of production; plainland for grains, hills for grazing, and coastal areas for fishing. Her mineral riches were considerable, and included beautiful stone for construction; her silver deposits were certainly a tremendous asset, and augured well for her future development. Unfortunately mining is an industry which, to be efficient, requires considerable capital outlay: furthermore, the organisation of a suitable labour force presents especial difficulties; the deposits are usually located in desolate, agriculturally poor, hence sparsely populated country, and the conditions of work are not so pleasant as readily to attract to it an adequate supply of voluntary labour; above all, the successful exploitation of the deposits depends on the development of trade to market the end product.

From the point of view of maritime commerce Athens' geographical situation was promising, though by no means as favourable as that of sites such as Corinth or Byzantium. The archaeological record shows that there was some early fulfilment of this promise. Athenian vases of the so-called Geometric type, dating to a period as early as the ninth century B.C., have been found in quantity distributed over a restricted area from Boeotia to Aegina, and in smaller quantities further afield in the Cyclades, Thessaly, and Crete: Corinthian ware of the same period has been found at Athens.[2] But it would be unwise to assume on the basis of this evidence that trade played an important part in the Athenian economy at so early a time. At the beginning of the sixth century, when Athens first appears in the dim light of recorded history, it is above all as a land of farmers; and her economy, together with her social structure, is plunged in the midst of an agrarian crisis, the causes of which are wrapped in provoking obscurity.

II

THE BREAKDOWN OF THE
OLD ORDER

THE pattern of rural organisation in early Attica is a matter of conjecture, but later developments indicate that the arable land was divided among the citizens, not necessarily on a basis of equality, and the grazing land on the hillsides was common. It is possible that private ownership of the land was at some stage confined to an inner group within the citizen body, and that citizens of a lower social status (possibly due to their ancestors' late arrival on the scene) had a stake in the land only as members of a commune or clan. To the farming population the land was the home of the family, the resting-place of their ancestors and the livelihood of present and future generations: land was therefore not traditionally regarded as an article of merchandise, like trinkets or slaves, and it is very unlikely that it was subject to sale: at least as late as the sixth century B.C. there was a taboo upon its alienation from the family or clan.[1] Apart from the larger estates which were able to produce a surplus for exchange, the form of production was subsistence farming; each farm being more or less self-sufficient in grain and oil, and obtaining its milk, hides, and wool from such animals as the farm could support on the fallow during the winter, and which could be pastured on the hills for the rest of the year.

If Attica had been permanently isolated from the world, and her population had remained below the danger line of pressure on the carrying capacity of the land, reasonable stability could theoretically have been expected to continue indefinitely under the conditions outlined above; in that case both the need and the incentive to further economic progress would have been absent. In fact, when the sixth century opens, the majority of the Athenian citizens had apparently lost their land; many had lost their freedom, were subject to seizure by the rich, and were being sold abroad as chattels: poverty and the threat of civil war lay across the land.

This crisis was probably the result of a combination of factors,[2] prominent among which was the population pressure, or land hunger, common to early Greek states. It is to this cause that the great wave of Greek colonisation of the eighth and seventh centuries is attributed; and while Athens apparently played no significant part in the colonisation programme, it is difficult to believe that she was not subject to the same pressures. Even in a country with Greece's difficult communications, gross inequalities of population density would eventually tend to be ironed out either by voluntary emigration or by transportation, that is, by the transfer of slaves. Rather than assuming that Athens was, for some reason, exempt from population pressures common to other Greek states, we may believe that her population problem became acute at a later stage than elsewhere.

One answer to the problem of population pressing on resources is to intensify local production; and since a given area of land will yield a greater quantity of food by cultivation than by using it for grazing, there is a natural tendency in such circumstances to plough up land used previously for pasture: grazing animals compete with man for the grain available, and at a time of food shortage one may expect to find a reduction of livestock, especially cattle, and the survival on a large scale only of animals, such as goats, whose diet differs from that of man. A shift from a mainly pastoral to a mainly agricultural system of production would reveal itself in a change of diet from one based on meat to one based on cereals, and there is some evidence which would lead us to suspect such a change.[3]

The attempt to increase food production by bringing under the plough land of poor or marginal quality carries with it the danger of eventual soil exhaustion, since corn crops are suitable only for good-quality land. It is possible that a progressive deterioration of the Attic soil due to overcropping was a basic cause of her economic difficulties; but in addition she faced a constant danger of soil erosion due to bushfires, and to excessive inroads upon the timber resources of her hills, as well as to the depredations of grazing goats. The deforestation of the Attic hills, noted by Plato,[4] removed much of the protective cover which had helped to make them a catchment for rains: as a result water which had previously sunk into the ground, thence eventually to issue forth as springs, became torrents gullying away the surface of the hillsides and causing a succession of floods and droughts in the valleys below.

Soil erosion almost certainly was a factor constantly threatening the stability of Attica's rural economy; but the very permanence of the threat prevents us ascribing to it the immediate causes of the sixth-century crisis, since we have no reason to believe that the fertility of the Attic soil deteriorated suddenly at this point. The threat of a decline in total food production, and the pressure of increasing population, were long-term factors lying behind the immediate causes of the economic crisis: its outward manifestation was the state of rural indebtedness, the fact that 'the whole people was in debt to the rich', and that 'the poor, their wives and children, were actually enslaved to the rich and were called Dependants and Hectemors': the latter 'tilled the lands [of the rich] handing over one-sixth of the produce'; while debtors who could not meet their obligations were being sold abroad as slaves. The impression given is that of free peasant landholders being transformed into serfs, then losing the benefit even of these conditions, i.e. the protection of feudal patronage, and becoming an article of merchandise. It is clear from the accounts in both our secondary authorities that the chief grievance felt by the masses was the threat of their enslavement.

It is not difficult to imagine how the peasants had come to fall into debt, for peasant farming and indebtedness often go hand in hand: for many an Attic farmer the day had arrived when he found that his store of food was inadequate to maintain his household until the next harvest. When the last of his store was used, he must then have approached the rich man with the request that the latter advance to him sufficient food to last until the next crop was harvested, in consideration of a future delivery by the peasant. The transaction thus amounted to the peasant selling his cash crop before harvest. It is likely that the advance was secured by a bond on the peasant's person, as an additional security; but the advance was, in other regards, safe, since the delivery of that part of the crop which had already been paid for, would be the first call on the peasant's harvest. Come what may, the peasant would have to pay up at harvest, and his bond would be thus liquidated each year.

The advance would be made on the assumption that things would improve next year, whereas, in a succession of bad harvests, they would actually be worse. In a few years the small farmer would discover that not only was all his surplus sold before harvested, but an increasing amount of the grain needed for his own sustenance was sold as well; the deterioration of his position would be accelerated by the fact that the creditor, having the peasant entirely at his mercy, would be tempted to increase the severity of his terms, so that the situation would one day be reached when the peasant was a whole year behind with his deliveries, that is, when the whole of his harvest had theoretically to be paid to the creditor, leaving him nothing for his own support until next harvest.

When this state was reached, the land had effectively become the property of the creditor, since its whole produce was his, to dispose of as he pleased. The traditional taboo on the alienation of land from the family had thus become *de facto*, if not *de jure*, null and void. The peasant, having lost control of his land, had the alternative of getting out, and trying to eke out a precarious existence as a casual hand on someone else's estate, or staying where he was, on whatever terms the creditor chose to keep him. In the latter case the landlord's terms must needs be harsh, since he must support the peasant for a whole year in return for a harvest of problematical size: the peasant had in fact become a kind of servant, with all the limitations of freedom that are implied in the relationship between master and servant. It is reasonable to suppose that an arrangement was agreed upon whereby the servant should retain a fixed proportion of the produce, and should surrender the rest to his master. One-sixth is a credible figure for the proportion to be surrendered; thus the landlord received approximately 17% off his newly acquired property.

But the debtor could sink into a still worse position. If the productivity of the holding continued to deteriorate, a time would come when the proportion to be retained would not suffice to keep him and his family. In this situation he could only implore his master to forgo part, or all, of the sixth part to which he was entitled, and carry forward arrears to next year, in the hope that he could, by herculean labours, so increase the productivity of the holding as to pay more than one-sixth, and thus wipe out his arrears. From this point onwards the land-lord could at any time seize and sell the debtor for defaulting on a loan covered by personal security, or else he could let him fall deeper into his master's power with no real hope of ever redeeming either land or freedom.

This situation had been reached on many Attic farms per-haps long before the days of Solon. The peasant, sinking deeper into a morass of debts, was protected only by the theoretical possibility of freeing himself from debt, by the apathy, or respect for tradition, of the landlord, and by the deep-rooted prejudice against enslaving a fellow-citizen. By allowing the situation to slip on in this fashion the landlord was in fact not seeking his best financial advantage, in that he was maintaining a work-force of uneconomic proportions: but his reward was an extension of power. The reduction of free men to serfs by debt bondage in this way represents a primitive system of accumula-tion, not of money (for the land would probably be run at a bigger loss as part of the estate than it had been run as an inde-pendent farm), but of power and status. This was one of the most attractive commodities which the nobles could buy with their surplus before the increase in commercial activity in central Greece offered them a wider range of alternatives.

The deterioration of the peasants' position at the end of the seventh century was caused in the first instance by the drastic enforcement of a recently instituted code of law (the Draconic code), which gave official sanction to the practice of enslave-ment for debt in Attica. A reason for the enforcement of the code, and for its institution in the first place, may lie in the opening up of overseas trade to Attic ports on a much larger scale than hitherto; this in its turn may be attributed to the commercial development of Athens' neighbours, Megara, Corinth, and Aegina. As long as the nobles of the Attic plain had little to buy with their surplus, they were content to let things drift on the estate, using the distress of the smallholders to buttress their own feudal position with additional depen-dants. But as developing trade made available more goods, and the pursuit of material possessions became almost as important as old-fashioned prestige, so the incentive to leave the debt-slaves on the estate declined, and an increasing number of former yeomen found themselves seized for the slave market. To pay for the goods now reaching Athens outward cargoes were necessary, and these soon included not only food required in Attica but the Attic debt-slaves themselves.

It is worth noting that the export of surplus population was, in its own way, contributing to the useful functioning of the economy. Unemployment, when it occurs in an industrial society, is a blatant sign of sickness in the economy, and as such it compels at least recognition as a social problem, if not positive remedial action. But rural unemployment can lie concealed for generations, postponing and making more difficult any remedial action which may be possible. If the unit is a family, it has no simple way of deciding which of its members are redundant, nor would family loyalties allow such a decision. Unless there is an obvious economic alternative to farming, the rural population tends to stay put, disguising the extent of the redundancy by sharing out the returns, however meagre they may become. As a result a household may unwittingly run down its capital in various ways: in the Attic context this was done by borrowing on the security of future returns and by eating the equivalent of next year's crop. Concealed rural unemployment, which is the basic cause of these misfortunes, is a menace to peasant farming communities, and an important advantage conferred by industrialisation, even on a modest scale, is the possibility of drawing off unwanted rural labour into the towns. But the excess manpower of Attica had found few outlets either in local industry or migration. Remaining on the land in worsening conditions they had become accepted as a normal part of the landscape, so that they had acquired a legal status as Hectemors or as slaves. Nevertheless, when the economic incentive to remove some of this labour had asserted itself, the creditors had defied tradition by deporting unwanted members of the community by virtue of their legal status as debt-slaves. The motives of the landowners were entirely self-centred; but the logic which lay behind their actions was soundly based. If production could not be raised to match the requirements of the existing population, in some way or other consumption would have to be cut. The landowners, in whose hands power rested, were hardly likely to consider a cut in their own living standards, were in fact eager to improve them; but since the living standards of the lower orders were already at a minimum level, the obvious solution (from the landlords' point of view) was a cut in the number of consumers. It is not suggested that this was the conscious rationale of the creditors, but it was the logic behind their actions. In addition, the development of trade encouraged landowners to use more of their land for growing a cash crop of wine, and this was an incentive to reduce the number of workers, since vines require less labour than cereals.

Economic pressure thus devised a way to make the system work, in however inefficient and heartless a manner. But the enslavement and deportation of citizens, explicable as it might be in terms of economics, was an affront to traditional sentiment and violated the principle of the solidarity of the citizen group. Hence the growing clamour, based on non-economic grounds, to stop the enslavement and the deportations, irrespective of whether the practice had acted as a safety valve to the economy as a whole. This demand, and the more extreme demand for a reallocation of the land itself, were understandably resisted by the creditors; and a situation was reached which could become explosive if the victims of economic change found the will and organisation to offer active resistance. Even so, as long as the nobles could agree among themselves, and arms were kept out of the hands of the peasants, the economic misfortunes of a section of the community need not necessarily have disrupted social peace. But in 640 B.C. one of the petty dynasts of Attica had attempted to set himself up as master of the country. The *coup* was frustrated and the pretender's followers were destroyed only by calling out the armed peasantry. On subsequent, and perhaps repeated occasions, the latter were called upon to fight against the militia of nearby Megara. In consequence the danger increased that the weapons they had sharpened for use against external enemies, and once had used in an internal conflict, would eventually be employed in a civil war to redress their own economic grievances.[5] It was in response to this danger that, early in the sixth century, a mediator was appointed at Athens to resolve the impending crisis. Solon, to whom fell this difficult role, had already in his verses attacked the rapacity of the rich, to which class he himself belonged, and writing after his reforms he claimed that his proposals represented a genuine compromise between the conflicting rights and aims of his fellow citizens.

The main points of Solon's economic programme were: a complete cancellation of debts; a prohibition of loans on personal security; an official recognition that the rights and obligations of citizenship were related to rural income; regulations affecting the coinage, weights, and measures current in Attica; a ban on the export of all natural products except oil; and a series of laws apparently aimed at building up Athenian secondary industry by encouraging the immigration of skilled foreigners and the training of skilled artisans. These measures were accompanied by a series of enactments affecting the political and institutional arrangements.

The most controversial of Solon's economic reforms was that concerned with the cancellation of debts. Later writers no doubt felt a contradiction between the tradition of his wisdom and moderation, and this frontal assault on the rights of property. It would have been surprising if none had felt the temptation to re-edit this part of Solon's work, in view of the unpleasant ideas which might be evoked in the minds of later reformers: thus Plutarch mentions the view of the fourth-century writer Androtion, that Solon did not actually cancel debts but only reduced the rate of interest by a kind of devaluation of the currency; a view which is rejected by modern scholars.[6]

An immediate consequence of the debt cancellation was that the serfs and slaves who had been recruited from the ranks of Athenian citizens were freed: the status of Hectemor ceased to exist forthwith in Attica, and henceforth we find the land worked only by native freemen and foreign slaves. It is believed by many scholars, though it is not stated in the sources, that the rehabilitation of the fallen peasants included the return to them of the farms which they had lost through the operation of the laws of debt.[7] The remission of debts rescued the peasants from the position into which they had sunk; the prohibition of loans on personal security was intended to stop the same process recurring. Nevertheless, the overall effect of the measures was not likely to be an unmixed gain for the peasants. The availability of credit is an important, often an indispensable element in a peasant economy: but after Solon's time few landlords would be anxious to extend further loans even on the security of land. It is interesting to speculate about the fate of the subsistence farmer who, after Solon's legislation, found himself without sufficient food to last through to harvest. In spite of the severe jolt to credit, some landlords would still perhaps be prepared to advance food against future delivery, even though the advance could no longer be secured by a bond on the person. But the terms would be strict, and it is most unlikely that a debtor would be allowed to sink so deeply into debt that he was a whole year behind with delivery, so that there was no real chance of repayment. The restriction of credit, implied by the prohibitio n of personal security, meant that in the long run the subsistence farm had to make ends meet. A farmer who failed would either have to reduce the size of the household or, in the last resort, dispose of the farm. Once he had quitted farming, he would find it hard to get back. The prohibition would stop him borrowing at all if he had no other security to offer but his body; his only possible status on the land in future would be that of the hired labourer, to be dismissed when redundant. Thus one long-term result of the prohibition clause, though not one necessarily intended by Solon, was to clear unwanted labour off the land and to keep it off. The peasants were now safe from the danger of enslavement and deportation for debt; but they could still find themselves forced off the land if their labour was surplus. In that case they would still have to be supported from the resources of Attica, and the natural tendency was for them to drift to city or port in search of work. But the organisational change was to be significant for the social and political development of Athens. A large number of dissatisfied peasants, when scattered over a hundred estates, was likely to be a less serious danger to the *status quo* than the same number combining, under urban conditions, into a pressure group. The remission of debts was not a prelude to a period of social harmony but to an era of internal strife in which the city population appears for the first time as a political force of increasingly formidable dimensions.

Solon's programme included an arrangement whereby he precisely linked political, military, and social status with farm income, expressed in terms of the measures of capacity which he himself introduced. His laws recognised as entitled to the full privileges of citizenship and burdens of military service the following categories of free-born Athenians:

Zeugitae	Those whose land produced at least 200 measures of 'dry' or 'wet' produce.
Knights	Those whose land produced at least 300 measures of 'dry' or 'wet' produce.
Pentakosiomedimni	Those whose land produced at least 500 measures of 'dry' or 'wet' produce.

By 'dry' produce is meant grains, and the measure used was termed a medimnus: by 'wet' produce is meant wine or oil, and the measure was a metretes. The Zeugitae served in the army as hoplites (heavy armed troops), and provided their own equipment. The Knights provided their own horses, as did the Pentakosiomedimni, and both probably provided a squire. Solon's enactment perhaps merely recognised a traditional practice whereby the expenses of defence were roughly divided in accordance with real income among those who had a stake in the country.

The Greek measures may be converted as follows:

200 medimni =	285 bushels	= about 17,000 lb. (of grain).
200 metretae =	1,700 imperial gallons =	17,000 lb. (of water).

The equalisation, for assessment purposes, of a metretes to a medimnus was on a basis of weight alone. The measures used were new, but were set to come into a fixed ratio with the traditional system used in Corinth and Euboea.

These figures shed significant light on the state of the rural economy in Solon's time: it is notable that only three products are taken into account; and the amounts specified are some evidence of the level of contemporary farm income in real terms. It is interesting to compare the nutritive values of the three commodities: the relation of oil, grain, and wine, in terms of digestible calories, is that of 10:5:1; *i.e.* 1 lb. of oil is equivalent in food value to 2 lb. of grain or 10 lb. of wine. In other words a farmer who (theoretically) furnished his whole complement of produce in oil could feed twice as many men as the farmer who grew only grain, and ten times the number of men as the wine grower of equal status to himself.[8] In subsistence farming the chief aim is to grow enough food for consumption on the farm, consequently highly nutritious crops, especially cereals, have priority: in commercial farming the incentive to grow any particular crop will depend on the reigning prices in relation to the cost of production and the comparative yield. In the conditions of Attica a rough estimate of comparative yield would be about 500 lb. of grain per acre, compared with 100 lb. of oil. Since 1 lb. of oil has the nutritive value of 2 lb. of grain, the relation of grain to oil from the point of view of nutrition plus yield is of the order of 5 to 2: that is, grain is more than twice as attractive a crop as oil, if the price of both is equal by weight.

The estimates of yield have been reached in the following way.

Since much of Attica's arable land is unsuitable for wheat, the main crop was barley, the yield of which is rather higher under the same conditions of growth. With a sixteen-inch rainfall, poor cultivation methods and seed selection, high susceptibility to disease, and a shortage of manure, the yield could not be high.[9] Recent statistics for the whole of Greece, including land above the fertility of Attica, and taking into account crop rotation, better technique, and systematic fertilisation, showed a yield of only 9·8 bushels per acre in 1927–8 (the yield has since climbed with the help of imported fertilisers). It is possible that there has been a general loss in fertility since ancient times, but this would be offset by the improved techniques of soil conservation today; given the farming conditions of Solon's time, with reliance on fallowing to conserve moisture, and a chronic shortage of manure, we must assume that the yield in sixth-century Attica was significantly below that for modern Greece. Since the latter has only recently risen above 10 bushels per acre, we are safe in assuming an average yield of not more than 8 bushels for Attica in Solon's time.[10]

There are grave difficulties in estimating the yield of 'liquid' crops for the following reasons: the proportion of vines to olives is unknown; the yield of olives shows enormous variations from year to year, as well as varying in accordance with the age of the trees; the yield of vines is very variable, depending not only on the fertility of the soil but also on the selection of stock and the ability to resist diseases and the depredations of pests. Nevertheless, the margin of error is not so extreme as not to rule out certain possibilities. Glotz[11] seems to postulate a yield of about 200 gallons of wine per acre, which seems high: we can hardly expect the ancient yield to have been much above half that of modern times, taking into account the greatly improved selection of stock; without irrigation this would give a figure of about 100 to 150 gallons per acre.

The yield of oil would be not more than one-tenth that of wine. Modern statistics of oil production, which must form the basis of calculation, are compiled on the yield of crops grown in cultivated groves, whereas much of Attica's olive crop was probably scattered over the hillsides on the poorest soil. Even in modern conditions the yield would scarcely average above three-quarters of a ton, and the oil will amount to about a seventh of this weight, *i.e.* about 20 gallons to the acre. It is impossible to estimate the average yield in Attica with anything like certainty, but we are probably safe in assuming the yield of oil per acre in a 'normal' season as not more than 10 gallons.[12]

If we now return to the assessments of Solon, we see that on the basis of the above estimate a Zeugites would need about 36 sown acres of grain to produce his assessed figure, if he grew only grain: if he fallowed every alternate year he would need a total acreage of at least 70 acres. If he grew only wine, he would need 10 to 15 acres in vineyards. If he grew only olives he would need over 150 acres of land to produce his total assessment. From these figures it is clear that the farmers' main income came from the grain and vine crops. We can be sure that no Zeugites gained his entire, or even his main source of income from olives: a farm of 150 acres or more would be enormous by Athenian standards[13] and unmanageable by a small household. The disadvantage of olives as a cash crop lies in their low and delayed yield, and in the fact that the trees can easily be damaged or lost. Only a high price incentive would make them preferable to vines for commercial farming, and this implies a developed market economy which did not exist in Solon's time. Grain was the basic crop, but vines were an excellent sideline on the farms, because the vintage occurs when labour is free from tending the grain crop; the latter has been harvested, and the labourers are available for other work, by August, while the vintage does not begin before September. Vines were a natural complement to grain in Greek farming, and we should expect most farms to grow both, as Hesiod did in Boeotia.

Solon's assessment took into account only farm income, and the implication is that the level of economic activity outside the farming sector was insignificant. Trade had presumably not progressed very far in Attica, consequently we must assume that at this stage commercial farming had hardly begun to replace subsistence farming: some cash crops there were, principally wine, but they were a small proportion of total output. This picture was to be radically altered by the increase in trading activity during the sixth century, and a rise in the demand for cash crops was to allow marginal land, which had struggled to produce a bread crop, to produce a wine crop for sale. It will be seen from the above calculations of yield that this could mean the replacement of a grain crop of less than 500 lb. per acre by a wine crop of over 1,000 lb.; if the grain crop required fallowing in alternate years, the substitution would mean more than quadrupling the yield by weight. Whether the heavier wine crop was more valuable economically, would of course depend on the level of prices once a secure system of exchange had been built up. If an assured market for liquid cash crops could be found, this would not only intensify production on the traditional farm land, but would also increase the total farming area by making profitable use of the sloping land which was unsuitable for cereals (hence for subsistence farming), but well adapted to vine and olive cultivation. The development of foreign trade was a key to Athenian economic progress, and Solon has been credited with an attempt at least to remove one of the hindrances to this development.

His most important contribution in this regard was to issue what was probably the first Athenian official coinage. Some doubt has been cast upon this claim by numismatists who would date the first Athenian coins into the second quarter of the sixth century,[14] but it seems preferable to accept the literary evidence, bearing in mind that the date of Solon's reforms is itself subject to controversy. Our authorities certainly believed that coinage had been in circulation in Athens before Solon's time, and this coinage had been on the standard of the earliest known Greek system, that is, the coinage struck in Aegina from late in the seventh century. This system had since been rivalled by a newer coinage system in use in Euboea and Corinth, and it was on the standard of this system that the Athenian coins were now struck. The names of the old denominations, talent, mina, and drachma, were all retained, but whereas the old mina had been equal in weight to 70 drachmas, it was, in the new Athenian currency, equal in weight to 100 drachmas. If the mina had remained of constant weight itself, the change would have meant that the same quantity of silver was divided into a larger number of smaller coins. However, Aristotle stated that Solon altered the relationship between the mina and the talent, the largest unit of currency: this relationship, which had stood at 60 to 1, stood in the new Athenian currency at 63 to 1.

Difficulties in the interpretation of these statements arise mainly from the double use of the terms mina and talent as terms both of weight and value. A lightening took place not only of the drachma but also to a much smaller extent, of the currency mina also: if the talent remained of constant weight, as it seems to have done, henceforth the same quantity of silver was divided up into a larger number of minas, as currency, than minas as denominations of weight: a mina as currency, that is, a mina's worth of drachmas, would now have a 5% higher value as legal tender than a mina's weight of bar silver: this margin of 5% was most probably the calculated cost of minting, spread over the whole currency. Thus, in so far as Solon issued coins whose stamped value as currency was slightly higher than their value by weight as bullion, he can be said, in this very limited sense, to have issued a token coinage.

This retention by the treasury of a margin of profit on issued coinage should be regarded as an entirely separate matter from the question of the lightening of the drachma. The latter can hardly be considered as a debasement of the coinage, as it has sometimes been described (assuming that there was previously in existence an Attic coinage to debase), for the quality of the silver was unchanged. The Solonian issue marks a milestone in Athenian economic history in the first place, because it was the first general issue of Athenian coinage which was put out by the Athenian state as such: thus the state was, by legal and administrative action, impinging upon the mercantile activities of its members.

The advantages of coinage over bullion for commercial transactions are at least two: the stamp shows that each piece of silver has been tested for quality of metal and need not be tested again; secondly, the device of milling, or, failing this, of spreading the design over the whole face of the coin, ensures that it is of standard size and has not been reduced by chipping. The result is that payment can be quickly effected, because the sum owing can conveniently be reckoned in terms of specie of standard quality and weight. The weight or size of any coin is immaterial (assuming that it is not too bulky to handle) provided that it is standard, and acceptable as between two trading groups. Difficulties occur when trade develops between two groups or spheres of commerce, which have evolved separate specie with a weight ratio which does not make for easy conversion. Each group naturally hopes to be paid for any excess of exports over imports in terms of its own specie, if possible; if it is forced to accept payment in specie with an awkward ratio to its own, there may well be difficulties in disposing of it in the home market. If the stamped value was the same as the conventional value by weight, foreign coinage could be disposed of as bullion; but if, as in the case of the Solonian currency, there was an over-valuation of specie over bullion to cover minting costs, then the disposal of coinage as bullion would mean a loss to the trader who accepted it.

It is likely that the over-riding consideration in the fixing of currency weight would be the direction of overseas trade; any export of Athenian currency must be in denominations easily interchangeable with Athenian overseas customers or creditors.[15] The coins which were current in Attica in the pre-Solonian era were of a standard associated with the great trading state of Aegina (the so-called Pheidonian standard): the currency issued by Solon was of the so-called Euboic standard, equivalent in weight to that minted in Corinth. Whether or not Athens had carried on much direct trade with Aegina, she evidently had formed part of the Aeginetan trading sphere, as is hardly surprising considering her geographical position. The

Solonian currency therefore meant, in terms of foreign trade, a state recognition of her greater interest in the Corinthian sphere. The new currency helped to smooth the way for increased contact with the rich Corinthian trade with the Greek settlements in Italy and Sicily.

The most important part of Solon's economic programme was his cancellation of debts, but we know so little about the operation of this measure that it is hard to estimate its effects upon the later economy. What is certain is that his reforms were a prelude to a period of intense social discord: it is also a period of some commercial development, and we may reasonably assume that the readjustment of the economy to this development was partly responsible for the social tension.

Our belief that Athenian trade expanded at this time is based largely on the archaeological record, which shows a sudden increase in the level of Athenian exports to the north-east and to the west. This is the conclusion drawn from an analysis of the distribution of Athenian Black Figure pottery,[16] and although the distribution of pottery is not in itself a sure index to the volume of general trade, it is the best direct evidence available. In the early sixth century Athenian pots appear in greatly increased numbers in Greece proper, for the first time in the Black Sea area, and for the first time in any quantity in the west. The sudden appearance of Athenian pottery in western sites which had hitherto shown only Corinthian ware suggests that the pots were taken along the usual trade routes by Corinthian shippers, and the implied increase in commercial co-operation between Corinth and Athens is consistent with Solon's measures to put out an Athenian coinage on the Corinthian standard.

We may connect this increase in trading activity with the capture by Athens of the offshore island of Salamis from Megara in the first half of the century. Intermittent fighting for the possession of this island seems to have gone on between the two states for some time, and while the island was in Megarian occupation, Phaleron, the port of Athens, was too unsafe to become a great centre of exchange. The capture of Salamis seems to have eased the position considerably, and to have brought the consumer market of the developing city into much closer contact with foreign trade. It is possible that a rapid increase in the trade flowing through Phaleron had an unsettling effect on other parts of the country, especially the area of the east coast, where trading ships from Euboea and Thessaly had been accustomed to call.[17] It may be significant that the period of development for Phaleron was apparently one of decline for Prasiae on the east coast of Attica, and that the same period saw the beginning of the decline of the great trading cities of Chalcis and Eretria on the other side of the straits. Whether or not trade was at this time drawn away from the eastern ports, it is clear that east Attica was, by 560 B.C., a centre of discontent and the home of a revolutionary movement.

The years following Solon's reforms were a period of discord in Attica, during which our authorities distinguish three groups or parties fighting for the political control of the state. The parties are referred to as the Pediakoi (the men of the Plain); the Paraloi (the men of the Coast); and the Hyperakrioi (the men beyond the Hills), or alternatively as the Diakrioi (the men of the Hills). Of these parties the last mentioned is said to have been the last formed, and is identified as the personal following of the hero of Salamis, Peisistratus himself. The party drew its strength from the lower orders of the free population; among its supporters were said to be men ruined by Solon's reforms and men of 'impure' descent. This description might refer to immigrants or their descendants, to illegitimate children, or to those who had, for some reason, been cast out of the family unit. In any case they would be landless, since only Athenian citizens could own land in Attica, and hence naturally belonged to the lower social and economic strata of the community.

The evidence refers to the supporters of Peisistratus as to an economic section of the community. But the traditions are in agreement in assigning to them a local habitat, as is indicated by the names by which they are known. The basis of party divisions is made explicit in Aristotle, who says that each party took its name from the area of land which it farmed. There is, however, considerable doubt about the precise areas denoted by the terms used to label the parties. The 'Plain' almost certainly refers to the Athenian plain proper, that is the central plain of Attica on which stood the city of Athens. A chance reference in Thucydides suggests that the 'Coast' was a term locally used to denote the south-east area of Attica, and this may well be the area denoted in this context. The term Hyper-akrioi (men beyond the Hills) perhaps refers to the inhabitants of the northern and eastern parts of Attica, which lie the other side of Mount Hymettus, regarded from the point of view of Athens. This is also the area defined as the Diakria in the Lexicon of Hesychius, and it includes Brauron, the home of Peisistratus.[18]

The struggle of the three factions no doubt reflects a conflict of regional interests, as well as a clash of personal ambitions between local despots. But it is significant that Athens, the stronghold of the 'Plain' faction, had a divided allegiance: the success of Peisistratus was ultimately due to the fact that his partisans not only held the home territory around Brauron, but were to be found in strength within the city of Athens itself. The faction had not only a territorial basis but also a political appeal which cut across the traditional territorial allegiance. But the spearhead of Peisistratus' support inside Athens was probably the migrants from his own part of the country: the rural population was on the move, and the men who drifted off the land and into the city in search of work were forming new pressure groups. The regional conflict was as old as the time when Athens first began to try to enforce its writ beyond the mountain ranges; it was the rural depression of the sixth century which transformed the nature of the conflict, and in so doing hastened the end of the old order.

The rate of population growth in Athens during the first half of the century was such as to attract the notice even of ancient writers quite uninterested in such matters as demography; it was also a problem of concern to both Solon and Peisistratus.[19] The evidence of an increase in trade indicates the probability of some improvement in the urban food supply, hence the possibility that the economy of the city was able to absorb a limited number of new arrivals. These consisted of foreign immigrants, who were officially encouraged by Solon to settle in Attica; of Athenian ex-slaves, who had been repatriated; and above all of surplus labour from the country areas.

A gradual move to the cities by elements surplus to the requirements of the farming community is a normal sign of economic advance, though its effects on the institutional arrangements can be disturbing. The rural immigrants are brought into contact in the cities with strangers who have quite different, often startling, attitudes to locally accepted custom, at the very time when the break-up of the traditional pattern of life is opening the door to new ideas of change, of individualism, and above all, of open competition for the privileges which have hitherto been distributed by an unquestioned, because accepted, custom.

Such ideas may be slow to affect institutions during a situation of slow, or 'normal' economic development, that is, when the diminishing farming share in population goes hand in hand with the expansion of the urban demand for labour, so that the newcomer to the city can fairly easily be absorbed in an existing, or smoothly developing, economic and social pattern. A much more perilous situation occurs when the drift to the city is at a rate significantly higher than that justified by its expanding economic activity; that is, when people flock to the city not because their labour is required there but because they have nowhere else to go. This is the situation when the food supply, or the livelihood, of a part of the rural population becomes inadequate for its support.

This had been the case even in the pre-Solonian period, but the problem of rural over-population had been kept within manageable proportions by the enslavement and deportation of ruined farmers. By ending the deportations Solon had complicated the problem. It was the city of Athens which now was to receive that excess rural population which previously would have been removed by deportation. In this way the rural problem was transferred to the city: but since economic conditions in Athens itself were not sufficiently elastic to absorb, at a tolerable standard of living, a rapid intake of labour from the country and from abroad, the result was an explosive situation within the developing city.

In Athens a leader soon appeared to champion the cause of the new urban proletariat. The hero of the war against Megara, Peisistratus, was a figure of national stature, who commanded more than a regional following. Thus there fell on the shoulders of the ambitious squire the mantle of the social reformer. On the loyalty of his local following in east Attica Peisistratus could place reasonable reliance, for their interests were, in the main, his own. But the support which he drew from the city population was dependent on his finding quick solutions for its economic and social disabilities. For the moment, however, the tide was running in his favour, and in 560, after a vote in the popular assembly had been carried, granting him a personal bodyguard, with their help he seized the Acropolis, and formally took over control of the city and the state.

III

ECONOMIC DEVELOPMENT UNDER
PEISISTRATUS

THE precarious nature of Peisistratus' hold on power is shown by the fact that he was twice ousted by his rivals; on the first occasion within a year of his original *coup d'état*. Presumably the support he enjoyed from the city population was fitful and unreliable, since no dramatic solution of their economic disabilities was readily available to him. A possible, perhaps an obvious line of policy lay in confiscation of land, and resettlement on small allotments: whether Peisistratus tried to carry out such a policy during the early stages of his regime we do not know; it had, in any case, fatal drawbacks as far as the immediate future was concerned. While the Tyranny was still shaky there were obvious political disadvantages in sharpening opposition and welding disaffected sections of the community into a solid opposition: from the economic point of view such a policy was likely to do more harm than good for some time to come: it was hardly likely to *increase* the food supply of Attica, on which the city was still mainly dependent, and in its operation, was almost certain to decrease it by adding an element of uncertainty and chaos to an already delicate and difficult situation: the number of large estates was limited and their acreage comparatively small; a resettlement scheme, even if successfully carried out, would satisfy only an insignificant percentage of the landless, while it drove into destitution, and violence, those who had been dispossessed. On the other hand it was by no means certain that the majority of the urban poor wanted to go back to the country: after their experience of city life many of them probably preferred to stay, and were prepared to back any leader who, they believed, could make available to them a livelihood in the city; if Peisistratus could not do this for them, another Tyrant might be found who could. A resettlement scheme could perhaps help to reduce urban poverty in the long run, but in this case the really fatal objection to it was that it required time to make its effects felt: on the other hand, to raise living standards in the city by providing employment or welfare payments was a task which demanded both time and money, and in both of these commodities Peisistratus was, for the moment, deficient.

It is said that he was driven out of the capital by a coalition of his political opponents, the Plain and the Coast. From Athens he withdrew, most probably, to his own part of the country, and within a few years was back as Tyrant once more, this time after an arrangement with the leader of the Coast party. In 556 he was again driven out, and this time he left the country altogether and was absent for ten years. In 546 he landed at Marathon, overcame local resistance north-east of Athens, and was joined by supporters from both town and country; returning in triumph into Athens he established a regime which was to last for thirty-six years.

The literary evidence of Peisistratus' exiles and restorations is so meagre and fanciful that it would be unwise to draw any but the broadest conclusions from the details which accompany them. Nevertheless, the importance of the role played by the city of Athens is noticeable at all stages. In each case Athens was the target: once in possession of the city the control of the state was apparently assured, in spite of the fact that the struggle was closely bound up with the ambitions of local dynasts, each controlling a section of the countryside. The later policy of the Tyrant was concerned to combat this local rivalry, just as the institution of the Panathenaic festival[1] seems to have been intended, by honouring the historic unification of Attica, to discourage the centrifugal tendency which lay at the heart of the local struggle for power. The anxiety of the exile to get to Athens, apparently even before returning to his local stronghold to collect forces, is evidence of the decisive influence it already exerted in Attic affairs, although the city as such was not identified with any of the three parties recognised by later Greek historians. Its support was evidently vital for an intending ruler, and from this it follows that the city's social and economic troubles called for priority consideration by him, and could be neglected only at his peril. The Solonian crisis had been largely agrarian; the present crisis was predominantly urban, in the sense that it was urban grievances which first demanded the attention of any government aspiring to the city population's important backing. The crisis of Peisistratus was thus different in kind from that of Solon. The latter had been mainly concerned with the rehabilitation of the countryside: the former laid a priority on finding some solution to the problem of urban poverty and underemployment. The lesson of how governments could be made and unmade in the city overnight must have been an alarming one for budding leaders, both local and national. It drove home the conclusion that, irrespective of the good of the country as a whole, the satisfaction of the wants of the urban population must come first: if the latter could not be given land outside the city, or did not want to go to it, then living standards had somehow to be maintained or improved within the city either by providing employment or by straight welfare payments.

A programme that would satisfy the most urgent needs of the urban proletariat needed for its support a supply of ready money, a commodity in which the traditional aristocracy was deficient. The wealth of the landowners was tied up in their farms, and in credit to their dependants; it was not easy for them to lay hands on ready cash, even if they wished to invest it in humouring those whom they regarded as a good-for-nothing mob, and whose interests were opposed to their own. It is at this point that we find a new type of leader emerging in Attica, as in other states of central Greece.[2] These men are not necessarily large landowners, or at least they do not rely for their political power on their possession of land. The feature which they have in common is money; and although contemporary writers knew that the old aristocracy were also rich, the wealth of these 'new' people seemed somehow of a different order. Their wealth was in liquid capital, in possessions that were, unlike land, freely bought and sold; they were in fact the successful representatives of a new commercial class. The historian Thucydides was not concerned to analyse the causes of Tyranny in Greece; but he notes *en passant* that as an institution it regularly coincided with a situation in which wealth was accumulated.[3] In the long term the rich landowner was perhaps in a stronger position than the merchant with liquid capital; but in the short term the latter afforded its owner a powerful political lever, since it was he who was in a position to satisfy quickly the demands of the urban population, hence to win their immediate allegiance. In farming, most of the profits tend to be reinvested in the maintenance of property and the acquisition of livestock;[4] it is only by constant improvement that the capital of a farm can be prevented from depreciating. But the position of the entrepreneur was quite different. It was unlikely that he would want to extend his investment by buying or building another ship; he would naturally sail with his own vessel, and it would be folly to hand it over to an employee, in case he lost both cargo and ship. There were no obvious reinvestment demands on the trader or pirate once he brought his last cargo home and settled down in the city: hence the incentive to spend money freely, and the unfortunate impression thereby given of a desire for vulgar ostentation. It is therefore no surprise to find the entrepreneur to the fore in political situations which put a premium on the possession of ready cash. For the first time in Attica's history political power comes to depend largely on leadership of the city commoners, and is not necessarily connected with traditional social prestige based on land ownership. The power of the Tyrants rested on their control of the city, and this in turn depended on their possession of the means to satisfy the urban population's crying demands, as well as the means to hire private armies to support their ambitions on the level of *Realpolitik*.

Peisistratus' power in Attica, originally resting, like that of any other squire, on the support of his local retainers, had reached challenging heights by reason of his national military prestige and his flirtation with the lower economic elements of the city. The first two regimes which he inaugurated were both short-lived, not only because of the opposition of the other Attic dynasts (for this was a more or less constant factor), but also because he could not hold the support of the city; presumably because he was not in a position to do very much to relieve their difficulties quickly. After his second return, which concluded ten years' exile, his regime is stable, and he is able to put into effect grandiose schemes for the betterment of Athenian conditions at home, and in their relations with the outside world. It is therefore of interest to consider the evidence of his activities during his exile, and to determine in what respect his position was so much stronger in 546 than it had been ten or fifteen years previously.

Our knowledge of Peisistratus' activities during this period is mainly derived from the accounts in Herodotus and Aristotle. The former writes as follows: 'Peisistratus travelled to Eretria, where he discussed the position with his sons. The opinion of Hippias, that an attempt should be made to restore the Tyranny, was that which prevailed; they thereupon set about collecting contributions from cities which were under some sort of moral obligation to them, and many provided large sums of money, the contribution of the Thebans being the largest. Then, to put it briefly, there was some lapse of time, and the stage was reached when all their preparations for return were complete. Mercenary troops from Argos moved up from the Peloponnesus, and the Peisistratids were joined by a volunteer from Naxos, whose name was Lygdamis: the latter was extremely keen, and brought along with him both money and men. Ten years after their expulsion they crossed from their base at Eretria and arrived back on Attic soil.'

The account of Aristotle is as follows: 'After this, and following his second expulsion, Peisistratus first colonised a place known as Rhaekelos, near the Thermaic Gulf. From there he went to the region around Pangaeus, where he made money and was able to hire some troops. After a lapse of about ten years he returned to Eretria and only then did he attempt to get back his rule by force. He received assistance from many quarters, more especially from the Thebans, from Lygdamis of Naxos, and from the Knights who still controlled the affairs of Eretria.'

A surprising feature of these accounts is the breadth of overseas support which was forthcoming for the deposed ruler. Aristotle notes (in a later passage) that help was given by Argos because Peisistratus had taken, as his second wife, a lady of that city. The support of Lygdamis was likewise linked with the latter's own ambitions to rule Naxos. But such statements do little to explain the assistance: the state of Argos, as such, could ill afford to hazard its fighting men for a sentimental attachment: Lygdamis might have considered it better to concentrate his men and money on satisfying his own ambitions first: we have no reason given to explain the support of the Thebans or that of the Eretrians. The combination of forces drawn from cities with such diverse interests can best be explained by assuming that these forces were not far removed from mercenaries; in the case of the Argive troops this was explicitly stated by Herodotus, and the latter went on to stress the dependence of Peisistratus, during his regime, on the support of hired foreign troops. Both Aristotle and Herodotus lay stress on the economic strength of Peisistratus' organisation and its importance for his career. It was only after ten years of work, which had mainly been spent in making money in the north-east of Greece, that the deposed ruler was in a position to make a renewed bid for power.

Rhaekelos has been identified as a place to the north-west of Chalcidice: east of the promontory lay the mouth of the river Strymon and the silver-mining region around Mount Pangaeus. It was his activities in this area which were the source of Peisistratus' wealth.[5]

Peisistratus had been unable to maintain control over Athens by virtue either of his local following or his national prestige: from the account in Herodotus it appears that on his second expulsion he doubted the value of even attempting another return. Ten years later he comes back from his colonising venture a rich man, receives support from many sides, and establishes a rule so stable that he is able to bequeath it to his sons on his death. The power of money in righting his political fortunes has drawn from modern historians a crop of speculations in which Peisistratus appears as a merchant prince riding to power on the backs of the trading classes, whose political influence at this juncture is assumed in order to explain his success. Yet our evidence does not suggest that Peisistratus was *primarily* a trader, though it must be conceded that, to make any mining venture a success, he must presumably have interested himself in the marketing of the product. The question at issue, however, is whether there was at this time in Attica a powerful pressure group made up of traders and manufacturers, as a cohesive section of the community. For this there is no evidence, and the lowly position of the trading classes at Athens in later times, when commerce was far more highly developed, seems strongly against it.

The problem is to discover what is the connexion between the success of Peisistratus' bid and the economic conditions in which it was carried out. Now the money made by him in the north-east was, it is reasonable to suppose, drawn from exploitation of the silver mines there. Mining is an industry which requires for its successful organisation the application of both technical skill and capital to assemble the equipment and workforce, and to maintain it until the product is prepared for the market. The advantage of Peisistratus over the natives of the district was perhaps that, when he fled from his homeland, he almost certainly took with him sufficient capital to lighten the burden of his exile: possibly he himself possessed, or, more probably, had with him men who possessed the technical skill to organise the industry—a skill developed in the mines of Attica. To take advantage of these assets he needed to get possession in some way of the fields, and this, in his adventurous style, he was able to do. It is perhaps significant that the Asian power whose influence had dominated the Greek fringe of Asia Minor for more than a century, was now in difficulties and its power contracting under pressure from the Persians. The return home of Peisistratus as a rich colonialist coincided exactly with the final collapse of the Lydian kingdom and the beginning of Persian domination in this area: in view of the later support which Persia afforded to the Tyrant's son, it is conceivable that Peisistratus himself in his venture had received some assistance from the Persians.

However his wealth was gained, it is fairly clear that it was this significant improvement in his finances which made him again a formidable challenger for political power in Attica, even in face of the massed wealth of the aristocratic land-holders. What distinguished his position from theirs was that his wealth was in coin, bullion, or credit which could easily be turned into money and goods; unlike the Alcmaeonids, he was in a position to throw all his wealth into a gamble for power by paying soldiers and buying support. The nobles who opposed him could muster in physical combat only their local following; to sell their own estates and hire outside troops to fight their battles would no doubt have seemed to them the idea of a lunatic.

No doubt the sea-traders of Attica, and those who made a living from industry, were more in sympathy with an adventurer like Peisistratus, whose interests were to some extent their own. But their support was not decisive. Among the factors which made possible the Tyranny we must reckon the disunity and financial difficulties of the nobles, the turbulent mood of the swollen city populace, and above all the economic power of Peisistratus himself, possessing the resources to equip a formidable private army, and also to satisfy the most urgent needs of the urban poor. The nobles were beaten down on two fronts: first, they were unaccustomed to dealing with an urban concentration of desperate men who owed no allegiance and accorded no respect to a local dynast: men who could not be threatened with eviction or dragged before the squire, acting in the capacity of the local justice: men who, uprooted from their local traditions and habits of obedience, were ready material to back the most reckless of schemes, brushing aside habits of behaviour hitherto accepted without question. The frightening phenomenon of a numerically powerful urban pressure group was something new in Attic politics. At the opening of the fifth century the urban population is already a formidable force, to be consulted or appeased if necessary; whereas in Solon's time the struggle had been between the squires and their yeomen, and had hinged on the use of land. It was the time of Peisistratus which saw the passing of the old order, and, in the process of change, the opening of the way to autocracy by the man who could exploit the temporary confusion.

But secondly, even this was not decisive for the triumph of Peisistratus, whose victory was, in the first instance, won in the country demes outside Athens itself. The urban confusion enabled him to bid for state-wide power, but the victory was won on the field of battle. The militia who opposed him were simply the hastily levied local yeomanry called from their farms by such nobles as chose to combine, and they went down before the first professional force to be seen in Attica: heterogeneous, but, no doubt, well armed, and above all, properly organised in the service of one leader.

By means of his mercenary troops Peisistratus had the means of coercing any opposition he might find in the city; he had already destroyed in open battle the power of rival Attic dynasts. During his lifetime he seems to have met little serious challenge to his authority from the great families, and was apparently able to persuade some of them at least to co-operate with him in the administration.[6] Nevertheless, the power which they had been accustomed to exercise in their local areas was always a potentially serious threat to central rule, and this was in the end to be the undoing of the dynasty he founded. Against this threat he protected himself by his private army, and by taking as hostages junior members of these families : in addition he sapped their local authority in a way which was to have important consequences for the constitutional development of Attica. Hitherto the nobles had almost certainly had the right of dealing out justice in the areas of their local influence: it is possible that a citizen was able to appeal from this judgement to the Areopagus in the case of serious charges, or else to the popular court, if this was indeed set into operation by Solon. But in practice the fact that a citizen could be hailed before the Bench of the local gentry meant that the latter's displeasure must be avoided at almost any cost, and this was without doubt a factor which had greatly strengthened the authority of the landed aristocracy. It was precisely this authority which was undermined by the measures that Peisistratus took to appoint circuit judges responsible to the central government, that is, to himself. Local authority was thus replaced by that of the central government; the justice that Peisistratus had once dealt out at Brauron he now, through his appointees, dealt out through the length and breadth of Attica. At the same time every act which served to strengthen the hand of the central executive in Athens meant a moral strengthening of the position of the capital in relation to the rest of Attica. The day was fast approaching, if it had not already arrived, when it would be everywhere assumed that whoever was master of the capital was master of the country. For this reason the goodwill, or at least the co-operation of the city dwellers was becoming an increasingly important element in Attic politics: a ruler could choose either to hold them down by force, or to some extent to take them into political partnership, realising that their goodwill and support, if it could be secured, would be a formidable bulwark against the ambitions of rival nobles from the country areas.

Peisistratus' policy towards the city population seems to have been a compromise between repression and demagogy. The story is told by Aristotle of how the Tyrant disarmed the populace by a trick, and this story perhaps reflects a sound tradition of how he kept control of the city within his hands by making his mercenary army the only armed force in existence in Attica. Hitherto the local dynasts had kept law and order in their own districts: henceforth security was to be the responsibility of a full-time force of men who were not members of the citizen body or subject to any loyalty save to the central executive. The repressive powers invoked by Peisistratus, and expressed through his control of a private army, had no constitutional authority, so that the Solonian constitution continued to function superficially intact. The novel institution of paid, foreign security forces seems to have gained acceptance with the Athenians, and the institution survived into Periclean Athens. Repressive powers against the city commoners seem rarely to have been invoked and all our authorities agree on the mild and 'democratic' nature of the regime. Terror does not seem to have been a prominent feature of the policy of Peisistratus; on the other hand there is clear evidence that he sought to gain the support of the masses by concessions. By a curious paradox it appears that it was this demagogic attitude on his part that was to lead in the end to the evolution of a democratic form of government.

The peculiar difficulties of pacifying the city populace at this time have already been pointed out. The poorer elements from the country, who had moved into the city in search of better conditions, had abandoned their traditional institutional background; their old social and religious grouping in the brotherhoods and clans, presided over by the nobles, had given them a framework within which their obedience could be unhesitatingly expected. But the new milieu of the city provided an atmosphere inimical to such implicit habits of behaviour: while minds were beginning to leave the groove in which they had moved for so long, economic scarcity, and the fierce competition for a living in the city, removed both the inhibitions and the sense of security people may have retained from their semi-feudal background. Furthermore, such people had a much better opportunity to organise, or be organised by their own leaders, than had those who stayed on their holdings, or in rural employment, in virtual isolation. To keep them under control by force was a difficult, though not an impossible task; for a well-equipped force of soldiers could still hope to ride down the rabble. But there is a point beyond which people will not allow themselves easily to be intimidated, and it was strongly in the interests of Peisistratus that he should not allow poverty and hunger to reach this point. Thus the problem of political control (which was the Tyrant's first consideration) assumed an economic form, and the force of circumstances drove him to influence and encourage the economic development of the country. It was a condition of preserving his rule that he should somehow maintain, and if possible better the living standards of the city populace, and the more politically important the capital became in the affairs of Attica, the higher the priority that had to be given to ameliorating the economic lot of its inhabitants. It is to be noted that there was a somewhat disheartening side to this problem. The greater the efforts made to improve their lot (whether by rural resettlement, urban employment, or some other device to improve the distribution of wealth), the more intractable the problem was liable to become; for the improvement in urban opportunities and conditions would attract more and more people from the country to share in the benefits. The probability therefore existed that the problem would continue in spite of all efforts to overcome it; for better or worse, Attica now had to live with the prospect of supporting a city population whose numbers exceeded the food potential of the surrounding Attic countryside. Peisistratus' greatest efforts were directed to dealing with this problem, and since many of the city dwellers were non-agricultural workers, it was natural that his efforts did much to benefit trading and manufacturing interests. This circumstance is essentially the basis of the modern theory that Peisistratus was himself a conscious champion of such interests because it was the trading classes which supplied his main backing.[7] This theory can be set aside as quite unproved, as well as highly improbable, and this analysis would rather indicate that, to Peisistratus himself, the support of such interests was no less incidental and unforeseen than the trend to democracy, to which he was also lending momentum.

Those who choose to live in a city must accept the fact that they are dependent for their food upon the countryside; in conditions of free exchange the size of a city must therefore be limited by the surpluses of its rural surroundings, and to command these surpluses the city dwellers must have sufficient money to persuade the farmers to grow food for sale to them: (this system may of course be extended into the field of overseas trade so that a city can be fed from topsoil outside its own political frontiers). Nevertheless, once a system of food importation to a city has been established, the population of the city may swell out of proportion to the food available to it, since the extent neither of the importation, nor of the population that is to consume it, is known to those who leave the country to make their home in town. When population reaches a point beyond the capacity of the city's resources to support it, theoretically the surplus population could be expected to return to the country. In fact this is not always the case, for a variety of reasons; prominent among these is the fact that there is in the city *some* food and work, even if it is inadequate to go round; this is then likely to encourage competition between people for what is available, rather than to force a 'proper' percentage to withdraw in favour of their more fortunate fellows. In practice it is commonly the role of the city to absorb surplus rural population rather than vice versa.

The essence of the problem facing Peisistratus was to bring the population of the capital, and the economic resources of the countryside into a tolerable relationship with each other; more food must be brought into the city, while, if possible, surplus city population was moved back to the country. Neither of these courses would necessarily do much to solve the economic problem of poverty which lay at the root of the matter, but they would promote political stability by reducing the threat of political agitation in the most vulnerable quarter, that is, within Athens itself. The underlying problem of economic want could hardly be solved by changes in the distribution of population, but only by increasing the total quantity of production. Since the total arable area was already being farmed, primary production could only be increased by extending the farming area to non-arable land, and producing goods for sale, that is, goods to be exchanged for food, rather than food itself. A long-term solution of Attica's economic misfortunes thus lay in an increase in trade. How far this was realised by Peisistratus is very doubtful, although the logic of his own policies drove him to implement policies which tended in this direction.

We may consider the famous agricultural resettlement policy of Peisistratus as one which combined political with economic aims: under this scheme money was advanced to poorer elements in the city to help them settle on the land. In Aristotle's opinion the chief aim of the measure was to get people out of the city (where their concentration was politically dangerous), into the country, where they were scattered in small pockets; by directing their efforts to their private welfare Peisistratus hoped to distract them from public affairs. At the same time this resulted in an increase of his income, for he levied a 10% tax on the value of their production.[8]

It has been suggested that a quantity of farming land came to be available for resettlement in this way because opposing nobles fled from Attica, abandoning their estates. The evidence is a statement of Herodotus: 'Some of the Athenians had fallen in battle, and others of them were in exile.' We should naturally hesitate to read too much into this remark, in view of the fact that representatives of several noble families are known to have held offices of state under the Peisistratids. Of those who fled, perhaps many returned and regained possession of their land: the amount of land made available by the exiles is difficult to estimate, but it is doubtful whether it was large enough to make much difference to the urban population. In any case the local yeomen who had worked the estates of the exiles, would have been the first to take possession of their land, and the problem of evicting them in favour of town dwellers would have been an unenviable one. The problem of urban poverty could hardly have been much affected by such a resettlement scheme as this, because the labourers who had formerly worked the confiscated farms would, if driven off the land, presumably have drifted to the city to take the place of the resettled poor; in addition, the chance of getting free land would have attracted into the city needy country people at a greater rate than the city people were being resettled. The end result would more probably be a rise than a fall in city population.

It is possible that loans were made not so much to settle farmers on allotments which had formed part of a cultivated estate (*i.e.*, on arable land), as to establish farms on newly cleared ground. The latter could be found in any quantity only on the hillsides, on old grazing land;[9] this would not be suitable for grains, but rather for vines or olives. If this was the case, the allotments could be quite small; but capital would be required by the settler to tide him over the years before his vines and trees were in full bearing. A scheme of this nature would have the advantage of getting more people on the land without the disruption of production caused by dispossessing those who had formerly owned, or tilled, the soil; and it would have been sound economics, in that it would have increased the total volume of production. The difficulty of the scheme was, of course, the fact that this was not subsistence farming, which could directly fill empty stomachs: if the crop was wine, it could be converted into food only by the alchemy of trade. In fact, any approach to the problem of increasing the real wealth of Attica involved the further problem of increasing the volume of trade, so that the product could be advantageously marketed, and it is to this aspect of Peisistratus' work that we must now turn.

Any account of Attic trade development is forced to rely to a great extent on the archaeological evidence available to us, in default of direct literary accounts, but certain conclusions in support of the archaeological evidence seem to follow from the record of Athenian political activity at this time.

The quantity of Attic Black Figure pottery dated to the years 560 to 520 seems to surpass that of any previous period; the pots are found in the Aegean islands of Chios, Lesbos, and Cyprus; in Asia Minor; in the Black Sea area; in Egypt; in Sicily and in Etruria.[10] Much of this ware is of high artistic quality and changed hands more for its intrinsic value as works of art or decoration than as containers for marketed produce. During this period begins also the export of Red Figure pottery, at first side by side with Black Figure, and eventually replacing it. The technical excellence of this ware is convincing evidence of the growth of a highly skilled artisan class at Athens; presumably city dwellers, whose livelihood and interests were no longer necessarily and primarily rural, but depended in the first instance on the exchange of goods via trade. Apart from ornamental ware, much pottery has been found which was clearly designed only as utility containers for liquid products, especially oil and wine. It was perhaps at this time that a suburb of Athens came to be known as Kerameikos, after the pottery industry which it housed: at the same time potters as a professional group were probably attaining a higher economic level in the city community, as is indicated by the increasing quantity of their dedicatory inscriptions on the Acropolis.[11]

The archaeological evidence suggests an increase in the total volume of Attic overseas trade, and proves that the trading area served by Attic goods widened during this half-century. If the overall total of Attic trade increased, this implies a change in the economic pattern of Attic society in favour of the craftsmen who contributed to it, and the entrepreneurs who conducted it. It is possible to detect signs of a transformation in Attic society in the agitation for political reform which appeared in the immediate post-Peisistratid era; but the process of change was of necessity gradual. In contrast, the effect on her external relations was dramatic. The extension of trade to new areas, hitherto the preserve of other powers, and the total increase in trade abroad brought Attic nationals into competition with the traders of other countries; and while such competition need not necessarily be of a hostile character, the very fact that the citizens of Athens were being drawn increasingly into economic association with other states meant inevitably that the Attic state as such would eventually have to take up some kind of working attitude to the activities of its nationals abroad.

Hitherto Attica can hardly be said to have had a foreign policy, since her concerns were not primarily affected by events much further afield than Megara; it is from this time that her relations to states outside her immediate vicinity begin to be defined. It would be absurd to suggest that the conduct of her external policy was decided now, or later, by the traders themselves, however important their activities actually were to the economic well-being of the state. Policy was at this time made by Peisistratus himself, and that he allowed economic considerations to affect the policies he pursued is almost certainly due to the fact that he had himself been convinced, by his own experience, of the importance of the economic factor, both in the winning and the holding of political power. Although he may have personally despised the entrepreneurs as a class, as a ruler whose authority depended not on acknowledged tradition but on results, he was bound to take special note of the opportunities, and the difficulties, of extending Attic trade. Neither a democracy, in which the traders were always a tiny minority, nor certainly a land-owning aristocracy, would have been prepared to consider long-term commercial interests in the way that Peisistratus could. No previous Attic government would have been at all likely to consider raising forces and risking money to support a distant commercial adventure from which, in a free society, the main benefit would accrue to the traders themselves. But the Tyrant was answerable to no man, and the risks that he had himself incurred in his struggle for political power through economic advancement, we now see the state of Attica itself incurring under his leadership. If money and trade had helped to make him great among Athenians, the same formula applied on a larger scale, and backed by the resources of the state, could result in greater security for his personal role at home, and increased authority for the Attic state itself abroad.

The archaeological record shows that there was a general expansion of Attic trade during the reign of Peisistratus: in particular there seems to have been a dramatic increase in Attic trade with the west, as a result of which Attic ware practically ousted Corinthian from many of its traditional markets there. Nevertheless, the ships which carried the ware may still have been Corinthian, and the increase in the incidence of Attic ware in traditionally Corinthian preserves may simply mean that there was a sharp increase in the volume of Attic trade with Corinth, following on the capture of Salamis. Corinth, by her position on the isthmus, was able to offer excellent marketing facilities for the exchange of the products of east and west, and much of the Attic ware was no doubt disposed of at the isthmus for re-export in Corinthian vessels to Italy and Sicily, with which Corinth was firmly linked by traditional commercial goodwill.

The developing Attic trade with the Aegean islands and the

north-east raised problems of a different kind, since on this route it was Attic ships which carried their native products (and probably Corinthian ware as well). This brought Attic seamen into increasing contact with the peoples of these areas, and because the marketing of the cargoes brought to Attica affected people at home outside the narrow circle of traders, an increasing proportion of Athenians was brought, by their interests as consumers, into contact with the problems of foreign relations. When foreign trade was negligible, the traders could simply be disowned if they found themselves in trouble abroad: but as trade developed, and became of greater concern to Attic consumers, more support for the traders operating abroad could be expected from home, and at the same time those citizens who enriched themselves by trade could begin to form the nucleus of a pressure group. While it would be easy to exaggerate the influence of the latter, the conditions of Peisistratus' administration provided unusually favourable conditions for its activity: although the Tyrant himself was no trader by inclination, all our literary authorities agree that his power had a strong economic basis; money was the backbone of his, as of other Greek Tyrannies. Since the success of the regime depended on alleviating the poverty which was at the bottom of the Attic recurring crises, schemes which offered opportunities of overcoming that poverty could hope to gain support not only from adventurous private elements in Attica but also from the government itself; a support which a traditional feudal regime, based on landownership, would never have given.

In consequence of these factors, accounts of extensive activities in the Aegean carried on by Attic nationals and supported by the Attic state, for the first time begin to appear in our literary authorities. Among the most spectacular achievements of Peisistratus' reign was the seizure, by Attica, of Sigeion, in the Troad, from Mytilene, and the installation of the Tyrant's son as governor. Sigeion is situated on the west coast of northern Asia Minor, south-west of Troy and south of the Hellespont; the importance of the place to Attic seamen seems clearly to have been due to the fact that it lay within convenient distance of the entrance to the straits. Its possession did not give Attic settlers control over the passage of the straits, but it was a valuable resting and supply base from which foreign cargo ships could be plundered, and it was excellently situated for a trading post. It is likely that Attic ships preferred to break cargo here to avoid the difficult run through the narrows, and the hostile attentions of the Megarian colonies Byzantium and Chalcedon at the Bosporus. The carrying trade between the entrance to the straits and the Black Sea ports was in all probability well organised by the local settlers, as is suggested by the wealth of, for instance, the enterprising city of Cyzicus: if that is so, the precious grain cargoes, for which the Attic ships had come, were available for sale in the Troad, and it was not essential to force a passage of the straits or compete with local carriers; the fewer the trading interests that Athenians offended the better, as far as they were concerned: at this early stage of their commercial development it is more reasonable to assume that they pursued a more cautious line of action than that of sailing, at the cost of whatever opposition, to the sources of supply, in order to get the grain at the cheapest price.

This was not the first time that Attic settlers had tried to hold Sigeion: our sources speak of a protracted struggle which dates back to the turn of the century, and in which the chief obstacle to Attic settlement of the place was the hostility of the commercial city of Mytilene.[12] Before the time of the Tyranny no doubt the Athenians engaged in the struggle had relied entirely on their own resources, it is highly unlikely that any form of state taxation was levied on the citizenry at home to support their cause, and even more unlikely that the Attic squires sent their armed yeomanry across the sea to do battle for it. But for the first time under the regime of Peisistratus money, ships, and armed men could be supplied by the home government, and it is this factor which probably clinched the struggle. This, the first Attic imperial venture in distant seas, was to set a precedent for decades of Athenian development.

On the other side of the Hellespont Attic settlers were already entrenched. Herodotus tells a curious story of the arrival in Attica of a native deputation from the Thracian Chersonese, the isthmus which forms the northern shore of the straits. Their aim was to find a champion who would help them to resist the hostile attentions of their neighbours; this call was answered by Miltiades, and when he had thus chivalrously shouldered the colonist's burden, the native Dolonci, in gratitude 'made him Tyrant'.

Miltiades was of the Philaid family, a line of squires whose writ had run in the Brauron area of eastern Attica, and which had therefore been local rivals, possibly allies, of the Peisistratids. The family of Miltiades continued to hold the Chersonese until the Persian invasion in the fifth century, and we hear of their unsuccessful attempt to capture Lampsacus, on the other side of the straits. Although Herodotus represents Miltiades' reason for leaving Athens as his dissatisfaction with Peisistratus' rule, there can be little doubt that this imperialist venture was carried out with the latter's approval; volunteers from Attica accompanied the departing colonialist. By this settlement the home country reduced the burden of its overpopulation, for the venture came at the time before the expansion of the trade under the Tyranny could have significantly increased the demand for labour in the city.

The position of the settlement, its proximity to Sigeion across the straits, and the attempt to expand to Lampsacus all suggest an organised effort to obtain control of the straits themselves, and the motive for this must be connected with trade: either the settlers wished to safeguard and extend their own trade, or else they wished to enrich themselves at the expense of others' trade, by tolls or piracy. That the Athenian overseas settlements maintained close touch with the home government is implied by Herodotus, who evidently considered the settlements as Athenian possessions rather than as independent states giving priority to their own local interests. Contact between the Hellespont and Attica was facilitated by the winning of staging points. By assisting his ally Lygdamis to become ruler of Naxos, in the Cyclades, Peisistratus gained for Athenian galleys a useful haven and a supply point. By his 'purification' of the nearby island of Delos, he demonstrated that this, the traditional centre of Ionic settlers in the Aegean, was under his effective, if not openly under his administrative control.

This level of overseas expansion is a surprising achievement in a comparatively short period, and set Athens on the road to imperialism. The geographical position of the dependencies she established, points to the supposition that her aims were primarily commercial, since all were conveniently situated for the trading run between Attica and the Hellespont, or Athens and Miletus: this supposition is confirmed by the witness of the archaeological record, and by the evidence we possess bearing on the changing pattern of Attic development at home. No doubt some of the overseas settlements were also agricultural, *e.g.*, that in the Thracian Chersonese, but in this case the cash crop produced there was almost certainly intended for the Athenian market, and its agricultural development was directly related to the needs of Athenian trade.

We are not informed by our literary authorities about the commodities exchanged in this trade, yet all we know of Attic economic development so far points to the conclusion that the basis of Athenian imports was grain and some fish; timber for shipbuilding was also important, and this may explain why Athens, at this early stage of her commercial development, traded with far-away Cyprus. Overseas expansion required a considerable fleet of ships for purposes of transport and defence; but their construction was a costly investment, which could easily turn out to be a dead loss. It was not sufficient merely to provide for the transport of goods to home ports; the loaded ships were a tempting target, and the problem of protecting them rose in direct relation to the value of their cargoes. It is not certain that Athens possessed any state fleet before the time of Peisistratus, but if she did, its purpose was probably confined to patrolling the coasts of Attica.[13] It was left to the entrepreneurs to provide both ships and protection for them on the high seas.

In the first half of the sixth century any war fleet that Athens possessed probably consisted mainly of the combined shipping of the traders: but Peisistratus himself, as a man with overseas interests in his private capacity, must have kept up a private fleet. The latter would be either overtly or covertly supported from state revenue, and was at his disposal in either a private or a governmental capacity. With the blurring of the distinction between the activities of Peisistratus the individual and Peisistratus the ruler, it is easy to imagine the idea becoming accepted that the government of Athens should employ public funds to maintain a fleet of warships for the protection not only of the homeland but also of friendly bases and communications across the sea. By the turn of the century Athens had at its disposal at least fifty ships,[14] and the foundation for future maritime expansion was already laid. The construction of a war fleet in the face of harsh economic difficulties, perhaps at a severe temporary cost to the economy and living standard of Attica, must be accounted as among the most striking achievements of the regime.

As for the exports which were exchanged for the precious grain and timber we can be certain only that pots, and their contents, were among them. Apart from the luxury trade in ornamental vases, the plain amphorae, which the archaeologist's spade has unearthed in such quantities, are mute evidence to the export of Attic oil, wine, and possibly grain itself. If this evidence is considered in connexion with what we know of Peisistratus' resettlement policy, it is clear that the economic tendency here implied is that of increasing the level of overall production by the raising of cash crops for sale in the city and overseas; that is to say, by superimposing upon the existing system of subsistence farming a degree of commercial farming which was calculated to employ under-exploited resources of land and people.

In addition to exporting pottery, wine, and oil, it would be surprising if she failed to continue the lucrative slave trade, except that now the slaves were no longer Attic-born but kidnapped from the islands. An important commodity of export was silver, usually in the form of minted coins: from the point of view of her internal economy, the labour-intensive industry of mining helped to draw into productive activity manpower which had been under-employed: externally, the export of silver enabled Attica to run an unfavourable balance of trade (to import more goods than she exported).

The products which formed the basis of that trade can reasonably be surmised: but any estimate of the terms or balance of trade can be little more than guesswork. The effects of this trade on her external relations have been discussed: it remains to give some estimate of the internal balance-sheet shown by her economic development programme.

In assessing the sources of revenue available to Peisistratus it is hardly worth while attempting to distinguish those which were due to him in his private capacity, and those due in his capacity as head of the state: in his expenditures we must assume that he, like other Greek Tyrants, did not scruple to use public money for his private schemes,[15] and thereby rendered meaningless any theoretical distinction between his public and private income. We must therefore take into account the wealth which flowed into his family from their overseas possessions near the Strymon: these had provided the strength of Peisistratus' final bid for power, and continued to support his position once he had won it.

The main source of his public revenue was the direct tax of 10% (or 5%) levied on agricultural production. This was possibly the first example of direct taxation in Attica, and if the rate was ever indeed 10% the burden on farmers could have been heavy if they did not adapt their habits to take account of the innovation. In effect the tax went more than halfway to reducing the whole landowning population to the old status of Hectemors, and it seems plausible that, as Sandys suggested, the tax was reduced to 5% by Hippias. Even so the total revenue theoretically made available to the central government was by contemporary standards enormous.[16]

The third main source of regular revenue was from state land. The extent of the latter was perhaps increased substantially by Peisistratus through confiscation, and it included the mining land of south-east Attica. At what stage the silver mines in this area had begun to be exploited is quite obscure: we know for certain only that a rich vein of silver was being tapped there early in the fifth century. This vein was, however, almost certainly well below the surface; from the richness of the yield we may assume that it lay at the second level of argentiferous ore, and hence that the higher, and poorer, level had been worked through in earlier times; the antiquity of the Laureion workings was asserted by Xenophon.[17] For this reason it seems likely that the mines were being worked in the mid-sixth century, and we have some grounds for suspecting that Peisistratus drew a substantial part of his revenue from mining. We have noted his active interest in the overseas territory near Mount Pangaeus, and the income he drew from thence; it is hard to believe that this income was derived from other sources than the mines there. If so, one can hardly assume that Peisistratus overlooked the metallic resources of his homeland once he was firmly in the saddle, and it is tempting to associate the wealth of his regime, as expressed in the issue of the large tetradrachm pieces, with the exploitation of the Laureion mines which apparently was under way about this period. Mining was an industry with unique possibilities, since a market for the end product was assured by the demands of the state treasury; mining, however, requires considerable capital investment, since there may be a considerable time-lag between sinking a shaft and reaping the profits. Perhaps a shortage of capital had been the main inhibiting factor so far; but the direct tax on farming supplied an unprecedented flow of capital to the central government, and this was perhaps made available in the form of loans not only to small farmers but also to prospectors. This hypothesis would at least explain the capitalisation and development of the Attic mining industry, which was a fact by the early fifth century.

In addition to direct taxation and income from state property, it is likely that indirect taxation was levied in the form of tolls and customs dues. We have no evidence that this was so, but since this was such a normal feature of public finance elsewhere in Greece, there is a high degree of probability that the method was employed at Athens too; in view of the great increase in the volume of trade, one may assume that tolls were one of the most important sources of revenue to the Tyrants. A lively income was also collected in court fines, and this income was heavily increased by making jurisdiction all over Attica the sole preserve of the state. A form of taxation in the form of unpaid service was perhaps required from all citizens, as it had been in Solon's time: it was perhaps during the Tyranny that assessment ceased to be reckoned solely on the basis of agricultural production, in order to draw upon resident aliens, who could own no land and accordingly would otherwise have been exempt from taxation and service. In case of need the government could call upon the ships of the merchants for purposes of defence, and in addition, the system of the naucraries was reorganised by Peisistratus.[18] Under this system, in later times an individual or a group of individuals with shipping interests, was compelled to provide a ship for the fleet at their own expense. During the Tyranny the first move was made to the provision of a true Attic war fleet; what had been hitherto mainly the collective shipping of the Attic merchants, mobilised in case of state need, now became a fleet.

Against these revenues in money and service must be set the ambitious programme of expenditure which Peisistratus was able to undertake. The largest single item of a recurring nature was the upkeep of his private army—the bodyguard formed from the mercenary troops with which he had invaded Attica. Many of the latter were dismissed once the country had been pacified, and we hear no more of Theban or Argive soldiers in Athens. But the Scythians remained, and eventually the employment of these bowmen as security troops or policemen became an accepted feature of democratic Athens. But in the first instance they were employed by Peisistratus not to apprehend those guilty of breaches of civil law, but to maintain the regime against internal opposition. It would have been in many ways preferable to recruit such forces from the citizen militia, and almost certainly cheaper, but Peisistratus had evidently no desire to put arms into the hands of his own countrymen: as was normally the case in Tyrannies, the bodyguard was not recruited from, but was designed against the citizens.[19] The Scythian archers, pictures of whom now begin to appear on Attic vases, were a drain on state resources which Peisistratus evidently thought unavoidable in view of the internal tension: in spite of the favourable comments by later Greek, and by modern historians, on his regime, the threat of counter-revolution was never so far away that terror could be entirely dispensed with.

In addition to the costs of maintaining internal security were the costs of external defence. The latter were not a heavy drain on government funds; Attica was not attacked by land during Peisistratus' rule, and there was, fortunately for the regime, no reason or excuse for the squires to mobilise the local militia based on the clans.[20] The adventurous policy pursued overseas paid for itself in terms of plunder and cheap food imports: it is true that the profits from the latter went into the pockets of the entrepreneurs (including Peisistratus himself), but the cost of the expeditions was likewise borne by them. We have assumed that some of the general revenue raised by taxation was utilised by Peisistratus for private commercial ventures abroad: the effect of this would be not only to increase his private fortune, but also to assist very considerably the economic development of Attic industry by increasing the quantity of goods exchanged. The pool of urban unemployment which was the result of rural

E

poverty, was thus reduced in so far as the increase of trade necessitated an expansion in the work-force of secondary industry: an increased demand for artisans to produce export pottery, and for seamen to carry it, helped to lower economic and political tension in town and port. In those rural areas which were within convenient distance of the ports, the increased demand for export agricultural products meant the possibility of an increase in farmers' incomes, since wine and oil can be grown on land unsuitable for bread crops, and the yield can be, under favourable conditions of exchange, much more profitable. The expansion of trade, while incidentally filling Peisistratus' private purse, also acted to improve economic conditions not only in the city but also in some parts of the country.

Another aspect of the struggle against poverty was the agricultural scheme which has been discussed above. In effect this was an investment of government capital in rural development by way of loans to small farmers; in the long run the scheme was no drain on public revenue, unless the farmer failed to produce the goods or was unable to market them, and the simultaneous expansion of trade reduced the probability of the latter eventuality. Apart from the hypothetical repayment of the loan, the intensive resettlement of the land meant an increase in total productivity, of which a substantial fraction was returned to the treasury in the form of taxation. It is worth noting that this is the first time that public investment in the land was found necessary, or even practicable: in earlier times it had been the squires themselves who had supplied the loans, and thereby increased the circle of their dependants. The end of this practice had been brought about not only by the demonstrable unwisdom of the policy (the inability of the debtor to repay), but also by the competition for investment capital in trade. Solon, by his law forbidding loans on personal security, had recognised that this form of investment had dried up: but as the increase of trade quickened the demand for rural products, the policy of unsecured rural loans once more became economically practicable, and the state took over the role previously played by private investment.

Agricultural resettlement and the expansion of trade were policies whose long-term effects could go far to solve Attica's economic difficulties. But to achieve something like political stability, drastic short-term methods were also required: if the hungry and unemployed could not be immediately absorbed into productive industry, at least they must be fed. A foretaste of the welfare legislation which was to be so prominent a feature of democratic Athens was an act passed by Peisistratus and ordering that those citizens crippled in war should be maintained at public expense.[21] Just as the squires had lost to the government their role of ruler, creditor, and judge, so too the state took over the responsibility of caring, however inadequately, for its dependants.

Nevertheless, it was no part of Peisistratus' policy to give away money for nothing. The unprecedented amount of capital at his disposal enabled him to undertake an ambitious programme of investment in public construction. Some of his projects were of a generally productive nature from the point of view of Attic long-term development, but our authorities are naturally concerned to mention only his more spectacular buildings, some of which were non-utilitarian in function. The Peisistratids certainly did much to improve Attica's harbour facilities. Very notable was the successful project to improve the water-supply of the city, the construction of the famous fountain of nine springs, and this fact alone, even if we lacked confirmatory evidence, would suggest a significant increase in city population at the time, with all its implications for economic development. Aristotle suggested[22] that the leading motive behind the whole programme of public works was to keep the people too busy to make political mischief, and this judgement is by no means so naïve as it might at first appear. Measures which are economically enlightened can still be brought into being by motives which are primarily non-economic: it was in fact in the interest of Peisistratus, whose rule rested, not on an accepted basis of custom but on force, that the poor should be kept busy, even if the work they did was of little economic advantage to himself or the community.

We therefore find the government launching a programme of works which included the construction of buildings of little utilitarian value. The greatest monuments to the Tyranny were the temple of Athena on the Acropolis, and (the unfinished) temple of Zeus. Money was also spent on a less permanent, but equally spectacular project, the embellishment of the great city festivals. It is to be noted that this served other ends than merely to give employment: the transfer of the Dionysiac festival from rural Eleutherae to Athens gave public recognition to the fact that the peasant culture of the countryside had found a new, and more splendid home in the city. Hitherto, the cultural, as well as the economic centre of the peasantry, had been the village, over which the squire presided as a matter of course; once more the local aristocracy found its functions, and privileges, replaced by the central administration: where men's political and cultural adherence had been local, now it was national. It is a matter of interest that a festival singled out for especial celebration in the city was that in honour of Dionysus: subsistence farming centred on the production of grains, of which Demeter was the spiritual symbol, but wine is a product typical of commercial farming, and its habitat is normally not the plains, stronghold of aristocratic tradition, but the hillsides. The inauguration of the Great Panathenaic festival in all its splendour likewise symbolised the union of Attica, with Athens its undoubted leader, and Peisistratus the head of a centralised government: it would be hard to over-estimate the value of this union, and of the acceptance of it, for the development of the country. The festivals thus served as a type of propaganda for the regime, dazzling the masses and outshining the tarnished splendour of local despots as the moon outshines the stars. A similar effect was produced by the brilliance of the court which assembled around the Tyrant—singers, artists, poetasters attracted by his patronage. But irrespective of the motives behind this policy, its practice revealed a new note of luxury in Athenian life; the cult of leisure and the pursuit of refined enjoyment by its more fortunate members.

The general trends of development under the Peisistratids are clear enough, although many details are necessarily obscure. There is evidence of city growth, penetration of overseas domains, a diffusion of Attic trade abroad and increasing Attic prosperity at home. The struggle against poverty was far from over, but the development of trade indicated a way in which, given favourable conditions, it could be overcome. Within Attica the distribution of wealth had been forcibly altered by taxing the farmers and reallocating some of the income thus obtained to non-agricultural workers. It was the farmers who, through taxation, built the new roads and temples and employed urban labour on productive and unproductive projects. The traders, with their profits, were building the ships necessary to an increase in the volume of trade and the consequent specialisation of rural production which was to be the basis of Athenian wealth. At the same time the accumulation of capital at the centre made possible a widening programme of investment both in agriculture and mining.

Capital investment is a characteristic feature of the Tyranny at Athens; but not only was much progress made towards solving the chronic problem of inadequate capital accumulation and underinvestment; the redistribution of income at home through public works programmes, although a temporary measure aimed at political stability, was to have important consequences in the trend towards equalising living standards. Economically an important result was to stimulate city demand for the products of the countryside, and hence to encourage rural productivity by increasing the local market; politically it paved the way for an egalitarian, if not a democratic society. An important achievement of the regime was to increase rural productivity by loaning the necessary capital for development; and although the problem of capital formation was not entirely overcome under the Tyranny, the first, and most difficult steps, were taken towards solving it. The taxation of the farming community was a desperate measure which must have reduced their already meagre living standards in the first instance: the policy was practicable only because capital was being simultaneously diverted into trade expansion, as well as in increasing local demand so that what farmers lost as a class they regained (though not necessarily as individuals) by the expansion of the market for cash crops which could be easily and economically produced. The worst sufferers were subsistence farmers in the outback of Attica, since they paid the same taxes as those living near the city or port but, by reason of their remoteness, were in a poor position to profit by raising cash crops for sale in town or abroad.

It is not surprising that such men should have received the worst treatment at Peisistratus' hands, for the more remote they were from the capital, the less important was their political influence. It was not pleasant for the ruler to find opposition to himself in the country, but it was much better than meeting opposition in the city, the control of which was vital for the existence of the regime. One of the most striking features of the Tyranny was the acceptance of this novel principle that city interests were paramount; that what was good for Athens was good for Attica; and that, in fact, Athens *was* Attica in the emotional, mystical sense symbolised by the Panathenaic festival. It should be noted that the success of the whole programme turned on the fact that, although all Attica contributed to the capital raised by the regime, much of the investment was concentrated on Athens and the ports which fed her. This investment programme was economically sound, since capital was being mainly applied at the point where it could do most good rather than frittered away at a number of points. Yet only an authoritarian regime could have carried out the programme which Peisistratus undertook, and the successful operation of the principle of dictatorship was not a pleasant lesson to be written into the history of a state which was to aspire to democracy. Politically, the authoritarian methods used inevitably involved a self-perpetuating system of repression, reaction against which was a continual danger to the regime itself. Economically the preferential treatment given to city interests was calculated to attract to the town the most enterprising spirits of the countryside and to induce them to abandon farming, the basic industry of the state. It was good that the city should be able to absorb surplus labour from the country, but there is a limit to the beneficial operation of this process and this limit is reached when the rural economy itself, on which the city depends, begins to be damaged by the drain on its resources and by the neglect of its owners. That day was still far distant when Peisistratus died, but the policy to which he showed the way, of giving automatic priority to city interests, was to have ominous effects on later Attic development. The eager use which demagogues were to make of it, and the accelerated pace of its operation were, a century later, to reach their own fantastic climax when Pericles was to abandon the rural industry of the Attic countryside in the interests of defending the city of Athens.

IV

THE NEW ORDER

IN spite of the economic progress which the Peisistratid administration had made possible, its authority rested on decidedly insecure foundations. The direct taxation levied on the farming population could hardly fail to alienate its sympathies even if, as seems likely, the rate was reduced by Hippias. Those settlers who had received government loans were faced with a bitter struggle to meet their obligations of capital repayment, together with interest and taxation; the majority were probably working newly planted land, and the waiting period before the farms became fully productive was a critical one. However, we are hardly justified in assuming that rural conditions were aggravated by depressed food prices due to foreign imports. While this may be true of certain local areas, especially those near city and port, it was not true of the farming area as a whole. Much of Attica's grain land was too far from the city market to be seriously affected, and the increasing number of non-subsistence farmlets producing wine and oil assured the grain farmers of an expanding local market for their product. But the future of the non-subsistence farmer was a precarious one. Those on the land who were opening up new agricultural areas, or were turning marginal grain land into vineyards, were in effect building up their own capital and the capital of Attica as a whole; their efforts were directed into investment in the future of the country rather than into present consumption. Yet amid their harsh conditions they had, unless specially exempted, to pay taxes for the development of the city, and to them it must often have seemed that their main efforts went to feed the tax-collector and the middleman.

Fortunately for the Peisistratids, both the topography of

Attica and the rivalry of her petty dynasts made improbable a sufficient degree of rural solidarity to topple the government. Provided that the support of the city population could be kept, the regime was reasonably safe against internal opposition. To protect it against external intervention the government seems to have relied mainly on paid foreign soldiers. The old Attic militia, drawn from the farming population and officered by the squires, was not a force on which the Tyrants could call with any assurance: those members of the population who resided permanently in the city (as opposed to those farmers who kept up a home there) were exempt from military service under the Solonian constitution, and we know of no administrative organisation provided by the Tyrants to recruit them. Ultimately the regime depended on hired security troops to protect it from outside invaders as well as from the Athenians themselves.

As long as urban conditions were kept tolerable, the issue might never be pressed, and later writers comment on the mild and enlightened atmosphere of Peisistratid rule. But after the assassination of Hipparchus the situation deteriorated, and repression increased: many citizens were put to death, and Hippias himself began to prepare the way for possible withdrawal abroad if the situation should demand it. But the fall of the regime, when it came, was brought about by outside intervention led by an exiled member of the Athenian aristocracy.

The Alcmaeonids were among the most distinguished of the Attic squires. Although they had at one time been in alliance with Peisistratus, they had subsequently helped to engineer his expulsion, and had themselves been exiled after the latter's final restoration. When the Alcmaeonids finally returned to Attica they, like the Peisistratids, came back richer than when they had left. Although their position rested on their farms in Attica, they seem to have succeeded in improving their financial position even when they were cut off from them. How they were able to do this remains something of a mystery; of their activities abroad we know only that they contracted for the rebuilding of the temple at Delphi which had been destroyed by fire in 548 B.C. It is easy to believe, as Aristotle suggests, that they enriched themselves from this venture, and it would have been rather unbusinesslike on their part if they had failed to profit from it. But the fact that they were able to undertake the contract at all implies that they were not without wealth and influence, even in exile, and it is difficult to believe that this wealth could have been derived from their farms in Attica at the time. The family had a record of association in ventures overseas, even in distant Lydia, and this suggests that for some time previously their economic activities had not been confined to farming their own land. With their wealth, however gained, they were in a position to raise troops for an invasion of Attica. In addition their peculiar position at Delphi enabled them to exercise indirect pressure on the representatives of other states which sent to consult the oracle.

Their first attempt was a failure: after seizing a centre of resistance in the Attic countryside they were forced to withdraw outside its frontiers. Whatever feelings the Attic farmers might have towards the regime, they evidently failed to display tremendous enthusiasm for a foreign invading force which, if successful, could be expected to do little but change the ruling dynasty.[1]

The Alcmaeonids' second attempt was on a more ambitious scale. Realising that the real key to Attica lay in the control of Athens, they aimed their assault at the capital by a sea landing at Phaleron. At this point it is not possible to separate the machinations of the Alcmaeonids from the vagaries of Spartan external policy. The Alcmaeonid leader Cleisthenes was supported by a force of Spartan soldiers; and both Aristotle and Plutarch believed that the influence of Delphi had induced the Spartan government to support the venture; but no doubt the payment which Cleisthenes was able to offer was an important factor in gaining the support of their troops. Whatever the motive behind the Spartan intervention, its failure was a blot upon their national prestige. It was the riders of Thessaly, said to be a thousand in number, who drove the invading forces into the sea. Once more the regime was saved, and the Attic peasantry had the disagreeable spectacle of their fate being decided by the clash of foreign armies on Attic soil, each directed or instigated by an Attic dynast.

The third attack on Athens was a full-scale assault led by one of the Spartan kings, Cleomenes. The presence of the latter suggests that this invasion was no longer an attempted *coup* by a would-be ruler backed by a force of subsidised allies, but a war of Sparta against Athens. The influence of Cleisthenes and the Alcmaeonids was now marginal, and Cleomenes was not necessarily committed to restoring them to their estates, much less to imposing Cleisthenes as head of the Athenian state in place of Hippias. The invasion was by land, presumably with the blessing of Megara: this time the issue was decided in favour of the invader by the defeat and withdrawal of the Thessalians.

Abandoned by its allies the regime was isolated in its own land. The Spartan force pushed on to the city of Athens, apparently without serious resistance, and was joined by some sections of the Attic people. After some negotiation the Peisistratids agreed to withdraw from the country and left for their property at Sigeion in the Troad.

Their withdrawal left Attica in a situation possibly unique in her history. A country which had hitherto been divided in the local allegiances its people owed to the various ruling families was now for administrative and practical purposes a unity. Yet this unity was the result of two generations of authoritarian rule from the centre: with the fall of the regime the danger existed that the country could again be divided by the centrifugal pull of the Attic dynasts. Sufficient time had elapsed to enable the economy of the country to be geared to its new political pattern, that is to say that more of the land was being used for cash crops, the disposal of which required freedom of movement and trade between districts, and between Athens and the outside world. If Attica had returned to its old pattern of political power this economic trend would have been reversed, the result would have been an inevitable degree of economic chaos in the countryside, and the city of Athens would have lost some of its reason for existence as the administrative and economic centre of the country.

One factor working against any tendency to return to the old division of Attica was the attitude of the city dwellers themselves. It appears to be a phenomenon of general validity that once economic or political conditions result in the collection of a city populace, there is the utmost reluctance on the part of the latter to abandon the town, even when the conditions which brought about this situation are no longer in operation. The population of Athens had a strong vested interest in the maintenance of centralised government, since on it depended the system of internal and external exchange of goods which fed the city, and any interruption of trade would have brought home to the city folk a realisation of the dependence. The political influence of the urban population was an important, probably a decisive factor in deciding the course of events. It might therefore have been expected that the fall of the Tyranny would result not in disintegration, but rather in the establishment of a new centralised government by a successor to the Peisistratids. This was almost certainly the intention of Cleisthenes in hazarding his life and fortune to attempt a return. But once the Spartan troops had occupied the city, a struggle for power developed between members of two rival families. The details of this struggle between Cleisthenes, the Alcmaeonid, and Isagoras are known to us only in briefest outline. Apparently Cleisthenes was being worsted when he finally had recourse to a political weapon of incalculable consequences, the support of the city population itself. This was indeed a strange *volte-face* for an aristocratic leader, yet it was a logical consequence of Cleisthenes' past actions: again and again he had been drawn into imitation of Peisistratus' own career. The appeal for popular support recalls the policy, followed by the Tyrants, of conciliating the city populace as far as possible. But whereas Peisistratus had been able to follow a policy in which conciliation was balanced with repression, the latter was hardly within Cleisthenes' power. Peisistratus had kept effective control of the situation by his hired troops, and the conciliation which he practised was by way of being a minimum concession to avoid the dangers of an internal explosion. Cleisthenes, however, had no mercenaries under his command, and owed his return to a foreign army whose deployment was quite out of his control: indeed it was Isagoras whom the Spartans were disposed to support. Hence the concessions which Cleisthenes had to offer to enlist popular support were many times greater than those envisaged by Peisistratus. The ultimate price was in fact the continuance of the economic benefits bestowed upon the city by the Tyrants, without the repression which had made possible the economic reorganisation involved.

The tussle between the adherents of Isagoras and Cleisthenes seems to have continued for three years after the expulsion of

Hippias. The Spartan troops had long since returned home, and the logic which drove Cleisthenes to embrace the popular cause perhaps provoked Isagoras to a rival programme of concessions. At any rate he appears to have achieved considerable success and was elected Archon in the year 508. At this stage Cleisthenes seems to have appealed for support over the head of his rival, now the chief magistrate: by this appeal against elected authority he set himself against the constitution of Solon, and as a last resort offered a series of amendments to it which apparently conferred upon the city populace supreme control over the affairs of the whole country.

A curious factor in the situation was the inaction of the rural population: throughout the crisis the appeal of the two leaders was to the city, neither seems to have called out the armed manpower of his local following. Perhaps neither of the leaders could count on support from their family estates large enough to affect the dangerous situation in the city. For the first time Attica was seeing the counterplay of political leaders who were forced to cajole and guide, rather than command their following. The economic development of Athens which the Tyranny had promoted, had incidentally raised up a giant which a shaky government was in no position to control. The collecting of a large urban pressure group without traditions of implicit obedience to aristocratic leadership coincided, on the fall of the Peisistratids, with a power vacuum at the centre of urban administration. It was less than a century since Attica had presented a feudal aspect of decentralised control by a ruling squirarchy: now by contrast the squires, no longer tied to their traditional estates, were outbidding each other in grotesque competition for the support of the urban masses. Whatever solution was reached it could only be favourable to the latter, unless massive outside intervention could quell the city populace, and a new regime of oppression could be inaugurated with the help of a new security force.

An appeal of Isagoras to Sparta for troops did not go unanswered. The Spartan king himself ordered the banishment of Cleisthenes and a number of other Athenians: a small Spartan force entered the city and proceeded to carry out a purge said to involve seven hundred Attic families: at the same time new constitutional proposals were put forward. For the first time during the crisis the forces of popular resistance were now effectively mobilised, and an ugly situation developed, with Isagoras, the chief magistrate, together with the Spartan troops, being blockaded in the Acropolis. A massacre was avoided when, after two days, the Spartans agreed to withdraw, leaving the followers of Isagoras to their fate. The Archon himself escaped with the Spartans; his followers were arrested and killed. Cleisthenes and other exiles were recalled, and the stage was set for a political settlement in favour of the city populace which, by a successful resort to violence against its own elected magistrate, had for the first time demonstrated the decisive nature of its power.

Even if Cleisthenes nursed hopes of becoming a Tyrant himself after the fashion of Peisistratus, the fate of Isagoras' supporters was a clear warning to step cautiously in his dealings with the mob, at least temporarily in the ascendant. The essence of the problem which underlay any settlement was how to maintain the centralised administration of Attica, without which chaos would result, while at the same time keeping some kind of order and control in Athens, and persuading the farmers in the country to go on producing for the city market. A prolonged period of chaos in the city was likely to induce farmers to return to subsistence farming, and this would have spelt ruin for the city; both because essential food would not have been forthcoming from the Attic countryside, and because the flow of exports, hence of imports, would have dried up. The only practical alternatives seemed to be the reconquest of Athens by an external force, or a reconciliation between the dissident local dynasts on the one hand and the turbulent city population on the other. The first of these alternatives had been unsuccessfully attempted by Isagoras: with the departure of the Spartans there appeared to be no immediate possibility of a solution imposed from without. The most pressing task facing Cleisthenes, or any other would-be ruler, was the restoration of law and order in the city after the ominous precedent set by the forcible expulsion of the chief magistrate and the liquidation of his supporters.

Second in importance only to the problem of restoring law and order was that of getting the administration of Attica running smoothly again. Whatever success the Peisistratids had achieved in this field they owed to the strength of their central-ised administration, its monopoly of power, and its ruthlessness in carrying out decisions made at the centre. If the only forces at the disposal of the government were now citizen forces, some degree of power must be returned to the people; consent rather than repression must be the keynote of the new administration. This involved a serious danger that measures beneficial to the economy, but unpopular with the people, would lapse; *e.g.* the taxation imposed on primary production, which had yielded the capital needed to build up the country's resources. We lose sight of taxation at this point and the probability is that it was a casualty of the democratic regime. Yet possibly a greater danger was the centrifugal impulse induced by local patriotism and dynastic intrigue. The loyalty of the rural peasant was prima-rily to his deme, clan, or brotherhood, rather than to the state as such. If repression was no longer a practicable policy, the unity of Attica could ultimately be preserved only by a constitution which enlisted the co-operation of the whole citizen body; above all, the mass of urban dwellers, whose allegiance was un-certain, must be drawn into co-operation with the peasants and the gentry, on whom they ultimately depended for most of their food.

Before the citizen body could be usefully organised at all, a new definition of citizenship was necessary. Traditionally a citizen was one who owned a share in the land of Attica, a definition natural to a state still in a condition of subsistence agriculture. This situation had already been outdated by the course of events, and the assumption that land ownership was an essential qualification for full citizen rights was no longer realistic. Soon after the expulsion of Hippias an attempt had been made to purge the citizen body of those who were regarded as not having a proper claim to full citizen rights: reversing this policy Cleisthenes now admitted formally to the citizen body many new members, including new settlers and ex-slaves. The fundamental question was thus settled in favour of those who had been struggling on the margin of full citizenship, those whose claims the establishment had hitherto failed to recognise. The policy of Cleisthenes in according them full citizen rights and duties was a recognition in law of the changed social and economic pattern of Attic society, and meant that henceforth the control of the state would be shared between both the rural and the urban populations.

Recognition of a new principle of citizenship was only the first move in a programme of constitutional reform. In Athens, as in Sparta, the ultimate right of law-making had been at least theoretically in the hands of a popular assembly of all the citizens. From the time of Cleisthenes the popular assembly becomes truly sovereign in the sense that its approval to motions submitted to it is not always a formality. During the Tyranny the function of the assembly had been rather to allow decisions already reached to become known to as many people as possible, since the vast majority of the citizens could not read any published decree. The removal of the central authority of the Tyrants gave the assembly an opportunity of using its traditional privilege in a way which enabled it actually to influence them. Few would have been so hardy or so silly as to dispute any decision put before them by Peisistratus, with his armed bodyguard around him to 'keep order'; but once the Tyranny was no more, and the bodyguard dispersed, the situation was transformed. As before, the decisions or proposals would come from a ruling body, but their acceptance would no longer be automatic.

Membership of the assembly was open to all citizens, hence the importance of Cleisthenes' formal enfranchisement of those whose status had hitherto been ambiguous. On the other hand participation in its proceedings was clearly open, as a regular thing, only to those dwelling in or near the city; yet its decisions were binding on the whole state. Thus the unified administration of the state was able to be maintained in this way, the heirs to final central power being (at least in theory) the citizens of Athens itself. Dwellers in the countryside of Attica, in Eleusis or Marathon, would possibly never have accepted a state of things in which decisions affecting them were made in Athens, if it had not been for the memory of the strong central control to which they had been accustomed during the Tyranny. Yet in the spirit of conciliation which underlay the Cleisthenic programme, safeguards were built into the new constitution to give maximum protection to local rural interests.

The assembly had been accustomed to give a simple vote on measures already prepared for it. In place of the departed

67

Tyrant some new authority was required to carry out the task of preparing measures for submission to the assembly; but if the latter was to do more than passively receive legislation (*i.e.*, act as a forum of publication) if indeed it was to consider each motion laid before it, a body was required to act as a steering committee. There is no reason to suppose that it was intended to formulate policy: this would remain in the hands of the chief magistrates, drawn from the wealthiest classes, the landed gentry who were still regarded as the state's natural leaders. A committee drawn from the whole citizen body was a symbol of the reconciliation between the various class and local interests of Attica: in exercising its important function of preparing business for the assembly, it was in an excellent position to safeguard the interests of all sections of the community which it represented.

The steering committee, or Council, established by Cleisthenes was recruited on the basis of a redivision, or redefinition, of the citizen population in accordance with its existing geographical distribution. The new arrangements recognised three main areas of population—the area of the greater city, that of the coast, and that of the hinterland: each of these areas was divided into ten sections (the so-called trittyes), and ten new 'tribes' were constituted, each containing one section from the three areas. Thus the urban (including the landless) population was drawn into the framework of responsibility for the conduct of affairs. Its importance was recognised in that it was represented in every tribe, but for constitutional purposes its solidarity was broken, since it was to be in a minority in each one: each tribe was to nominate 50 members annually for the Council, making the enormous total of 500 members in all.

The new constitution thus gave overt protection and representation to rural interests, though in practice the urban members of each tribal delegation would be in a stronger position in debate, through their greater familiarity with the workings of the constitution. On the other hand the urban members of the Council themselves could hardly be expected to act without advice, and the rapid turnover of their membership made it unlikely that they would have much opportunity of organising themselves during their year of office into a strong pressure group. Thus in the committee which was to act as a brake on the assembly, both urban and upper-class interests could be expected to be well protected.

It seems that the heirs to the power of the departed Tyrant were neither the assembly nor the Council; although both these bodies were bastions of the coming democracy, in that they had at their disposal constitutional power which, if still largely theoretical, could yet be called into action if the situation one day demanded it. In a sense they supplied a safety valve, so that the violent surge of popular feeling which had resulted in Isagoras' overthrow, would in future find outlet in constitutional and bloodless action. The power vacuum left by Hippias was filled by individuals, all drawn from that class of men who were traditionally experienced in government. A feature of Cleisthenes' settlement was the revival of the powers of the Archons, the old chief magistrates whose powers had been in eclipse during the Tyranny. The nine Archons, who were annually elected by the assembly, were still chosen only from the top property classes. From the ex-archons was recruited the supreme court of the Areopagus. Thus by the terms of Cleisthenes' constitution, the political initiative remained in the hands of the old aristocracy: the rule of one family all over Attica had been overthrown: in its place was set constitutional rule by the gentry acting in agreement both with each other and with the urban populace. The form of the constitution was democratic, its practice aristocratic; yet the rule of the land-owning aristocrats now rested on a degree of consent. In the last resort it depended on the support of the new militia, which was recruited on the basis of the new tribes, each tribe contributing one regiment. The townsfolk were thus distributed among all the regiments, and these continued to be commanded by the rural gentry. To some extent then the solidarity of the urban block was broken down for military, as well as for electoral purposes. In any case no arms were put into the hands of the urban proletariat: only hoplites and horsemen were recruited, and the assessments of Solon, now perhaps converted into money terms,[2] were still used to fix a minimum income qualification for military service.

From one point of view Cleisthenes' reforms can be described as conservative, in that they left the real power in the hands of the old ruling families, acting with the support of the middle economic group. On the other hand the reforms mark a great step forward; for the new constitution enabled the centralised administration of the state to continue, with the consent of the urban populace and without the repression found necessary by the Tyrants. This constitution, although leaving leadership in the hands of the nobles, yet provided a political framework within which the changing economic organisation of the state was able to function. It likewise provided the means for peaceful adaptation of the constitution to keep it in line with future developments. The citizens of Athens could claim that they were sovereign over the affairs of Attica, so that Athens already had the form of a democracy. The limitation of the highest magistracy to the gentry, and the local influence which the latter still possessed over their humbler fellow citizens, ensured that for a long time to come the sovereignty of the people would be limited mainly to choosing between policies put forward by rival aristocrats. Yet the day might come when they would dare to reject all this advice, and elect to follow the leadership of one of their own number. In Cleisthenes' lifetime that day was still distant, but when it arrived, the aristocratic support which his constitution now enjoyed would certainly be revised. But before then the economic changes ushered in by the Tyranny, and now able to continue, would so have progressed as to transform the structure of Athenian society in a way perhaps inconceivable to an observer of the sixth century.

V

THE PREPARATIONS FOR WAR

URING the troubled times of Solon and Peisistratus economic problems had loomed so large, and so obviously influenced political actions, that they had forced their way even on to the pages of the Greek historians. For the thirty years which followed the expulsion of Hippias we have practically no literary evidence directly concerned with the economic development of Athens. Our knowledge of that development is based on the archaeological record, such as it is, and on deductions drawn from the external activities of the Athenians during this period. In the narrative of these years the power of Persia assumes a role of increasing importance.

Before the fall of the Tyranny an incident had occurred in north-east Greece which illustrates the interest of the Athenian government in the control of this region. The Thracian Chersonese, commanding the Hellespont, had been governed autocratically by the Athenian *émigré* Miltiades. After his death, and the death of his successor, the younger Miltiades left Athens with the help of the Peisistratids and became the new ruler of the Chersonese: he was able to crush local opposition after his arrival, and to maintain his authority with the aid of hired Greek troops. The fact that a successor was sent from Athens by the Athenian government shows the dependence of the Chersonese administration on the home government, and the interest felt by the latter in maintaining its ties with the dependency. Like Hippias, Miltiades relied on a mercenary army, but there was little chance that this force could protect him from the authority of the Persian government, if it chose to intervene.

Persian power had reached the Aegean some thirty-six years before the fall of Hippias. In 523 a Persian naval force had driven out the ruler of Samos. In 514–13 the Persian king Darius took an army across the Bosporus into Europe, struck inland and crossed the Danube to invade Scythia. The entry of Persian power into the Aegean, and its control of the Greek-settled north-east, could not but affect the conduct of trade through the Hellespont, the interests of Athenian settlers, and the supply of food to Athens itself. The entry of a giant imperial power on to the scene was no doubt an alarming development to settlers and traders who now became dependent for the first time on Persian goodwill. On the other hand there was the hope of greater stability and an end of the chaos caused by inter-city feuds; at the same time a formidable sea force was in being (the Phoenician) which could effectively put down piracy. There was apparently no reason why Greek settlements near the Hellespont should necessarily have to fear Persian authority. The Persian government had so far shown no inclination to submerge the subject peoples as national groups by denying them their own cultural identity or spiritual aspirations.[1] The Persian government showed no interest in restricting or mani-pulating for its own special advantage, the sea-going traffic plying with its Aegean ports. As members of the Persian empire the Greek cities on the Ionian coast were enjoying considerable prosperity, and were in touch with markets far beyond the limits of the Greek world. In any case resistance to Persia was a highly dangerous business, and we might expect to find some co-operation on the part of the Greek traders and settlers' governments towards Persia.

Evidence for such co-operation is to be found in the report that the Athenian settler Miltiades fought in the king's service on the Danube expedition. Hippias had likewise allied himself by a marriage connexion with the ruler of Lampsacus. We have no evidence which would lead us to suppose that Athenian commerce was seriously affected before 510 B.C. by the great changes in the north-east ushered in by the arrival of Persian authority, and it might be expected that commercial risks would be lessened by the imposition of the *pax Persica* at sea. But the withdrawal of Hippias to Sigeion after his expulsion brought about a new and strange situation. The Athenian settlements in the Troad were now in the hands of a pretender government, bitterly opposed to the home government. Across the Hellespont was Miltiades, the former associate of Hippias, who had apparently enjoyed the latter's favour at home,[2] and had been helped to power in the Chersonese by Hippias. After the fall of the regime, Miltiades could hardly hope to be friendly with both Hippias and Athens: both the Athenian governments sought the support of Persia, and we find deputations from Athens waiting on the Persian court in 508 and again in 500 B.C. Persian preference was for Hippias, and when they came out openly in his favour, the home government in Athens was thereby automatically branded as illegal in Persian eyes and became the official enemy of the Great King. But in spite of Persian threats it is doubtful whether there was in 500 B.C. any serious intention of action to unseat the Athenian democratic government; at any rate some years passed before any such move was made. But the position of Athenian trade with the Hellespont was affected; Athenian traders no longer could safely operate near Sigeion.

The fall of the Peisistratid dynasty was followed by the loss of the miniature trading empire which Athens had built up during the regime, and before the full assertion of Persian authority in the Hellespontine region and along the coast of western Asia Minor. The restriction of Athenian influence overseas was also perhaps connected with a decline in her naval power. Ships which had belonged to Hippias and his associates presumably sailed away to Sigeion with him: in the chaos which followed the expulsion perhaps other Athenian ship-owners also staged a prudent withdrawal from the scene. In the case of entrepreneurs plying the Peiraeus – Hellespont route the situation became difficult when the two terminals were in the hands of powers hostile to each other, and a decline in the level of trade between Athens and the north-east may be indicated by the archaeological record, which shows a falling-off in the quantity of Athenian Black Figure vases found at Russian sites and dated to the period 510 to 480 B.C. The evidence, however, is far from conclusive.[3]

The urban section of the Attic population, which had increased during the commercial expansion of the Tyranny, depended for its sustenance on the transport of food from the country districts of Attica and from overseas. How far these arrangements had been shaken by the civil strife remains uncertain; but it may be significant that about the end of the sixth century, Athens, which under the Peisistratids had avoided a major clash with any mainland power, now begins to pursue an adventurous policy of aggrandisement at the expense of her neighbours. This was probably the moment when she accepted the alliance with Plataea, on the other side of her northern mountain frontier.[4] Her victory over the Theban forces which attacked Attica in consequence was followed by the annexation of Hysiae.[5] Athenian troops crossed to Euboea during the same campaign and annexed a strip of rich agricultural land to which an army of Athenian settlers was subsequently sent.[6] This planting of an agricultural colony at Chalcis marks a new departure in Athenian policy, the use of her land forces to increase her own farming area. It is also possible that the possession of Oropus dates from this time.

We can only guess what part was played in these ventures by the necessity to replace imported food by supplies grown nearer at hand. No doubt the causes for the Athenian actions were complex: as far as the war with Boeotia was concerned, there were probably long-standing causes of friction, *e.g.*, the rivalry of Attic and Boeotian shepherds and goatherds on the mountain pastures which separated their territories. The fact is that by the end of the century Athens was in a powerful position to assert her rights on land, for she now possessed a citizen militia force more formidable than ever before. This was the result of increased overall population; of improved economic conditions which enabled a higher percentage of the population, as compared with a century earlier, to equip themselves with hoplite gear; and, above all, of a more centralised administration, as a result of which a government in Athens was able to call on the resources of all Attica in a way that would have been impossible in the time of Solon.

The strength of Athens on land does not seem to have been matched by her strength at sea, and she found it hard to defend her coast against the raiding vessels of Aegina. Yet in 498 we find an Athenian expedition of 20 ships sailing across the Aegean to assist an Ionian revolt against Persia. An observer might well have regarded this expedition as insane for a state in Athens' position, and the motives which inspired it have never been satisfactorily explained in terms of logic. At any rate the consequences of the venture, which succeeded in burning the town of Sardis, were unfortunate for Athens. Whatever the original motives for the expedition, to the Persians the affair seemed an outrage, an act of vandalism typical of the sea raiders who infested the Aegean; and the origin of the raiders was marked down for punishment. To compound the problems of the Athenian government, their settlers were now seeking to occupy the islands of Lemnos and Imbros in the northern Aegean. In this operation Miltiades acted as the self-appointed agent of the home government, and thus declared himself openly the enemy of both Hippias and the Persians.[7] In due course he was driven from his dominion in the Chersonese and reached Athens as a refugee. Meantime across the Aegean the Ionian states, after laying the foundation for a promising experiment in federal organisation, were finally brought to heel at the battle of Lade in 494. The fate which befell Miletus was, as it turned out, to be rather convenient for Athens in the long run; but at the time she could only savour with unpleasant foreboding the prospects of a similar fate for herself. This fate seemed to be imminent in 490, when the Persian armament moved westwards across the Aegean and after landing in Euboea, destroyed the city of Eretria, which had eight years previously joined with Athens in the support of the Ionian rebels. In the event Athens was saved by her hoplite militia at Marathon, and no further attempts were made to extend Persian sovereignty to the Greek mainland for a decade. The Persians were very obliging enemies, and their destruction of Eretria, like that of Miletus, removed a powerful competitor from Athens' path, and left her in a strong position to work her will in Euboea, even though her settlers there had suffered temporary loss.

The years between 490 and 480 saw a great increase in Athenian sea power with important results for her future development. The failure of the Phoenician fleet to extend the *pax Persica* to the western Aegean left a somewhat confused situation there, in which conditions were more favourable for privateering than normal trading.[8] It is in the light of this fact that we may regard the Athenian raid on Paros, following the victory at Marathon. The aims of the raid, as mentioned by Herodotus, were frankly predatory; and the complete failure of the venture resulted in the punishment of its leader Miltiades. The incident is interesting as illustrating the apparently anarchic conditions at sea, conditions thoroughly bad for any economy based on overseas trade. We hear of desultory war with Aegina, in which Aeginetan vessels sail along the Attic coast, wreck the installations at Phaleron, and kidnap the sacred vessel on its way to Sunium. The lawless conditions prevailing at sea, the war with Aegina, and the long-term threat of Persian reprisals all played their part in persuading the democratic government at Athens in 484 to take the historic decision to build at public expense an armada of warships.

This decision must be seen in the context not only of the troubled conditions at sea, but also in the light of Athens' decline as a sea power since the Tyranny. The fleet of the Peisistratids had long since disintegrated, and had not been replaced by the democratic government, both because it failed to see the long-term advantages of protecting Athenian overseas commerce, and because it was reluctant to invest public money in the expensive equipment of a fleet: the hoplite democracy naturally preferred to rely mainly on its citizen land force. We do not know what force of warships Athens possessed before 484, but in all probability many of the ships on which she relied for defence were privately owned,[9] and such ships, although liable to be commandeered when required for defence purposes, were in fact often outside the effective control of the government. They were readily available for a supposedly lucrative raid, like that on Sardis or Paros, but when serious trouble threatened from Persia or Aegina, they were prudently absent. Furthermore, apart from ships built for privateering, most of the privately owned vessels were cargo ships, designed more for capacity than speed or manoeuvrability, and their reliance on sail made them an easy target for a fast oar-driven vessel. Until late in the sixth century the most powerful navies of Greece still relied on 50-oared galleys (pentekonters), but by 490 the conditions of sea warfare had been quite transformed by the introduction of triremes on a considerable scale. The latter achieved greater speed by the provision of increased motive power without lengthening the vessel to such an extent as to make it unmanoeuvrable and practically unseaworthy.[10] The triremes were in 484 B.C. the most modern and fastest ships afloat and their provision in any numbers would make Athens a formidable sea power overnight. The decision taken by Athens was to build 100 of these ships.[11]

A construction programme of these dimensions would entail the assembly of skilled craftsmen, the conveyance of timber, mainly from overseas, and the building of shelters for the ships,[12] for these would hardly be left afloat to ride out the winter seas: in addition to the hull there was a considerable quantity of equipment to be provided, some of which involved imported materials, e.g., linen and fibres for sails and ropes. Each ship would require a complement of oars amounting to about 200, including spares; i.e., at least 20,000 oars were needed for the new fleet. While the ships were being built, crews would have to be trained.

It was an accepted tradition at Athens that public money could be spent on coastal defence, and as recently as 494 a programme of building and fortification had been undertaken at the Peiraeus.[13] But the naval rearmament programme of ten years later called for an economic effort on a different scale, and involved the diversion of manpower and of material resources for years to come. It was to be a crash programme (our authorities believe that the fleet was in action within four years of the decision to commence building), but the maintenance of the ships and of their shore facilities was a long-term policy. The importing of the necessary materials, over and above what could be supplied from local resources, directly involved the Athenian democratic government, perhaps for the first time, in the problems of overseas commerce. Although the goods would be conveyed by private traders, the safety of the cargoes and hence the security of the shipping lanes, was now a matter of direct concern to the government, for a breakdown in the shipping services could have been fatal to the rearmament programme itself.

The ship-building programme was fully financed, according to our sources, by the proceeds of a new silver strike in the mines of Laureion. This mining area had apparently been worked since at least the time of Peisistratus, and it may seem strange that a major strike should have occurred in an area which had been under exploitation for over half a century. Three layers of argentiferous ore have been detected in these workings, each covered by a layer of limestone: the top, and least rich layer of ore, was probably tapped by open-cut methods in the sixth century after its presence had been revealed by surface erosion:

and it has been conjectured that the workings on the second layer were begun on a large scale about the time of the Persian invasion: (this would agree with the meagre references to its later workings, from which we learn that yield fell significantly later in the fifth century, but revived during the fourth century). The mining land was the sole property of the state, but was leased to small-scale operators under conditions of considerable obscurity. According to Aristotle the state gained a revenue of 100 talents ($=2\frac{1}{2}$ tons of silver) in 484, but we do not know how this revenue was obtained (whether by sale of leases, or tax on production, as seems to have been the case in the fourth century): nor do we know what percentage of the total silver yield it represents, nor whether it was an annual yield or an accumulated surplus. All we know for certain is that the actual income to the treasury arising out of the mining workings was at this time dramatically increased, and that for the rest of the century it remained an outstanding source of Athenian public income. The surest evidence for this is the noticeable acceleration of her development from this point: but the significance of the silver workings is attested in contemporary literature over and over again.[14]

The extraction and refining of the ore was an expensive business in terms of manpower, for even after the initial costs of driving the shafts and galleries, the ore had still to be extracted by primitive means (by child labour according to the size of the galleries uncovered), then crushed by hand, milled, washed, and smelted, before finally separating the silver from the lead in the remaining amalgam. Nevertheless, the under-employment of the free population, together with the low price of slaves, still made the production of silver on these conditions extremely profitable.

It can be said that the intensification of silver mining beginning about 484 marks a turning point in the development of Athens. Her basic economic disability was that, like other Greek states, her land was insufficient to supply her population with adequate sustenance: but her capital, *i.e.*, her topsoil, could not be increased except by the dangerous method of conquest. Silver mining provided an almost ideal solution to many of her troubles, since it offered a labour-intensive industry, producing a commodity in universal demand. A steady supply of home-produced silver could allow Athens to import more of the earth's products than she exported: once stamped with the official seal of the state it was the most acceptable means of payment for incoming cargoes, for tramp boats calling at the Peiraeus would in many cases prefer payment in currency to the limited range of cargoes which Athens could offer for sale. Oil and wine, the basic products of which she could produce a surplus, were in common supply generally in the Aegean, and needed to be transported a long way before they acquired a scarcity value. Apparently neither of these products was in particular demand in Egypt, one of the best sources of grain. Wine and oil were conveyed in pots, the material of which is practically indestructible; but, except at the site of Naukratis, Greek pottery has not been found there in any quantity dating to the period before 300 B.C. The hoards of Greek coins found in Egypt suggest rather that silver was the commodity which the Egyptians welcomed in exchange for their grain.[15] In the sixth century the chief supplier of silver from the Greek mainland seems to have been Aegina, which tapped the mines of Siphnos: but in the fifth century Athens has replaced Aegina as the chief source of supply. No doubt it was the demand for silver for overseas commerce which had induced the Athenians to accelerate the search for the ore, and the exploitation of the deposits.

The ancient authorities were concerned only to make the point that the capital for the new fleet was drawn from the exploitation of the state mines: they were not concerned with the economic implications of this exploitation. One implication has already been touched upon: since the main usefulness of silver is for exchange with other products, the Athenian diversion of effort towards silver mining implied an increase in the importance of trade in the economy. Secondly, in so far as accelerated silver production would increase the amount of money in circulation in the home market, it would affect the level of prices and wages in Athens, and this could have repercussions upon Athenian overseas trade. The net proceeds of the state mines went, in the form of refined ore, to the treasury for minting. The coins were then available to pay for the imported materials necessary for the new ships. Some of the money, however, went to pay for the cost of labour in Attica (the miners, shipwrights, crews, etc.), and this money was fed into the home economy. If the level of goods available to be bought in the home market had remained constant, the result would necessarily have been an eventual fall in the purchasing power of silver at Athens, since the same quantity of goods would have been covered by an increased quantity of money. It is quite likely that something of the sort happened, and that the progressive inflation of the Athenian drachma, of which we have evidence later in the century, seriously began about this time. The possibility has to be borne in mind because it affects our appreciation of the position of Athens with regard to external commerce. A rise in prices at Athens would increase the inducement to overseas traders to bring their goods for sale there. The increased supply of silver acted to draw towards Athens grain cargoes from abroad, and since the purchasing power of silver would not fall as quickly outside Attica as in it, the price structure favoured the overall development of Athenian overseas trade. An increase in the supply of overseas goods available would of course work to counteract the inflationary tendency of increased spending; in other words the increase in the supply of money resulted not merely in an adjustment of prices but also increased the quantity of goods available.

The external dangers facing Athens, which made rearmament a prudent policy, have already been mentioned. But this does not altogether explain her decision in 484 to use the money in this way. We know that the decision was not carried through the popular assembly without opposition: the alternative use suggested for the windfall was 'a distribution to the people'. To Aristotle the choice seemed one between long-term investment in defence, and immediate consumption. But perhaps this is misrepresenting the opposition. At least one other alternative lay before the assembly, and it is strange if it was never mentioned; that is to invest not in ships, which soon decay, but rather in those public buildings which provided the outstanding amenities of the Hellenic world. Persia, after all, was a long way away; she had made no hostile move against Athens for over five years; at Marathon it was the hoplites, not the ships, which had saved Athens. Aegina was certainly the more immediate threat, but it is strange that the hoplite democracy of Athens should sacrifice so much to build up the sea arm against her. The decision to choose triremes in preference to doles or temples was a historic one, and reflects a surprising conviction, on the part of the democracy, of the future importance of the sea arm, and, by implication, of sea-borne food imports. This decision, however it was reached, was to be the salvation of Athens in the coming conflict with Persia; and once the war was over, the ships, and the naval facilities she was now constructing, were to prove an asset beyond price in the race for the carrying trade of the Aegean.

VI

ATHENS AND THE DELIAN
CONFEDERACY

BY 480 B.C. the delicate network of trade with the north-east finally collapsed, as Persian forces moved across the Hellespont and down into the Greek peninsula, mopping up as they went. At the same time the fleets of the Persian empire swept the Aegean, keeping closely in touch with the land arm. By the early autumn Attica itself was occupied, and the Peisistratids, with their followers from exile, were ceremoniously repatriated by the occupying Persians: thus, after an exile lasting thirty years, and for a very brief space, the Tyranny was restored at Athens.

We are led by our sources to understand that the regime ruled over an empty land. Attica was for the most part evacuated; only the old were left behind, and a last-ditch garrison defended the Acropolis.[1] After the battle of Salamis, Mardonius apparently withdrew northwards for the winter, and returned in the spring for the second occupation. The Athenians thus claimed to have lost the best part of two harvests, as well as suffering enormous physical damage to their capital assets in the form of trees, buildings, and livestock, whether they slaughtered the latter or tried to evacuate them. The losses to property were such that Thucydides writes of the Athenian farmers as still recovering from them half a century later.[2]

For the rehabilitation of the rural economy after the war an urgent need was the replacement of stock losses, and the planting of trees, since the olive is so long in maturing. But as far as the cereal crops were concerned, no long-term damage was likely to be suffered, even if the cover crop was burned off: the chief damage to the economy was the immediate one of losing the harvests. Fortunately, the loss of the 480 harvest was probably far from complete. A good proportion of the crop could have been gathered before the Persian entry, although some disorganisation was probably experienced owing to early mobilisation and premature harvesting under the influence of panic. But the 479 cereal crop could have been completely lost to Athens if Mardonius was in occupation from the spring. It is difficult to believe that Athens gained much home-produced grain this year, and this raises the question of the source from which the Athenians got their food until the harvest of 478. Two of the places which are mentioned as reception centres for the evacuated population, Salamis and Aegina, were poor in food production, and Aegina was in fact a net importer. It is clear that the Athenian evacuees must have been fed on imported food, and in the transport conditions of Greece, this means food brought by sea. We hear of negotiations for bulk imports from Sicily,[3] but these were apparently abortive: the transfer of goods by private trading was not yet rivalled by the institution of economic aid. But however the food was transported, the dependence of the Athenians on shipping services for their survival was underlined as never before. If the fighting ships saved Athens, it was the merchant ships that kept her population alive through the war. But even after the end of hostilities, when the Athenians returned to their battered homeland, substantial imports of food, including oil, were needed for the period while the farms were recovering from the war damage. Before 480 food imports had been needed only to cover the requirements of excess population. After 479 war losses had probably brought about a temporary fall in population, but this fall was outweighed by the damage inflicted on the farming industry. If Athens began the war as a net importer of food, she ended it with a widened gap between her needs and her home production. While the resulting high level of demand increased the importance of the commercial sector of the economy, the losses suffered by the farming industry offered a diminished incentive for evacuees to return to it. The proportion of the Attic population engaged on food production obviously fell drastically during the war years, and even when the Persian fighting was over, circumstances prevented the restoration of the old proportions. A relative increase in the size, and in the economic and political importance of the urban population was to be a feature of Athens during the fifth century.

The brunt of the war damage was borne by the farming sector of the economy. The silver mines were intact and ready to resume production as soon as the necessary labour was available. Of the Athenian shipping pool, it was the warships which had been mainly exposed to the perils of war; and whatever losses of merchant ships had occurred had perhaps been more than replenished by the captured Persian hulks which fell as prizes of war into Greek hands. The output of the mines, the strength of her marine force, and the skill and enterprise of her sailors were the great assets of Athens in the post-war years. Fortunately for her the opportunities for turning these assets to advantage were unusually good.

The war had dislocated food production in varying degrees in all areas of Greece with the possible exception of the Peloponnese. This dislocation put a premium on the value of vital foodstuffs, and on the means of delivering them: this establishment of a seller's market for food brought profit in the first instance to the entrepreneur who could supply the necessary shipping services, and how this reacted upon the economy of the state will be discussed in the next chapter. But ships were a good investment not only from the purely economic, but also from the political point of view. The departure of the Phoenician navy put an end to the writ of Persia in the Aegean, and whichever state succeeded it as the arbiter of law and order on the sea lanes could obviously use this position for political advantage. Immediately after the war a key to the allegiance of the islands lay in relief supplies to tide over the critical shortages before a new harvest could be taken; and these supplies could be guaranteed only by the masters of the sea. But political advantage was not limited to the provision or withholding of relief supplies. In the field of direct action lay the possibilities of blackmail, or extortion, against those states which had not been already ruined by Persian occupation. This kind of action was described as the collection of war levies to cover the cost of continuing operations against the 'Barbarians'. We hear of Themistocles sailing from island to island to collect such levies. At Andros he was checked: at Paros he was successful: at Carystos in Euboea he collected, then subsequently landed and plundered the countryside. On this occasion his ships sailed across the Aegean to Rhodes, from which he extracted the sum of three talents.[4]

While circumstances thus offered unusual opportunities for maritime profit, the Athenians were in an exceptionally strong position to exploit them, backed as they were by the most recently constructed fleet in the Aegean: the naval programme launched by Themistocles was now about to yield high dividends. Rowing and directing the fleet were men of hard experience, many of whom had probably served their apprenticeship in pre-war mercantile ventures in the north-east. In years past they had been held up there by the competition of Miletus, by the intrigues of the Sigeion group, by the opposition of the Megarian colonies at the Bosporus, by the dominance of Persian land power, and by the threat of the powerful Phoenician fleet. After the battle of Mykale all these checks were reduced or eliminated. At a time when the demand for food in Greece was at a new peak, the road lay open to the sources of supply in the Black Sea area.

Athenian sailors were of course not the only ones to see the opportunities presenting themselves, and other maritime states allied to Athens were prepared to cash in on the situation. Under the cloak of the alliance a bitter struggle was already looming: how intense later historians believed this rivalry to be, is illustrated by Plutarch's highly coloured anecdote about Themistocles, who, according to the story, secretly proposed to set fire to the ships of other allied contingents.[5] A more sensible plan, and one more in keeping with the ways of this pragmatic Athenian, was not to sabotage the fleet, but to manipulate it to Athens' advantage. To see how such a thing was possible it is necessary briefly to consider the terms of association by which the allied contingents were banded together.

In the winter of 481 the representatives of a number of Greek states had assembled at the Corinthian isthmus to consider common action in face of the expected Persian invasion. Although the nucleus, or possibly the majority, of the assembled deputies represented Peloponnesian states, the assembly itself included a number of non-Peloponnesian cities, including Athens, which felt itself most closely threatened. This gathering, the aim of which was the formation of a common front against the invader, had the character of a Hellenic League, including, but wider than the Peloponnesian League, and acknowledging Spartan leadership. Members of the alliance were to have the same friends and enemies; hence Athens and Aegina were formally reconciled, and attempts were made to bring Argos, the traditional enemy of Sparta, into the League. The embassy to Syracuse to seek economic assistance for the war effort had been one of the League's first actions: the co-operation of the allies in economic matters is attested by the arrangements made for supporting the Athenian evacuees at Aegina and Troezen.

Unfortunately we do not know how the contributions of the allies to the common war effort were fixed; but presumably each state offered what its government felt it could, and should, contribute. But after the Greek victory at Salamis, states which had been neutral, or had collaborated with the Persians, were apparently drawn willy-nilly into the alliance and made to contribute. Mention has been made above of Themistocles' activities at Andros, Paros, Carystos, and Rhodes, and his attempts to levy compulsory contributions on these states; thus the future Confederacy of Delos had, even at this embryonic stage, consisted of voluntary and involuntary subscribers. In 479, at a general meeting of the confederates, it was agreed that a war effort on an ambitious scale should be sustained from the common resources of the Greek allies.

During the same year the membership and scope of the alliance were dramatically increased when, after an invitation from emissaries of Samos, the confederate fleet crossed the Aegean and defeated the Persians at Mykale. This victory was followed by a second Ionian revolt, in which the rebellious states looked for assistance to the confederates. At a meeting at Greek naval headquarters on Samos a decision was taken to receive the petitioning states into the alliance; the new adherents included the important islands of Samos, Chios, and Lesbos. According to Herodotus it was expressly stated, when they were accepted as allies, that they should stand by the alliance and not secede; the aim of this stipulation was to prevent them from withdrawing their support once the immediate Persian danger had passed away. Reinforced by its new allies, the confederate fleet sailed northwards to the Hellespont to cut off the Persian land retreat across the improvised bridges, but on reaching Abydos they found the bridges already down; the Peloponnesian contingents then withdrew from further operations of that year. At this point the Athenians took over command of the allied forces, already swollen by new adherents from cities in the Ionian and Hellespontine region which had joined in the revolt. At the head of the confederates the Athenian flotilla crossed the straits, besieged and finally captured the fortress of Sestos on the northern side. The allied fleet then dispersed for the winter.

Meanwhile, the Athenian administration at home was busily organising the repatriation of its evacuees and the restoration of the city's defences: all available labour was mobilised to the latter end. These defences were apparently not intended against the Persians, for it had been twice demonstrated that the homeland was not considered defensible from attacks from that quarter. In any case the Persian danger was over, and at a time when the problem of providing the most urgent necessities for the winter was still critical, the diversion of resources to a frantic rearmament programme could not fail to bring disquiet to those states which were the neighbours of Athens. Expressions of alarm, and proposals for general disarmament put to Athens by her neighbours were brushed aside. By the winter Athens and its main port were already fortresses that could be defended by a small number of home-service troops, freeing the rest for naval service overseas.

In the following year Athens continued her vigorous war effort at sea, still operating under Lacedaemonian leadership and within the framework of the grand alliance. The fleet sailed eastwards to Cyprus, which was possibly a Phoenician naval base, and gained local successes there: it sailed northwards, passed the Hellespont and the Propontis, and captured Byzantium from a Persian garrison. This city was a strategic prize of the first order: fifteen years before, its Greek population had fled, and the town had been burned down by the Phoenicians. By its recapture the allies were not so much liberating a Greek settlement as gaining a naval base which could be put to whatever use its new masters thought fit. The effort involved in its capture was fully justified by its military value in the continuing struggle against Persia: but whether or not the Athenian admirals realised it at the time, Byzantium was not only a strategic base but also a key to commercial progress in the hands of its owners. Generations of Athenian traders had found the way to the source of the products they needed blocked by the Megarian settlements at the entrance to the Black Sea; now at last the way was open. Athenian traders need no longer restrict their commercial ventures to the Aegean; they could sail direct to the sources of supply. Previously the problem had been the hostility of settlements in and beyond the Hellespont: now there was the possibility of so arranging matters that Athenian seamen might travel to the Black Sea ports along a route whose safety would be ensured not merely by the neutrality, but even by the organised co-operation, of the settlements on the sea lanes.

In 478–7 the Athenian commander in the north-east theatre of operations received a request from the Ionian, and other freshly liberated peoples, to take over the leadership of the confederate forces, in view of the unpopularity of the Spartan commander, Pausanias. The Athenians acceded to the request; Pausanias was recalled, and an officer was sent out to replace him. It now appeared that the allies' dissatisfaction was directed not at Pausanias personally, as had at first been suggested, but at Spartan leadership as such. The allies refused to accept Pausanias' replacement as leader: the Peloponnesian contingents thereupon formally withdrew from the entire operation. The Athenian officers were left in undisputed command of the remnants of the confederate fleet, and of its precious prizes of war.

Thus the independent Greek cities which had once, from the Athenians' point of view, barred the way from the Hellespont to the Black Sea, had first been destroyed by the Persians for their part in the Ionian revolt; they had then been liberated by the confederate fleet; and finally they fell, together with the leadership of the fleet, under the influence, actually under the control, of the Athenians. The incredible luck which had brought about this situation to the advantage of Athens is almost too good to be believed, and one may well suspect the Athenians on the spot of having nudged the arm of providence by tampering with the loyalty of the allied and liberated communities.[6] Nevertheless, it is the verdict of Thucydides that Athens' assumption of leadership was with the consent of the allies, and we lack the evidence to dispute this judgement. The relationship of Athens to the allies was that of leader to followers; it was soon to become that of master to servant, and the formal terms of the new confederacy were the instruments of the new servitude.

In the winter of 478 an inter-state conference was held at the island of Delos to discuss the future of the alliance, its aims, and its organisation. In our brief record of this momentous meeting the agreed aims are summed up in one curt sentence; 'to obtain compensation for losses received, by destroying the lands of the [Persian] king': the programme was practical, materialistic, aggressive; a concerted and indefinite plundering of the king's property (*i.e.*, his empire). There was no question of a land invasion with a view to conquest and liberation of the Asian hinterland. The League was to be primarily a naval venture; its aims amounted to a systematic policy of raiding against the ships and land bases of the Persian empire. The association between the allies was to be permanent: League policy was to be the responsibility of delegates at a synod at which the Athenian delegate was to preside: the finances of the League were to be a joint responsibility, each state contributing either ships or money: the financial contributions of states not supplying ships were to be fixed in each case by the Athenian representative. The administration of the League's finances was to be in the hands of a board of officials (the Hellenotamiae) appointed from the Athenians.

The congress thus confirmed Athens in her position of leadership; it established the framework of a permanent inter-state organisation, saddled the members with financial obligations of indefinite duration; and delivered into Athenian hands the control over the distribution of such burdens, and ultimately over the use to which the expected revenues were to be put.

The exact financial arrangements for the support of the allied cause are a matter of some dispute: we are for the most part dependent on the summary comments of Thucydides, echoed with some slight additions by Plutarch.[7] The total annual contributions to the League were assessed at the level of 460 talents, and whether this sum included the value of contributions in kind, including the ships themselves, or was the total cash contribution, is not stated by the literary authorities.

In 454 the treasury of the League was transferred from Delos to Athens, and one-sixtieth of the annual cash tribute collected was dedicated each year to the Goddess Athena. The surviving lists which record this quota show that at this time the cash contributions were coming in at a level substantially lower than 460 talents, in spite of the fact that the League now comprised many additional members who had joined since 477, and that important cities which had earlier contributed ships were now contributing cash. Thus, if the original assessment referred only to cash contributions, the conversion of ship-contributing to cash-contributing allies must have meant a corresponding increase in the monetary level, which would have brought it well above the level of the original assessment, unless the individual contributions had meanwhile been reduced. There is no mention of such a thing happening, and while an argument *ex silentio* has rarely much historical validity, in this case it is hard to believe that a gesture of such magnanimity as a voluntary reduction of tribute by Athens would not have been mentioned at some point by speakers in defence of Athens' imperial position.[8] We are almost certainly safe in assuming that no such reduction occurred, and we are accordingly left with the task of explaining why the level of tribute was not higher at the later date, for which we have controlling epigraphic evidence. Since our evidence refers to money actually collected, we must also take into account the probability that the total collected in any one year was likely to fall short of the assessment for that year, but in this case the gap between assessment and collection is too great to be explained merely in terms of temporary default of payment. Thucydides' figure of 460 talents as the original assessment has to be considered in relation to the epigraphic evidence which establishes that the collected amount even in 454 fell substantially below this level, and that therefore the total collected in 477 was by implication much lower again.

Before attempting to reconcile these figures, it would be interesting to discover how the figure of 460 talents was arrived at in the first instance. It has been suggested that the amount was simply the total obtained by adding together the maximum contributions which members were able to pay; and that this maximum was again based on the assessments made on the value of members' resources by the Persian administration some fifteen years previously.[9] This suggestion, however, raises fresh difficulties. In the first place some members of the Confederacy had never been tribute-paying subjects of the Persian empire; and in any case the recent war had violently affected the economic condition of many states as a result both of physical devastation and of detachment from the market facilities offered by the Persian empire. Secondly, it would seem very strange to equalise the new contributions to common defence with the old level of imperial tribute to the Great King; the two figures would be totally unconnected as far as the purposes of the payment were concerned. The suggestion that members simply transferred their payments from the Persian to the confederate treasury, seems altogether too facile, reflecting the hindsight of historians who saw in retrospect that by their 'liberation' the member states achieved little more than a transfer from one imperial domain to another. The equalisation of the confederate contributions to the old imperial tribute would have been a most tactless way of revealing this fact to members at the very outset of the League's history.

In describing how the initial level of contributions was set, Plutarch remarks that the Greeks used to pay contributions to the war effort even when the Spartans were leading the Confederacy, and that on this occasion they entrusted to Aristeides the responsibility of fixing their several contributions in accordance with the value (of their resources) and their ability to pay.[10] 'Ability to pay' seems to imply a maximum level consistent with the member's resources, and it is hard to imagine members agreeing to hand over to the common war chest such a sum, unless it was clear that the total thus raised would be barely adequate to carry out the purposes of the League for mutual protection. In other words, the combined total of the individual contributions must in the end be related to the minimum needs of the Confederacy as a whole, as they appeared at the time to members.

A few years later we hear of the allied fleet on active service at Eurymedon (467 B.C.), and on this occasion the size of the fleet is put by Plutarch at 200 vessels, by Diodorus at 300, of which Athens is said to have contributed 200 and the allies 100. We have no means of deciding which of these figures is correct, but at least they give us an idea of the naval strength thought to be available to the allies, and a fleet of 200 seems a reasonable estimate of the minimum adequate to patrol the Aegean at that particular time, and to safeguard members against sudden raids by the Phoenician fleet still in being. It must, however, be said that this was a year of high tension, when a maximum war effort was called for by the League, so that the 200 (300) probably included all reserves. There is no reason to suppose that a fleet of this size was sent into action every year.

We may now consider an argument advanced by the authors of *A.T.L.*[11] For the year 454 B.C., when the empire reached its greatest extent, they postulate an assessment of about 480 talents: of this total they estimate that about 400 talents was actually collected. From the figure of 480 talents they subtract the value of contributions from states which joined the League between 477 and 454, and states which were foundation members but were contributing ships at the outset of the Confederacy. The exact number of states in these categories, and the combined value of their contributions, does not admit of precise definition, but the authors make the reasonable estimate of at least 200 talents to cover the value of contributions made in 454 B.C. which cannot have appeared as a cash assessment in 477. They are therefore driven to the conclusion that of the original assessment of 460 talents only about a half was an assessment of cash contributions: the other half was the assessed value of contributions in ships. The cost of a new trireme in 483 B.C. is assumed by Aristotle to have been in the region of one talent, at the level of costs then prevailing at Athens.[12] If the authors of *A.T.L.* are right in their argument, it appears that the allies budgeted for a fleet of 200 to 300 warships, and calculated an annual recurrent cost of 200 to 250 talents.

The cash contributions were intended to cover the maintenance costs of the fleet, and perhaps to increase its size. The recurrent cost of keeping the ships at sea can be divided into two main sections; first, the cost of repair and replacement; and second, the maintenance cost of the crews. Under an arrangement such as that suggested above, the cost of repair and replacement is naturally included in the contribution of the states supplying the ships; and we should note that, as the proportion of the fleet contributed by other states fell, and that contributed by Athens rose, so the Athenian expenditure on repairs and replacements increased accordingly. As for the maintenance costs of the crews, personal service was an obligation assumed initially by all the allies: manpower was therefore available either from the ship-contributing allies, as part of their contribution, or from other allied states. The wage-hire element can therefore be ignored; the actual maintenance cost would be the sustenance of the crews. If the food of a seaman is calculated at 3 obols a day, the cost of keeping a trireme at sea was about a hundred drachmas a day. If the campaigning season averaged 90 days, each trireme could be expected to cost one and a half talents annually in running expenses (apart from repairs): a war fleet of 200 to 300 triremes would therefore theoretically require an annual budget of 300 to 375 talents. The actual cost, however, would generally be less. Our figures for the number of triremes at sea are taken from campaigns when a maximum effort was sustained: in normal years the number of ships sent out would be much smaller. Furthermore the marines were expected to live off the land in enemy territory; on the territory of friendly, but non-member states, provisions were perhaps supplied very much at bargain prices to such formidable callers; in some cases the confederate fleet may have levied an unofficial tribute in kind. The collection of the cash contributions was complicated by the fact that some member states also perhaps fulfilled their obligations in kind from time to time. This would help to explain the comparative lowness of the sums collected in cash, and the surprising fluctuations from year to year.[13]

At this point we may conveniently consider the general cost, to Athens, of her leadership of the Confederacy; and the profits which accrued to her by reason of it. The cost to Athens can be considered under four main heads: there was the expense of building and maintaining a large war fleet; of maintaining and enlarging the harbour facilities for its use; of improving the general defence of the state to face the increased peril of attack by a coalition of disaffected subjects or 'allies'; and lastly, of keeping on active, but unproductive, service, a large number of its citizens in the prime of life.

The exact size, and hence the cost, of the Athenian fleet from time to time cannot be easily estimated. We have the figures for the allied navy at Eurymedon (200 in Plutarch; 300 in Diodorus, of which 200 are said to be Athenian). Plutarch mentions that 60 triremes were kept in permanent readiness.

Pericles claimed in 431 B.C. that Athens had 300 triremes in sea-worthy condition. Aristotle and Plutarch agree in estimating the size of the Athenian fleet at Salamis at 100 ships; of these some were privately owned and were probably but improvised warships; (Herodotus put the number at 200 ships). Diodorus suggests that in the time of Cimon 20 new hulks were laid down each year.[14]

Of these numbers probably the most reliable is that quoted by Pericles at the beginning of the Peloponnesian war, as it forms part of a considered estimate of Athens' strength: since Pericles was attempting to hearten the Athenian people, we should assume that the number he quotes is a maximum. On the other hand, a comparison of the numbers here given can hardly give us a clear picture of Athenian naval construction, since, even if the numbers themselves are acceptable, certain complicating factors are quite unknown to us. When Pericles stated that Athens disposed of 300 seaworthy vessels, he certainly included ships fit only for training, communication, and home defence; *i.e.*, the front-line strength was much smaller. If the figure of 20 new ships constructed per year is accepted, this would be sufficient only to keep up to front-line strength a force of 100; but the addition of obsolescent, but still seaworthy, vessels to the reserve would increase the total naval force available, and steeply increase the maintenance costs. We can assume that some of the overall increase in the Athenian war fleet came from prizes of war, and in this case the additional vessels must be considered not as a cost but a gain to Athens. It seems on the whole clear that the Athenian naval strength increased between 477 and 431 from a minimum of 100 to a maximum of 300 triremes. If this is right, we must assume that even allowing for the additional strength supplied by prizes of war and confis-cation, Athens must have built at least 20 new triremes a year, as Diodorus says she did, to cover replacements to front-line strength and additions to the reserve.

At the level of costs prevailing in 483 the replacement of 20 triremes annually would have cost Athens about 20 talents: maintenance on the existing fleet would be a large item of ex-penditure. We can safely say that in money terms 30 talents would be a minimum annual estimate of the cost of replace-ments and repairs. In addition it should be noted that the cost

94

must have sharply risen in money terms. There is evidence of a general rise in wages and prices after the war, and by the end of the century the wage of an artisan had doubled. Since the tribute assessments stayed unchanged for many years, it is clear that during this period of monetary inflation the financial position of all the ship-contributing allies, whose contributions were assessed in real, not money terms, must have deteriorated *vis-à-vis* the cash-contributing members, the real value of whose contributions fell steadily with the decline in the value of money. In addition, the cost of building new triremes almost certainly rose in real, as well as in money, terms, since their construction became increasingly elaborate.[15]

In addition to building and maintaining ships, Athens was forced to undertake a heavy programme of public works in order to provide proper haven facilities for the confederate fleet.[16] We hear but little of this work on the Peiraeus: our authorities are mainly concerned with the spectacular building programme to wall off the harbour area against a land attack; but dockyards and mooring sheds were also needed. These public works of construction must be considered as a part of the general rearmament programme undertaken by Athens as soon as the Persian war finished: one of the most striking features of this programme was the entire rebuilding of the city walls, and the construction of the long walls linking Athens with the coast. Local material was used for these projects, in many cases the material actually consisted of salvage, including tomb stones. Thus the real cost to the state was the diversion of labour into non-food-producing activities like naval service and rearmament. The country had, in the pre-war era, suffered from a chronic under-employment of its human resources, and the temporary disorganisation of farming, due to enemy action, made it probably difficult, in the immediate post-war period, usefully to deploy on the land all the labour available. In that case the cost to Athens of rearmament was, in real terms, probably quite low: the real problem was organisational, to see that whatever food was available was spread in an orderly fashion through the working population. Assuming that the central government was strong enough to ensure such orderly distribution, the mobilisation of the work-force for rearmament was possibly more of a gain than a loss, in that it helped to provide

a system of distribution outside the traditional patterns of subsistence farming and open marketing, both of which had temporarily broken down under the impact of war. One aspect of
the organisational problem which the government had to face
was shortage of certain types of skilled labour, on which the
employment of unskilled labour depended. A hint of vigorous
attempts to break this bottleneck is given by Diodorus in his
account of Themistocles' measures to attract to Athens skilled
artisans from abroad by the offer of attractive conditions.[17]

Thus the costs to Athens of her leadership of the Confederacy
were, in the immediate post-war era, heavy in money terms: in
real terms they were much lighter. But two factors were against
her in the long run. The change in the value of money would
increase her real burden as the value of the cash contributions
fell, while the real costs of the ships rose. Secondly, as the farming industry of Attica recovered, and could use more labour, a
constant diversion of manpower to defence could prove increasingly expensive. The tendency which in fact developed
was for slaves to be imported to do the jobs that citizens once
had done: as a result Athens was forced to feed an increased
population out of the resources she had, or could acquire. We
must also take into account a cost which is incalculable in economic terms; that is, the cost of war casualties which were to
carry off some of the most valuable members of the community,
leaving widows and orphans dependent on public aid to survive. A consequence of this terrible drain on the community's
human resources was the later provision and extension of social
services at Athens, a significant by-product of her imperial
position.

So much for the costs of leadership. If the Confederacy was
to be profitable to Athens, the positive advantages to her would
have to be large enough to do more than cover the increased
costs, and we may now consider what concrete advantages she
gained by her leadership of the League.

If we are justified in considering the Athenian rearmament
drive as mainly a consequence of her membership of the Confederacy, then the most obvious and lasting of the gains thereby
accruing to her were the visible results of rearmament; the
ships, walls, buildings, and harbour improvements. These were
the main capital assets which resulted from her investment of

money and labour: how far the economic development of Athens was thereby assisted can be inferred only from our estimate of the economic return which these assets brought her. It is, however, quite clear that they also brought in a non-economic return in the form of power. This latter must be of interest in the economic reckoning, in so far as political power over other states might be turned to economic advantage. Apart from the visible assets resulting from rearmament, we may consider the material gains accruing to Athens under four main headings; the free services made available to Athens in her capacity as leader; the goods and money acquired by Athenian sailors and officials as a direct result of confederate action; the tribute which she collected; and the commercial advantages which her position conferred upon her.

Those allies who initially contributed ships certainly contributed crews to man them; to begin with, these ships were independent units which simply attached themselves to the allied fleet each spring. The development of the Confederacy saw a change in this system when some allies began first to contribute ships without crews, then later, money to finance ships: at this stage the allied contingents thus contributed ceased to have any independence and became mere accretions to the Athenian fleet. Thus the service element in allied naval contributions actually declined as the Confederacy progressed: on the other hand it seems to have become increasingly common for allies to contribute soldiers to the common cause.[18] Such contributions are of interest for the present purpose only in so far as they assisted in the economic betterment of Athens, and their assistance in this direction was indirect: by strengthening the Athenian power militarily they helped, among other things, to secure for Athens those commercial advantages which will be considered below. But there is one form of direct economic assistance afforded to Athens which is not described in so many words in the literary record, but can be reasonably inferred. This was the provision of free mooring facilities and of fresh water to Athenian ships while in allied ports, whether the ships were officially on confederate duty or not. It is also possible that provisions and repairs were provided for Athenian ships, payment for which was reckoned in lieu of tribute. If so, there was a clear gain to Athens, for the tribute was due to the coffers of the League, while the provisions went directly into the mouths of Athenian sailors.

We have already noted cases in which the allied fleet under Themistocles' leadership had used its power to exact forced contributions from the smaller Greek cities: the official aims of the Confederacy likewise included that of seeking compensation for war losses by plundering the territories of the Great King. Confederate patrols might thus be expected to pay for themselves in a lucky season, and we hear sporadically of the booty harvested by them. Plutarch illustrates the shrewdness of Cimon's financial judgement by recalling the division of Persian loot after the capture of Sestos and Byzantium: on this occasion the Athenians let the allies take the captured goods while they themselves kept the Persian prisoners: in the outcome the ransom paid for their return enabled Cimon not only to cover the expenses of the (Athenian) fleet for four months but also to send gold back to Athens: *i.e.*, the ransom more than covered the costs of the season's campaign.

After the battle of the Eurymedon, Cimon's men captured the camp of the Persian host 'full of all kinds of treasure'.[19] Theoretically the spoils of war belonged to the confederates as a whole, but we find no mention of the Athenian generals turning them over to the common war chest at Delos, nor of drawing the tributary allies into the distribution: the spoils in fact belonged from the beginning to those who won them, as we see from the anecdote of Cimon's division. All states which supplied ships could expect a share in the spoils of victories in which they had directly taken part; but the Athenians took the major share, both because they supplied the largest contingent and because they were the leaders; were in fact in charge of the distribution: accordingly, as ship-contributing were progressively replaced by cash-contributing, allies, so the Athenian share correspondingly increased.[20] It may be noted that in lucky seasons when booty more than covered the costs of campaigning, the money contributed by the allies for that purpose needed not to be touched, hence the rapid accumulation of the confederate financial reserve. Theoretically this reserve still belonged collectively to the allies: on the other hand the Athenian sailors would probably feel that the booty in any case belonged to those who had won it, and that if, by their bravery and skill, they had saved the confederate treasury the expense of their upkeep, then in some sense they had a moral right to the money thereby saved. Thus the Athenians, when successful in the field and on the sea, were not only able to enrich themselves year by year, but gradually established a moral, as well as a physical hold over the money accumulating in the common war chest.[21] The change was symbolised by the transfer in 454 of the League treasury from the island of Delos to the Acropolis of Athens.

But the spoils of war could be more valuable and spectacular than a few prisoners or trinkets. When Cimon gained possession of the Greek city of Phaselis (in Asia Minor), he imposed upon it a fine of 10 talents. When he had driven the Persians from the strategic coastal settlement of Eion, near the river Strymon in Thrace, he actually turned the land over to Athenian settlers for cultivation, and the rich surrounding country became an Athenian overseas possession. When he conquered the Greek island of Scyros, in the central Aegean, he enslaved its inhabitants and arranged for Athenian settlers to take over the land. Neither of these territories attained the status even of a tributary 'ally'; they became a simple extension of Athenian sovereignty across the sea. The manipulation of allied naval power to win overseas territory for Athens was among the most spectacular of the advantages accruing to her from her leadership of the Confederacy: the device of enslaving or expelling the native people and resettling the land with Athenian colonists was an attractive and profitable one to Athens. She had used the device before (in Euboea), but it was as head of the Confederacy that she was able to exploit this phase of imperialist policy in a big way, and as her hold on the League tightened so the chain of colonies increased. Their contribution to the general prosperity of Athens in the fifth century will be considered in the general context of imperial welfare.

The third great source of revenue available to Athens was the money contributed by the confederates to the fighting fund of the League. From the beginning this fund was, as we have seen, administered by a panel of officials drawn from the Athenians. The temptation to use this fund for Athenian rather than confederate purposes was understandably very great, yet one must be cautious in speaking of Athenian misuse of confederate money. We have no evidence that Athenian administration of the funds enabled Athens to make illicit use of them for her own purposes during the first twenty-seven years of the Confederacy. Since the aim of the fund was the strengthening of the allies' naval power, the maintenance of Athenian naval strength through the financial support of League members was an unforeseen, but technically not an improper result. There is no evidence from the earlier life of the League that the contributions were directly used to defray the capital cost of ships built in Attic dockyards; but if they were so used, this would not have run counter to the League's original aims, provided that the ships thus built were transferred to allied command and employed exclusively for allied protection. However, the allied high command soon became practically indistinguishable from the high command of Athens, and any obligation on her part to give account of her stewardship soon became a dead letter.

Contributions were intended to defray not only capital but also current costs, and it is stated by Plutarch at one point that Cimon paid Athenian sailors out of allied contributions. This is probably true even of the early period in the League's history. But it was a legitimate use of allied funds to finance the current expenditure of the Athenian section of the confederate fleet, provided, again, that the ships so financed were being used for League purposes; *i.e.*, to shield the confederates against the danger of Persian aggression. The allies could properly complain only if the confederate fleet which they were financing were put to uses other than those of collective defence, or collective reprisals, against Persia. Apparently in the early stages some contributions were made in the form of unmanned ships, and Athens supplied the crews: at a later stage she went further and hired foreign crews.

In any attempt to estimate the gain to Athens from the tribute, we must be careful to distinguish between the earlier and the later periods of the Confederacy. Before 454 B.C., when the allied treasury was transferred to Athens, we have no evidence of Athenian officials misappropriating funds in the interests of their own government. Athens had broken her covenant only in that she had, through the agency of the confederate high command, misapplied in her own interests the force available to the League. Before this time the confederate revenue directly contributed to Athenian economic progress only in so far as rearmament gave employment to Athenian residents and absorbed surplus labour there. The allied contributions helped towards a more efficient utilisation of Athenian manpower, even though the slack was taken up in generally non-productive industries, chiefly in war services. But the indirect advantages to the Athenian economy were more complex, and consisted primarily in the economic advantages secured to Athens by virtue of her increased bargaining power in international affairs, particularly in so far as increased political authority could be translated into commercial dominance. It was only from about 450 onwards that allied funds began to be fed directly into the Athenian economy.

In 449 B.C., almost thirty years after the foundation of the League, peace was finally concluded between Persia and Athens, acting on the League's behalf.[22] Since the war was now over, it could be argued that the confederate fleet was no longer needed. The main purpose for which it had been set up had been achieved,[23] and it was no longer practicable to seek further compensation at Persian expense by raiding her territories. It seems reasonable to assume that, once news was received of the peace treaty, the allies envisaged a suspension of payments for collective defence, and there is some reason to believe that for one year payment was suspended. The tribute quota lists for the fifteen years following the transfer of the treasury to Athens (454 B.C.) are all inscribed on one stele: but only fourteen such entries can be identified, nor is there sufficient remaining space to permit another full entry. The obvious inference is that no tribute was collected in the missing year, and this conjectured break in the collection is plausibly connected with the signing of the peace.[24]

Whether or not a suspension of payments did take place, as this attractive theory suggests, the coming of peace raised the question of how the accumulated surplus, now held at Athens, ought to be disposed of. According to the original intention of the founders, the League net surplus was a proper offset to war damage suffered by members; and it is therefore to this point that modern historians have assigned the famous invitation of Pericles to an all-Greek congress, the agenda of which was to include the restoration of the holy places damaged by the

Persians. In the event the congress was boycotted by other states and was never held. After this Athens, as a centre of major war damage, proceeded to use such portion of the allied funds as she thought fit for the restoration of her own sacred buildings. A decree was passed through the assembly that 5,000 talents in the public treasury, and drawn from allied contributions, should be earmarked for a public building fund.[25]

The existence of such a large capital reserve suggests that a high proportion of League income was not in fact being spent on the purposes for which it was contributed. Pericles claimed in 431 B.C. that 600 talents were coming in every year from the allies in the form of tribute, apart from other income. This figure is not confirmed by the quota lists, which record an income of less than 400 talents at this time (*A.T.L.* iii. p. 334). In his speech Pericles was discussing the liquid resources of Athens, expressed in cash and bullion, and we cannot suppose that he included in his figure an allowance for a non-cash item such as contribution in ships or service. If the quota lists correctly reflect the level of tribute, Thucydides (or Pericles) stands convicted of a gross error, and because it is so difficult to believe either that Thucydides would have committed such a blunder, or that he would have passed on a figure of transparent falsity, we are driven to conclude that Pericles included, under the heading of tribute, money which found no mention in the quota lists, *e.g.*, the payments made by Samos and Amphipolis.[26]

In the same speech Pericles referred to the financial reserve which Athens had built up in the pre-war years. The text of his statement (Thuc. ii. 13. 3) is unfortunately a subject of serious controversy: in the manuscripts on which the book texts of Thucydides are based, the relevant section reads as follows: '. . . there was at that time still on the Acropolis a reserve of 6,000 talents of coined silver (the largest sum which had been there at any time was 9,700 talents, from which money had been spent on the Propylaea of the Acropolis, on the other buildings, and on Potidaea).' This passage has been preserved in a very different form in a quotation (by a scholiast commenting on a passage of Aristophanes); this version is as follows: 'There had been on the Acropolis for some time a reserve of 6,000 talents of coined silver (the bulk of this, actually 5,700 talents, was still there; from this reserve money had been spent on the Propylaea, etc.').

It is this latter version which is preferred by the authors of *A.T.L.* According to their theory, between the years 449 and 435 B.C. the reserve was kept more or less stable at a level of 6,000 talents:[27] to support this view they adduce the decree of Callias which reveals that by 434 a total of 3,000 talents had been transferred to the Acropolis. This transfer is supposed to have been spread over the fifteen years, the normal annual surplus of 200 talents in the League fund replacing each year the money drawn from reserve to cover the costs of the public building programme. According to this view the figure of a 9,700 maximum is an error which had crept into the text. Gomme on the other hand defended the figure of 9,700 as a plausible one, which is supported elsewhere.[28] Declining to accept the theory that the Athenian reserve was kept stable at a level of 6,000 talents for fifteen years, he suggested that the maximum may in fact have reached the stated figure about 447 B.C., since in addition to the postulated 6,000 reserve on the Acropolis there may well have been over 3,000 talents in the public treasury of Athens. In the decree of Callias Gomme saw the authorisation of transfer of this amount from the public treasury to that of Athena on the Acropolis.

The rate of accumulation implied by these figures is at first sight quite astonishing. The figure of 6,000 talents is very high indeed, if we take into account the fact that the League funds had been tapped to finance the Athenian building programme (perhaps 2,000 talents had been spent in this way by 431 B.C.).[29] The figure of 6,000 is supported by the Papyrus decree, and, if this is correctly dated to 449 B.C., it follows that the unspent surplus had been at a level of nearly 200 talents a year during the period 477–449.

The original figure of 460 talents as the League's annual income had been fixed on the basis of the minimum figure compatible with security. We certainly have no reason to believe that costs fell during this period, nor is there any evidence that the confederate fleet was smaller, less well equipped, or less expensive to maintain at the later than at the earlier date. It is possible that Aristeides grossly overestimated the costs of the confederate fleet in the first place and set the level of contributions unnecessarily high. This, however, is contradicted by the whole tradition which praises his work, and shows the allies invariably appealing to it as a just assessment. If therefore 460 talents was a realistic assessment of the League's expenses, and Athens managed to meet the same (and in many cases increased) expenses on only a third of the assessed annual total, it follows that she was meeting League expenditure out of funds other than those derived from the tribute.

From the beginning Athenian warships were the mainstay of the League fleet, and if the original 460 talents included the value of the ships, then this figure had included a substantial contribution from Athens. As more and more of the allies switched the form of their contribution from ships to cash, Athens maintained the strength of the allied fleet by stepping up her own contribution accordingly: had she been logical in her accounting policy, she would have used only allied funds (drawing upon them through the Hellenotamiae), to build and maintain all those ships which she put into service over and above the number in her original contribution; for example, the Hellenotamiae should have transferred each year from the League to the Athenian public treasury a sum to cover rental costs involved in allied ships spending the winter in Athenian ports. By 450 B.C. we might have expected that the Athenian war fleet would consist of two divisions; one division being her own national fleet; the other being the property of the League, but based on the Peiraeus as its home port. All the expenses involved in the upkeep of the latter contingent should have been met from the tribute, and in order to keep the accounts straight, the two divisions would have necessarily been regarded as separate fleets.

There is no suggestion that such a distinction was ever contemplated at Athens. The ships contributed to the common defence of the League were in fact never regarded as belonging to the League at all; although the contributing state was prepared to put the ships under the control of the League commanders each year, the ships themselves remained indisputably the property of the contributors. Consequently, when Athens assumed responsibility for providing ships in lieu of those previously provided by other states (as the latter switched to cash contributions), she regarded the new ships as her own. The Hellenotamiae had every right to draw on the tribute for the capital cost of the new ships, but once the latter joined the fleet at Athens, there was no distinction made between these, and the warships financed by Athens herself. The maintenance of all the ships was carried out according to the trierarchic system,[30] whereby a wealthy member of the Athenian community was made responsible for the current expenses of a warship for one year. In this way internal revenue was subsidising League expenses.

The confusion between Athenian revenue and League resources had been inherent in the system from the beginning, since the latter fund had been fed from the former. But when Athens stepped up her contributions to cover those of other states, the confusion was intensified; it was no longer clear what part of the allied fleet was the property and the responsibility of the Athenian state; and while funds were being transferred from the League to the Athenian public treasury, Athenian internal income was being used to subsidise League projects. In these circumstances the distinction between the two treasuries became purely formal, and did not reflect at all the progress of the two accounts; the distinction had evidently lapsed by 431, for Pericles lumps the funds together as one reserve (though the private treasuries of the gods were always regarded as formally apart, and their contents were separately accounted for).

If the above argument is accepted, it is clear that the surplus in the League account must be regarded as an overall surplus in Athenian public finance; i.e., as the difference between the sum of the League funds plus Athenian public income on the one hand, and the public expenditure of Athens and the League on the other. The controversy about the maximum reached by the reserve at any one time is perhaps not of fundamental importance, since it would be determined not only by the current rates of accumulation and expenditure, but also by the extent of amalgamation of the two funds. The interesting figure is the level of the reserve in 431; in the immediately preceding period Athens had fully maintained routine expenditure on the fleet, had met exceptional and heavy calls on League funds for the operations at Samos and Potidaea, and apart from routine internal expenditure had carried the costs of the great public works programme. The extent of her reserve is eloquent testimony to the buoyancy of her internal revenue, which according to the implications of a statement of Xenophon[31] could have been as high as 400 talents a year. The figures cited above are in fact an indication not so much of Athens' canny management of League finances as of her general economic expansion.

So far we have considered only the direct economic advantages which accrued to Athens from her leadership of the League; the money, and the goods and services made available to her citizens individually, or to the state collectively, as a result of that leadership. But although these created favourable conditions for economic progress, the key to that progress lies rather in the field of international trade. The problem of Athenian commercial development has to be considered in a wider context, for the improvement in trading conditions became linked to a change in the pattern of home production, as a market economy developed. On the other hand, because commercial expansion overseas led to increased international friction, and the Athenian government began to use its economic power for political ends, economic progress led Athens into a series of new problems which threatened not only her economy, but her very existence.

VII

THE ECONOMIC CONDITIONS OF
IMPERIAL ATHENS

IN the whole field of Greek history there are few more controversial subjects than that of the conduct and development of
Athenian trade in the fifth century B.C. The abundant
quantities of Athenian pottery relating to this period, and found
at various sites, especially in South Russia, Italy and Sicily,
western Asia Minor, and the central Aegean area, and the large
quantities of foreign pottery found at Athens, prove that there
was a considerable exchange of plain ware, filled with the products of the earth, and of fine ceramics, between Athens and
the outside world. But the historical conclusions to be drawn
from all this ware are rather limited.[1] We can make inferences
about the geographical pattern of trade; about the comparative
importance of certain cities as suppliers of ceramics and their
contents; and about the importing habits of certain states. Such
inferences, based as they are upon a small sample of evidence,
must be considered speculative even as regards the trade in
ceramics. We are entitled to make surmises about the comparative level of trading activity in certain cities, but not about the
absolute level of trade. Even if we can prove that trade (in
certain products) was greater in one city than in another, this
information is not really important to the historian unless he
is satisfied that trade was of more than trivial importance to the
economy of one or both of them. In the case of fifth-century
Athens the archaeological evidence cannot tell us whether trade
was really important to her economy or not. We are forced
back upon the literary and epigraphic evidence, and it is the
meagreness of this evidence, and the extreme difficulty of drawing reliable conclusions from it, which has made the subject of
Athenian fifth-century trade so very controversial.[2]

We may begin with some more or less reliable figures. By the middle of the fourth century, Athens produced from her own soil about half a million bushels of grain (mostly barley) and imported about a million (mostly wheat).[3] The vital importance of food imports to the Athenian economy is asserted over and over again in contemporary literature, especially in speeches concerned with breaches of commercial law. This importance gained official recognition in a series of Athenian statutes which laid down restrictions on the export and re-export of grain from Attica, and which channelled Athenian investment into the financing of the grain trade.[4]

There is no doubt that foreign trade was vital to Athens by the middle of the fourth century,[5] and the evidence gives us a *terminus ante quem* for its period of growth. How far this evidence is applicable to the preceding century is quite obscure, but obviously we should not be justified in assuming, without further evidence, that it is so applicable. There are in fact a number of references, dating from the second half of the fifth century, which imply that by that time Athens was already a great centre of trade. Pericles, speaking in 430, claimed: 'The greatness of our city enables us to draw upon the produce of the whole world, so that the products of other lands are as familiar to us as those of our own.' A pamphlet penned by an unknown author (the *Old Oligarch*),[6] gives a vivid contemporary picture of Athens as a cosmopolitan city whose area of trade extended over Italy and Sicily, Cyprus, Egypt, Lydia, the Black Sea, and the Peloponnese; this city, as he claimed, was able not only to assure its own supplies, but also, owing to its domination of the Aegean trading area, to deny to other states supplies of strategic raw materials.

Such references as this certainly imply that by about 430 B.C. Athens was a great centre of maritime commerce. This impression is confirmed by data which suggest that the population of Athens increased sharply during the fifth century (see Chapter VIII). Since we have no reason to believe that the Athenian production of basic foodstuffs, that is, breadcrops, rose appreciably during this period, we must assume that the increase of population was matched by an increase in imports. We can illustrate this inferred increase by a known instance, which chance has preserved in the literary record, of a massive consignment of grain from Egypt, dating to 445 B.C.[7] But the most spectacular evidence of Athenian commercial growth in the fifth century is provided by the Peloponnesian war strategy of Pericles, which virtually led to the temporary abandonment of the Attic rural economy, and relied on foreign imports for the sustenance of the whole population.

We have positive evidence for the importance of overseas commerce to Athens in the fourth century, and we have strong presumptive evidence that much of this commercial growth had taken place between 480 and 430 B.C. It is for these vital fifty years that we are so much in the dark: the trend is clear, but the details are conjectural. Nevertheless, we can at least limit the areas of conjecture, and possibly dispel some of the darkness, by noting certain significant features of the Athenian situation, and of Athenian behaviour, during this period.

From the sixth century B.C. the growth of the Athenian urban population had outstripped the capacity of the surrounding countryside to satisfy its needs, and it had been a constant struggle to close the gap between home production and consumption of cereals by imports. This gap was immensely widened by the Persian wars, which for two years dislocated farm production in Attica, and reduced its productive capacity for a number of years. The shortage of seed and the loss of draught animals made it difficult to resume full production of cereals after the war. We must assume that many farm buildings had been destroyed, and that when the first post-war harvest was gathered there was a problem of storage, since building materials were in heavy demand for housing. Above all, many of the younger men, once evacuated from the farms, probably never went back. There were more attractive opportunities for enrichment in service with the fleet than in the back-breaking, and heart-breaking, task of getting a wrecked farm back into production. In the case of the wine crop there was a delay of several years to be faced before full production could be resumed: in the case of the olives the delay was of the order of twenty years.

Our sources give us no information about how the Athenian population was fed during these critical years, they do not even indicate the existence of a problem. Athens not only survived this bleak period, she emerges from it in a burst of accelerating vigour. There can be no doubt that during this period she drew heavily on outside sources of food; and it is rather probable that the economic connexions she forged at this time were those which stood her in good stead later on.

Some wheat surpluses were available in the pre-war period from Euboea and Thessaly, but war had disorganised production to various extents in both these areas, and both had fed armies of occupation. It seems reasonably certain that the bulk of the supplies which bridged the post-war gap came from outside the war area, that is, from Italy and Sicily, or from the north-east.

No doubt traders from mainland Greece sought grain cargoes from many centres, and some of these cargoes reached Athens. We have already noted the organised effort on a government-to-government basis to arrange supplies from Sicily during the war. Although these negotiations broke down, and the unsuccessful invasion of Sicily by Carthage probably brought about some temporary disorganisation of transport and production there, we have no reason to doubt that grain shipments from the west to mainland Greece were resumed in the early post-war period on a trader-to-trader basis. Whether any considerable volume of direct trading with Persian-controlled Egypt was possible at this time is more doubtful. After the war Athens mounted a vigorous offensive in the south and south-east Aegean, and we may find economic significance in the successive confederate naval activities at Cyprus (on the Egyptian corn route) in 478, 467, and 460, and in the subsequent Athenian intervention in Egypt itself. It is, however, only fair to say that this activity can be explained on purely strategic grounds: the importance of the economic factor in the planning of grand strategy must remain a matter for speculation.

The Persian inroad into Europe, shortlived though it was, disintegrated many of the pre-war trading connexions established overseas by the Greeks, and the decade which followed the war was vital for the formation of new patterns of trade. In commerce tradition and goodwill count for a good deal, and whoever is quickest to establish trading connexions in a new area has an excellent chance of maintaining them. Although we do not know which area helped most to relieve Athens' food shortage in the period 478–70, an examination of Athenian naval activity during this period seems to suggest that the north-east route was that to which Athens paid closest attention, while any consideration of conditions in this area would suggest likewise that here lay the greatest economic opportunities.

The speed with which Athens and the allies moved to seize Sestos and Byzantium was no doubt inspired by a desire to destroy Persian communications with Europe, and was dictated by obvious reasons of strategy. But both places are vital links in the supply route that stretches from the Black Sea to the Aegean: it is notable that the Athenians and the islanders, whose food supplies had been most dislocated by the war, were much more keen on clearing the Hellespont in 479 than were the Peloponnesians, whose food production at home had hardly been affected. It is also of interest to note that those Hellespontine states which were enrolled in the League at the earliest stage all lie on the most convenient route between the two outlets of the Propontis, a route which for the most part follows the European side: on the southern side, which lies off the main route, the Persians seem to have retained their hold longer.[8] The attack on Scyros in 476 appears to have been intended as a move to stamp out a nest of pirates preying on the north-east routes across the Aegean, and by this success Cimon was said by Plutarch to have liberated the Aegean. Athens drew some grain from the Egyptian area during the fifth century, and the number of Athenian coins dating from this period is evidence of the trading connexion.[9] Nevertheless, in the early post-war years Athenian naval efforts were mainly directed towards the Black Sea, and it is easy to imagine why this was so.

At the height of her pre-war commercial activity, Athens had penetrated this area as far as the Troad and the Thracian Chersonese, and had established friendly contacts in the islands en route. The settlement at Sigeion may be considered as a terminal for Athenian trade, and it is unlikely that her ships had sailed much beyond the entrance to the Propontis. At its eastern end, and barring entry to the Black Sea, stood the Megarian colonies of Byzantium and Chalcedon; the sea beyond had been almost a Milesian lake, dominated for trading purposes by the Milesian colonies at Sinope, Phasis, and Trapezus to the east; Panticapaeum, on the straits of Kerch; Tanais at the mouth of the Don; and Olbia, at the mouth of the Bug and the Dnieper. Before 480 an important factor limiting Athenian commercial opportunities here had been the established position of other powerful states, first Megara and Miletus, then later Persia and the Phoenicians. The war, however, not only curtailed Persian influence in the north-east, but it severely jolted the position of the Greek states established there. The richest of the pre-war commercial cities, Miletus, had been crippled by the failure of the Ionian revolt. Persian occupation of Byzantium and Chalcedon had eliminated Megarian influence in the area. Of the Greek maritime states which might have moved into the area, Eretria had been physically destroyed; the revolt and the war had dislocated the connexions and reduced the shipping of Lesbos and Samos which might, under happier circumstances, have succeeded Miletus; Naxos, potentially a formidable contender, was soon to be eliminated by Athenian action. Thus the naval programme, undertaken by Athens in the pre-war period, fitted her to challenge for mastery of the north-eastern waters at a time when the power of her potential rivals was in eclipse.

The most important naval concentration in the Aegean in the early post-war years was that provided by the Confederacy of Delos: it was confederate naval patrols which succeeded those of Phoenicia. But the organisation and deployment of confederate naval strength was in Athenian hands almost from the outset. This meant that the regulation of naval traffic across the Aegean lay in the power of Athens, if she cared to use the confederate fleet for that purpose. We are not entitled to assume that the Athenian government had any conscious intention of using this power for the benefit of Athenian traders; official policy aimed only at securing sufficient imports of food and other strategic materials. The emergence of Athens as the dominating Aegean naval power meant for Athenian traders two immediate advantages; first, the risk of molestation on the high seas was reduced because they could rely on the protection of friendly confederate patrols; and second, the eclipse of Megarian influence at the entrance of the Black Sea, and the end of Milesian dominance of the sources of supply allowed Athenian entrepreneurs to sail boldly through the Hellespont and the Bosporus to establish direct trading arrangements with exporters in the Euxine: having taken on cargo there, they could sail straight

for home with no breakage of cargo between Sinope or Panticapaeum and the Peiraeus. Once direct shipping links were
established between Athens and the Black Sea sources of supply,
the amount of cargo which could be conveyed to Athens by this
route was limited mainly by the shipping available to the
merchants, the effective demand at Athens, and the availability
of a return cargo.

Unfortunately for Athens, during the critical years following
the war, she evidently had available for export no worthwhile
cargoes of natural products with the exception of silver. We are
debarred from thinking of Athenian trade during this period
as of a simple barter of Russian grain for Athenian wine and
oil, because in fact Attica was in a much worse position to
produce these commodities than she was to produce grain.
Indeed on *a priori* grounds we might have expected her to be
exporting some of her early cereal harvests to import oil, rather
than vice versa. It is clear that whatever products she did export between 478 and 470 B.C., silver must have figured promi-
nently among them, and it is convenient here to recall that in
Egypt, while there are quantities of Athenian coins dating to
the sixth and fifth centuries, Athenian amphorae are hardly to
be found outside Naukratis. In south Russia likewise the amount
of Athenian pottery dated to the early decades of the fifth century shows a decline on that of the preceding century, and also
as compared with the later decades of the fifth century itself.[10]

In this connexion one aspect of Athenian activities may be
significant. In spite of her dependence on imported cereals,
during the fifth century she evidently made no serious attempt
to gain physical control of the chief sources of supply. Her naval
policy in the north-east, her intervention in the Egyptian delta,
and her diplomatic offensive in Sicily in 454 and 433, in so far
as they can be attributed to economic motives at all, seem to
have been designed to safeguard the routes rather than the
sources of supply. But in the case of silver she appears to have
achieved by her efforts a virtual monopoly in the Aegean area
from about 460 B.C. Ever since the growth of Carthaginian
power had denied the Spanish silver of Tartessus to the Samians
and Phocaeans, the chief sources of silver to the mainland
Greeks had been Siphnos, Laureion, Thasos, and the Thracian
mines around Mount Pangaeus; also, but perhaps to a smaller

extent, the deposits in the Troad.[11] Of the three main centres of production outside Attica itself, Siphnos and Thasos were members of the Confederacy from the beginning, though the latter preserved a disturbing independence which ended in open rebellion in 465. The gold and silver mines on the Thracian mainland were thought by Herodotus to have remained in native hands: but control at least over the marketing of the product was exercised from Thasos until her revolt. Athens made vigorous and repeated attempts to gain a foothold in this area by planting colonies at the mouth of the river Strymon, and it was her activities here that led to the open breach with Thasos over the issue of control of the mainland mines. The revolt of Thasos was crushed in 463, and whether or not Athenian soldiers occupied the Thracian mining areas, Athens certainly drew revenues from them from this time, and Thucydides the historian a generation later derived a private income from his interests there.[12]

We may draw conclusions about the pattern of trading activity from the fact that silver was the most valuable Athenian export in the post-war years, and from her energetic attempts to control the supply of silver in the Aegean area. The actual conduct of trade was throughout in private hands, and probably (in view of later conditions) many of the traders who landed food cargoes at the Peiraeus were foreigners. There is no evidence to suggest that at this period foreign (or even Athenian) merchant ships were induced by government action to bring their cargoes to the ports of Attica rather than elsewhere. We must assume that the magnet which drew them was economic. They landed cargoes at the Peiraeus because there they could exchange them for what they considered to be the most valuable return and the safest investment, that is, silver money. The post-war shortages all over the Aegean area must have led to an instability of prices: the price relationship between various commodities at the port marts would vary sharply in accordance with local shortages, though all would rise in terms of specie. The trader who converted his final cargo of the season to silver was playing safe: this was the only investment which would assure him an outward cargo next spring, for even if nothing worthwhile was available to be picked up on the outward run, he could always sail in ballast to the Black Sea or Egypt, and the silver itself was the surety for a good return cargo. The unsettled conditions and the widespread shortages which followed the war not only stimulated the flow of trade with the food-producing areas, they also increased the demand and enhanced the value of the precious metals which were the basis of whatever rudimentary credit existed in the Aegean trading sphere.

Athens was able to survive the critical post-war period so well in the first instance because she was able to pay for food imports with silver. But the leading position which she held in the Confederacy also helped her supply situation in the following way. While the fleet was on active service it was supported by confederate tribute, as well as by unofficial war levies (*e.g.*, at Carystos and Rhodes), and by the spoils of war when these were available. Apart from those sections of the captured treasure which were taken home for dedication, most of this money was spent on provisions and other goods at the port markets during the campaign. Neither the Athenian nor any other Greek navy, as far as we know, carried its own supply organisation. On a very short journey crews might carry their own rations, but the build of the triremes and the size of the crews precluded the possibility of carrying supplies for more than a day or two. While the fleet was at sea, the fighting ships were normally accompanied by supply ships, which were in most cases privately owned and which acted like camp followers to a land army.[13] The merchants who followed the fleet scoured the area for supplies and sold them to the commanders or crews of the warships, setting up their own market at each staging point. Money raised for the sustenance of the war effort thus passed through the hands of the merchants, who used it to finance further purchases; to this limited extent one might say that in Greek warfare trade literally followed the flag. The merchant ships might venture alone on their travels, so that they could be found where no warships were; but the reverse hardly applied. On long campaigns warships and merchant ships worked together as a matter of course and their functions were reciprocal.[14] Just as the merchant ships were needed by the warships to keep them supplied, so the latter by their presence protected the precious cargoes from pirates and enemy raiders. Both these categories were treated indifferently as pirates by the Athenians. The attack on Scyros is an illustration of confederate action against piracy, as it was claimed. The action against Naxos, which had an unenviable record for sea raiding, probably had similar overtones.[15]

From the beginning the Confederacy had not only a political but also an economic function (to seek retribution for war damage). But because the supply services of the fleet were left to private enterprise, much of the plunder, the levies, and the tribute found its way through the hands of the merchants who followed the fleet, and thus it provided the financial basis of the long-distance trade between the sources of food supply and mainland Greece. But as the service functions of the fighting and the merchant fleets were reciprocal, so to some extent were their aims. The naval commanders, in making their plans, were forced to take into account the supply problems of the merchants; just as an army cannot simply be marched across the desert, however desirable from the strategic point of view such a march might be. In practice the fleet is never found operating for long periods far away from convenient centres of food supply: it was almost certainly because of his practical experience as a navy man that the historian Thucydides stressed the importance of the economic basis of warfare.[16]

To some extent then the merchants did not simply follow the fleet, their problems influenced its plans and movements. The navy was directed to operational areas in accordance with the demands of grand strategy; but within the framework of that strategy the fleet necessarily cruised near centres of supply: these were the centres which most interested the merchants, not only for the day-to-day job of supplying the forces, but also for the lifting of the final cargo home. When the campaigning season was over, the cargo ships would load to their utmost capacity, their purchases financed by the proceeds of the season's trade. We should not doubt that the naval arm would lend any necessary co-operation in the securing of these vital cargoes: the admirals might not be interested in the entrepreneurs as persons, or in their private gains, but they could not be unmindful of the acute supply problems of their fellow-countrymen at home. The cheers which awaited the return of the venturers each year were not only for the fighting ships, but also for the straggling train of cargo boats which had followed them all the way from the operational areas.

In the early days of the League the national contingents of warships would be escorted by the merchant ships of the various cities: at the close of the season the fleet would split up, and merchant, as well as fighting ships would steer for home. But as more and more of the allies switched from contributing warships to furnishing money, and the confederate fleet became increasingly Athenian, the latter was still accompanied by an international mercantile force whose ties were increasingly centred on Athens. Instead of the various merchant contingents sailing home, more and more of them continued with the convoy, and the Peiraeus began to welcome not only its own fighting fleet but also the latter's international supply train. It was not merely the camaraderie engendered by the long campaign, and the fact that foreign merchants grew accustomed to working with the Athenian navy that drew them towards Athens, but the Peiraeus itself offered marketing opportunities which few ports could rival. Instead of sailing home with their cargoes and returning in spring to pick up the fresh convoy, more and more of these foreign traders began to dispose of their wares in Attica and to stay over winter near the great city.[17]

In this way Athenian commercial development was assisted by her leadership of the confederate fleet. But it would be an error to overstress its dependence upon that leadership; for while the Peiraeus was becoming increasingly a centre of Black Sea trade, Athenian commerce was developing even in areas where the confederate fleet did not operate, especially in Etruria and Sicily. By 470 B.C. Athenian production of grain and wine should largely have recovered from the war damage, and this recovery allowed Athens to rebuild her export trade in wine. Although the quality of Athenian wine and other natural products was not exceptional by Greek standards, the fact that trading ships of many nations put into the Peiraeus to discharge cargo gave Attic producers an opportunity to sell their goods to these traders for their outward cargoes in the spring. But the gain to the economy of Athens was not merely the simple one of obtaining a market for local produce. Because cargoes in excess of effective local demand were landed at the Peiraeus, that port gradually began to acquire the functions of an entrepot, and it was to adapt it for that purpose that public money was lavishly spent by Periclean Athens on commercial installations which included a Corn Exchange and an Exhibition Hall.

The knowledge that quantities of imported food were being regularly landed at the Peiraeus attracted to its market local traders from the whole surrounding area. It is clear that by the end of the fifth century at the latest, a pattern of trade had developed whereby smaller states preferred to buy grain imported in bulk to the Peiraeus rather than to try to deal with the sources direct, nor is it difficult to follow the logic of such a practice. It is true that the price would be higher, since the consumer was paying for the service as well as the wares. But unless the consumer lived closer to the source of supply than he did to Athens, or unless there was a huge difference between the price at Athens and that at the source, the disadvantages were outweighed by the advantages. The risk of total loss faced by the operator on the longer run was practically eliminated; a second serious risk was also removed, that of failing to find a suitable cargo in face of the priority which came to be accorded to ships bound for Athens. Because of the smaller distance, the trader could supply his home market at shorter notice, avoiding the danger of overstocking and having to dispose of his freight on a buyer's market. Furthermore, on the short run between the Peiraeus and his home port, the cargo could be lifted by lighter craft and a ship could make more journeys: it could take advantage of short bursts of fine weather rather than wait for the high season of assured calm, hence the sailing season could in practice be extended. In short, a pattern of trade whereby goods were regularly available from stock in a central position in the Aegean offered very great advantages for the smaller importing states; the risk was taken out of commerce, and a more intensive use of shipping became possible. The importance of the last-mentioned consideration becomes obvious when one remembers that the shipbuilding industry itself depended on imported materials. A network of trade radiating from a central point in the Aegean not only reduced the running costs of trade, it also reduced the capital stock necessary to conduct it.

The development of re-export, or transit, trade was not something new in the Aegean: Corinth, Megara, and Aegina owed a great deal of their prosperity to this form of commerce. Athens in fact was only developing further a pattern set by these great trading cities, and this development was undoubtedly assisted by her control of confederate shipping. Nevertheless, the building up of the Athenian network was probably a slow business, and we cannot date its various stages; but it did not exist in 480, and it is an accepted reality in the early fourth century.[18] The development of the Peiraeus as a great entrepot certainly preceded the Peloponnesian War, for it seems likely that during the war Athens imported in bulk grain supplies for her allies, and supplied them from stock. The evidence lies in the Methone decree;[19] in which the little town of Methone, in Macedonia, is permitted to import direct from the Black Sea after giving notice to this effect to the Athenian naval squadron stationed at the entrance to the Hellespont. The implication is that in wartime the allies purchased through Athens essential goods from the Black Sea area, and that this virtual Athenian monopoly was enforced by the inspection of cargoes at the straits. There is no evidence that Athens enforced a monopoly in peacetime; but the management of the allies' supplies in time of war clearly depended on a pool of merchant shipping being available to feed the market at Athens with the necessary bulk supplies. It does not seem at all likely that Athens would have been willing or able to improvise in wartime the implied network of supply, unless the arrangement was a continuation of commercial practices which had developed in time of peace. Whether or not the allies were compelled to buy through Athens, it seems that many states did in fact draw supplies through the Athenian market in the fifth century, as they did in the fourth. The development of the Athenian entrepot in face of the competition of cities like Corinth and Megara, which had preceded Athens in this line of business, can be attributed both to the enterprise with which Athenian traders seized their chances in the Black Sea area, and to the advantages accruing to Athens by reason of her leadership of the Confederacy.

It is evident that during the course of the fifth century a change had come over the attitude of the Athenian government towards trade. From the first half of the century there is no evidence that the government intervened to influence the course of trade, except by action to safeguard the routes from pirates and enemy raiders. If Athens can be said to have had a commercial policy at all, it was simply to keep alive the inward flow of vital materials; she took no action to secure special advantages for Athenian entrepreneurs nor to exclude those of other states. But after 450 B.C. there are some signs of a change in official policy. Diplomatic relations were fostered with the rulers of the Black Sea kingdom at the Cimmerian Bosporus, around the straits of Kerch, and arrangements seem to have been made to secure priority there for traders bringing freight to the port of Athens. Pericles himself sailed to the Black Sea with a squadron, and his visit was followed by the establishment of Athenian settlements at Amisus and Sinope on the south coast, and at Athenaeum and Nymphaeum on the straits of Kerch itself. In Macedonia, too, Athens seems to have secured a short-lived monopoly of shipping timber.[20]

In the late fifth century the author of the oligarchic pamphlet accused the Athenians of using their imperial position directly to control the trade of the allies. 'No city can escape the necessity for importing or exporting something, and this they cannot do unless they gain the consent of the rulers of the sea.' He followed this up by describing how Athens exercised a monopoly of shipbuilding materials. 'The Athenians alone among the Greeks and other nations are in a position to enrich themselves. For if a state is well endowed with timber for shipbuilding, where will they sell it to if they do not get permission from the ruler of the sea? Or supposing a state is rich in iron, bronze or flax, where will they dispose of it unless they can persuade him? These are the materials from which we get our ships; timber from one state, iron from another, wax from a third. Furthermore, they will not permit those competing with us to convey their goods anywhere else; or [if they do] the sea will be closed to them.'[21] Lest it be thought that the last statement was a flight of the writer's fancy, we may recall the passing of the Megarian decree at Athens shortly before the outbreak of war in 432: by this measure Megarians were excluded from the Athenian market and from every harbour in the Athenian empire.

It is quite clear that by 430 B.C. Athens was pursuing a policy of economic imperialism. Yet it must be noted that restrictions on trade concerned only strategic materials, including grain. It is in fact more likely that Athens used her economic position for political, or even strategic, purposes than vice versa. Her imperial position certainly gave impetus to her own commercial development, just as the latter, in its turn, strengthened her imperial position. But it is hard to believe that the encouragement of commerce was anything but an unforeseen by-product of imperial ambition, for the status of the traders themselves at Athens was politically insignificant, and many of them were not even Athenian citizens. On the available evidence we can only conclude that the trading pattern asserted itself without conscious government interference, and that it was only when the trading network was well developed that the Athenian leaders realised trade itself was a weapon which could be turned to political ends. How far commercial motives influenced Athenian official policy is quite obscure, for it is impossible to determine whether actions which impinged on commerce were consciously directed towards the ends they achieved. A difficult case is that of the Athenian regulation enforcing the use of her own coinage upon the whole empire. We have epigraphic evidence for this decree, but unfortunately it is uncertain whether it was passed early in the second half of the century, or whether it was a wartime measure.[22]

The effect of the measure was to compel the allies to pay their tribute to Athens each year in Athenian coined silver, since no other coinage was recognised as valid. But to obtain this coinage the allies obviously had to buy it directly or indirectly from Athens. To do this they were forced to sell their surplus products either to Athens or to states which sold to her. The result was a pattern of trade in which the Peiraeus provided a centre to which the allies exported their rural products in competition with each other: it is accordingly no mystery why Athenians, who made wine and grew wool, themselves drank the best Chian wine and wore the wool of Miletus. The allies' need to obtain Athenian currency, and the fact that their products, grown in similar climatic conditions, competed with each other, must have driven down the cost of their wares on the Athenian market and placed the Athenian consumers, and the traders buying for export, in an enviable position. This of course greatly enhanced the attractions of the market as a loading centre for outward voyages. However, the export market for Athenian silver was assured by the requirements of the tribute itself: Athenian coins were one of the best investments a trader could make; her coins were regarded not only as specie but also as a commodity for resale.[23]

From the allied states Athens imported a range of products which for the most part competed with home-produced commodities. Although she had great resources of marble in the quarries of Hymettus and Pentelicus, she imported the marble of Paros for sculpture: wine was a staple Athenian export to the Black Sea and perhaps to Egypt, but she herself imported the luxury wines of Lesbos, Chios, and Thasos. Attic soil supported the goats and sheep which clothed Athenians in their rough woollen garments, but an aristocrat like Alcibiades could wear the finer fabrics of Miletus. Linen was always a luxury commodity at Athens and Attic soil grew little flax; the latter requires soil and climatic conditions similar to those for grains, hence Greece drew its main supplies of flax from far afield, the north-east, Egypt, and Asia Minor. In spite of the expense, linen was used for sails, the Greeks having no worthwhile substitute, and the import of flax to Athens assumed a corresponding importance. In addition to the trade in staple commodities Athens, as befitted her position as a great entrepot, dealt in a range of luxury products from the whole Aegean trading area; dairy products and chariots from Sicily, silphium from Cyrenaica, fruits from Euboea, fine weapons from the Black Sea, gold from India, and beautiful furniture from Miletus, incense from Syria, and horses from Thessaly.

Among Athens' more noteworthy imports were slaves. In Solon's time the slave element in the population of Attica was drawn from the economically, hence socially, degraded section of the citizen population: in fifth-century Athens the large slave population was entirely foreign; public opinion did not favour the enslavement of Greek, nor did the law allow enslavement of Athenian citizens. A slave market was held regularly at Athens, and the taxes levied thereon formed a regular source of revenue to the treasury. The sources of supply were probably various; prisoners of war and the victims of kidnapping were busily fed into the markets overseas. The state police at Athens were, from Peisistratus' time, always recruited from imported Scythian slaves, who thus formed an important element in government administration. The Attic mines absorbed a constant flow of servile labour on a fairly large scale: owing to the gruesome conditions of their employment there, it was possibly more economic to work them to death and replace the capital asset than to try to prolong their life by more humane treatment. Some idea of the numbers employed can be imagined from the work force of 1,000 leased by Nicias, and from Xenophon's suggestion for purchasing 10,000 slaves as an investment in mining.[24] Industrial slaves, apart from those employed in mining, probably did not constitute an important element in the population, the case of Lysias who employed 120 slaves in his workshop is probably quite exceptional: an unspecified, but probably large number of slaves were employed in domestic service in Athens. The import of slave labour to Athens on a considerable scale had important consequences for the whole economy of Attica: for the slaves were not only producers but also consumers. From the point of view of interstate commerce it is clear that they formed a significant element in the balance of payments between Athens and the allies, as well as between Athens and the sources of supply outside the empire; although Athens probably re-exported some slaves, she was a net importer on a considerable scale.

The large volume of imported goods which reached the Athenian market in the fifth century was paid for by the export of primary products and of services; secondary production contributed to the export programme mainly through ceramics and coined silver, and the gap between the value of what Athens bought and what she sold abroad was closed by so-called invisible exports. Olive oil and wine became the staple rural products of her export programme as soon as her rural production recovered from the war losses. The quality of neither was exceptional by Aegean standards, and both products were freely available from other trading states of Greece; the success of Athenian traders in disposing of their home products in markets where the greatest demand existed, in Egypt, the western states, and the Black Sea area, was in some cases very greatly affected, as we have noted, by non-commercial factors connected with Athenian marine dominance. But this is not true of the Athenian penetration of the western market, for her success there had preceded the development of her naval power, and we can only speculate on the causes of her successful challenge to Corinthian and Milesian ware in the sixth century in one of their traditional areas of trade. Athens was favoured by nature in comparison with many of her competitors in the field of rural produce, for the latter required an ancillary ceramic industry to package its goods, and the clay deposits across the Aegean were of varying economic value: fortunately for Athens those of Attica were of unusually high quality. The tradition of a ceramic cottage industry for the internal market had in its turn called forth the skills which, when given their chance on the international market, won a brilliant name for Athenian pottery over the whole Aegean area. With the increase in the demand for Attic containers came an impetus to the development of a non-utilitarian, or fine pottery industry which won an honoured place of its own among the export products of Athens.

In addition to wine and oil, honey and scent were carried abroad in Attic pots, as market-gardening assumed an increasingly important place in the Athenian economy. She exported wool, and perhaps some woven textiles, and some building-stone. But the most valuable of all her export products continued to be coined money: whereas she imported grain to re-export it, she exported money in order to re-import it via the tribute. Thus the path of Athenian economic progress lay along the route that led from the mines of Laureion, via the trading cities of the Aegean, and back to the temple of the goddess in Athens.

Although the main economic aim of Athenian official policy was the simple one of keeping up the flow of vital goods, trade was regarded by Athenian governments as itself a source of revenue for the state. The attitude of Greek governments to taxation must not in any way be confused with that of many modern governments. There was no thought, as far as we know, of maintaining a balance between the private and public sector of the economy, nor of mopping up surplus spending power and channelling capital into long-term productive investment. To the best of our knowledge taxation on a national scale originated with Peisistratus, who extended to the whole country the levy he previously laid on the tenants of his own estates. In the case of the Tyrants there was the desire to make a profit on taxation, *i.e.*, the surplus left over after payment of the security troops and other expenses of control. For the young democracy there was no point in trying to make a profit, and when state revenue actually exceeded expenditure, as happened after the Laureion silver strike, the first inclination was to distribute the surplus among the citizens. In Periclean Athens for the first time the principle of building up a capital fund became accepted, and the desire to 'make a profit' returned to public life. Traditionally taxes had been levied on rural production, since this had been considered the only real source of wealth. As Athens developed into a commercial state, trade became the milking cow of public revenue. By this happy solution the public revenues of Athens were multiplied and the profits of commercial enterprise were distributed throughout the entire citizen body.

Market dues and taxes on transit trade were a normal feature of Greek public finance, and they are reckoned among the three major sources of income by the author of the *Economics*.[25] Reference to such taxes at Athens appear in literature rarely, but they leave no doubt that such duties existed there: the scarcity and obscurity of the references make it impossible to reach any definitive conclusions about the way they operated, let alone the income which they earned for the public revenue. Since the greater part of Athenian trade was sea-borne it is understandable that our meagre knowledge of the system is mainly concerned with harbour or customs duties; we do not know when these duties were first instituted, but in a passage of Andocides, dating from the fourth century, we find certain reference to a 2% *ad valorem* duty on goods entering and leaving the Peiraeus. There are references in Aristophanes and Xenophon to a duty of 1% levied at the Peiraeus, and it has been suggested that the 2% duty was the result of an increase in the earlier duty of 1%. But Aristophanes, in a passage only two lines earlier, mentions the existence of 'lots of one per cents', implying that the harbour dues mentioned by Xenophon may be quite separate from the customs dues mentioned by later writers. A fragment of the comic writer Eupolis says that 'the taxes must be paid before embarkation' and this suggests a passenger tax, which may be identical with the conjectured dock dues.[26] The revenue drawn from customs dues by other Greek states was at times very large, the outstanding case being that of Hellenistic Rhodes, with an income of a million drachmas from this source; and we may draw conclusions about the state of Athenian revenues accordingly. The only statistics we possess refer to the end of the fifth century, when Athens had lost the war and her empire. At this time the 2% tax was leased for 30–36 talents, and if we allow for the effects of contraband, this implies a port turnover of about 2,000 talents, or about twelve million drachmas. If we postulate a population figure for Athens of about a quarter of a million people, the *per capita* turnover is not very impressive for a commercial centre, and some historians have doubted the validity of the figure.[27]

By the transit dues, the Athenian state was able to draw off a steady stream of revenue not only from its own merchants but also from the trade of others, in so far as that trade was channelled through the Peiraeus. The impost could have had a depressing effect on trade by keeping foreign entrepreneurs away; but this danger was outweighed by the advantages offered by the Peiraeus as an entrepot, and by the fact that customs duties were payable in other Aegean ports. These revenues gave the state funds from which it was able to contribute to further economic growth by capital improvements and by utilising under-employed labour. But the gains accruing to the state from trade were not confined to indirect taxation. Since all merchants conveying goods to Athens received equal protection and marketing facilities irrespective of their nationality, it was natural for foreign merchants to base their activities on the Peiraeus rather than on their native ports. In this way Athens gained the benefit of their skill, capital, and enterprise: in addition the foreigners were obliged to pay a poll tax for the privilege of living in Athens. They were also (like Athenian citizens) subject to 'calls' (liturgies) to finance public festivals, and were expected to make 'gifts' (epidoseis) to the public purse in time of need. The revenue drawn from the resident aliens in direct taxation was evidently quite considerable, and Busolt has estimated it at 20 talents in the fourth century.[28] To the Athenians, in contrast to some modern attitudes, it seemed axiomatic that foreigners brought wealth to the country: 'For the more people who visit us, or settle here, obviously the greater the volume of imports and exports, of sales, rents, and taxes.'[29] Such people not only increased the flow of consumption goods, they helped to build up Athens' stock of capital by bringing their own ships and money for investment; the profits earned by this capital benefited the citizen community as a whole through that proportion of earnings which was directed to the treasury via taxation, and distributed to the citizens via the welfare services.

But while Athens was importing the services of foreigners to help man the commercial sector, she was exporting the services of citizens via the armed forces. Athenian marines, who increasingly formed the bulk of the confederate navy, were technically in the employment of the League and were sustained from its resources. Athenian services were likewise exported through the financing of foreign trade; as the latter developed, there began to emerge that pattern of credit which we know to have been in full operation by the fourth century: capital was made available to finance the purchase of outward cargo on the security of cargo and ship, and the terms of the loan included an insurance cover.[30] A vital benefit which Athens gained from her imperial position was the opportunity to sell not only her goods but also her services: she sold the services of her ports for trading; of her men as marines; of her money for credit; even of her jurors for litigation; for in the case of legal disputes arising out of contracts made at Athens, or of serious political charges, the case was heard at Athens rather than in the courts of the allied states themselves.[31] This bringing of judicial disputes to Athens was one of the more remarkable ways of drawing to the city the foreigners who contributed to Athenian revenue, and the *Old Oligarch* was impressed with its economic implications.[32] 'The Athenian people get the following benefits from the fact that the allies conduct their cases in Athens: (*a*) there is increased revenue from the 1 % duty at the Peiraeus; (*b*) business conditions are improved for those with apartments to let; (*c*) the same applies to people who hire out animals or slaves and (*d*) the town criers also benefit.' While the demand for Athenian facilities was being thus quaintly stimulated at home, a small army of Athenian officials was going abroad at confederate expense with various supervisory functions; guards, overseers, and taxation officers.[33]

The development of inter-state trade was sufficient to provide Periclean Athens with her essential food imports (grains and fish), with the raw materials of her shipbuilding industry, and with a mass of luxury items from within and without the empire; including fine wool, leather, textiles, cheese, wine, and slaves for domestic service: in return Athens exported silver, wine, oil, honey, scent, pottery, and services. Her invisible exports included profits on transit trade; tourist trade; court revenues from allied states engaged in litigation at Athens; the return on foreign investment (*e.g.*, the mines in Thrace which were the source of Thucydides' wealth); and the revenues she drew from aliens for the privilege of living in or operating from Athens. The extension of trade and credit enriched the community by making possible a more intensive use of its natural resources: a measure of her economic growth was the increase in the value of the goods and services which that community provided. This in its turn resulted in an accumulation of capital in the state treasury and in private hands: the possession of this surplus gave Athens a key to further economic development. In the public sector the capital was spent on armaments, welfare, and (mainly non-utilitarian) public buildings. In the private sector there was no real attempt to increase the scale of production in industry, with the possible exception of armaments: a cottage-type industry, sustained by family and domestic workers, remained the basis of the manufacturing sector, and even large construction enterprises were leased by the state to a mass of small contractors, each providing his own human and animal helpers. At the end of the fifth century, as in its early decades, the basis of Attic production was peasant agriculture and mining. The value of Attic primary products was enhanced by the stimulation of the overseas demand for them, and the rise in demand naturally resulted in an increase in the level of production to meet it. In the case of the mining industry higher production was achieved mainly by an increase in the (slave) labour force. In the agricultural sector production was expanded, and its value enhanced, by improved efficiency resulting mainly from greater specialisation in the commodities produced. How this came about can best be demonstrated by examining the pattern of Athenian agriculture as it developed under the stimulus of trade: we can get some idea of the extent of this development by contrasting the conditions which prevailed in the sixth century with those of Periclean Athens.

The establishment of a market at Athens, and the conversion of the Peiraeus into an international entrepot, enabled commercial farming to spread in Attica, and to a certain extent to replace subsistence farming: the extent of this replacement was limited only by the costs of transport between the farms and the market. The most general trend of change in the pattern of farm production was from 'dry' to 'wet'; or from grain to wine and oil. It may be assumed that in Attica a given area should normally be expected to return twice the weight of wine as of grain: if farmers fallowed in alternate years a switch from grain to wine would mean more than a quadrupling of the net product. Needless to say, the commercial attractiveness of the two crops would depend on the reigning prices. In a self-regulating market an increase in the output of wine could be expected to result in a fall in its price relative to grain, if the market were fed by domestic production only: this would not necessarily be so if domestic production were only one of the market's sources of supply. In the case of fifth-century Athens our statistics as to prices are small and unreliable, and the situation is complicated by a general decline in the value of money, assisted no doubt by the release of tribute into the economy after 447, and the disorganisation of production during the war years. This inflationary trend is shown by an apparent rise in money wages towards the end of the century, and by a decline in the value of silver (the metal of currency) relative to gold.[34] If we ignore the change in money value and consider only the relation between the prices of rural products, we note that, on the admittedly shaky evidence we possess, between 600 and 420 B.C. the price of wine actually improved threefold in relation to that of grain. This estimate is based on the consideration that grain and wine were accepted as of equal value by weight in the earlier period; that is, a measure (medimnus) of grain was held to be equivalent to 1 drachma, or to about $8\frac{1}{2}$ gallons of wine. In the time of Aristophanes, when the price of grain had risen to between 2 and 3 drachmas, 1 obol (one-sixth of a drachma) could buy 3 kotulae (about $1\frac{1}{4}$ pints) of wine, *i.e.*, rather less than 1 drachma per gallon. If we average the price of grain at $2\frac{1}{2}$ drachmas per measure, it follows that a measure of grain was now equivalent in value to less than 3 gallons of wine. What has been said of wine production applies even more to that of oil. Whereas, in the Solonian reckoning, a measure of grain was equated in value to about $8\frac{1}{2}$ gallons of oil, by the end of the fifth century it was equivalent to about 2 gallons only.[35]

The movement of prices thus favoured the substitution of

viticulture, and to an even greater extent, of olive growing, for grain cropping, except in conditions especially favourable to the latter. This is not to imply that grain production became a depressed industry. An increase in demand was ensured by the expansion of population; and, in the case of consumers who bought through the Athenian market, the landed price of foreign grain was not so low as to debar home producers from taking advantage of this expansion: *i.e.*, although the price at Athens, and the Peiraeus, was heavily influenced by imported food, the cost of the latter evidently allowed efficient home producers in the vicinity of the market to compete, and to receive a return attractive enough to encourage them to continue producing: (in the case of producers living far from city and port the competition of imports was far less, since the cost of hauling the imported food overland was prohibitive). The tendency was for good plain land everywhere in Attica to stay in grain production, and for poorer land in touch with the market to switch. Thus while the pattern of rural production adjusted itself to market demand, the overall increase in the volume, and the value, of farm output, coincided with a decline in the proportion of that output represented by grain. As marginal land switched to vines, the subsistence farmer in the Athenian plain came gradually to be replaced by the commercial grower, planning his output in accordance with market requirements. An example of a commercial farmer was Pericles himself, who caused his estate to be run entirely on a commercial basis, and, like a good economist, ordered his own supplies through the market;[36] an increasingly familiar figure in Athens was the peasant trudging to market to sell his grapes and buy flour.[37]

As the urban population increased, the rising demand for land, hence the improvement in land values, would tend to reduce the average size of the farms in the vicinity of the city. Vine and olive orchards can, unlike subsistence or grain farms, be profitably worked in small holdings, even in tiny allotments which the owner can work in his spare time. There was thus a tendency for farmlets to spring up near the city, and it became increasingly possible for families to live in the country near Athens on a tiny block of land, while the breadwinner could increase his income by working as an employed labourer in city or port. As the olive harvest falls in mid-winter, when shipping was tied up in Greece, conditions favoured such a distribution of labour in every way.

The combination of a change in the pattern of production and a decrease in the average size of the farms resulted in a much more intensive cultivation of the farm area, and consequently an increase in the real wealth available. How this increase in wealth was distributed among the community is a different matter, which will be discussed below: it would be rash to assume that the whole increase was retained by the growers. At this point it is sufficient to point out that, in general, specialisation (in primary production) leads to an increase in the national product, since it implies the more efficient employment of the resources available: subsistence farming on the other hand implies an attempt to wrest from the soil products which it is not necessarily best fitted to produce.

The trend to specialisation was in all cases limited by geographical considerations and transport costs. As trade increased, and the market for wine and oil became assured at the same time as did the supply of imported grain, the trend to specialisation went furthest in areas in closest touch with city and ports. The more remote from the market was the farm, the less it would be affected by the trend.[38] Since Attica had poor land communications and no usefully navigable rivers, there was no chance of subsistence farming disappearing in the remoter areas. But in the case of land within easy reach of Athens and the Peiraeus, that is, most of the Athenian plain, the availability of a market at which produce could be exchanged for imported goods meant the beginning of the end of subsistence farming: unless the farm could produce good crops of wheat of comparable quality to that available from abroad, it would be foolish and wasteful to grow one's own bread when the land could be producing liquid crops which could be exchanged on advantageous terms for imported grains. In addition, the land around Athens is more suited for barley than wheat, and the former is not suitable for bread-making; at any rate the Athenians, like most people, seem never to have eaten barley if wheat was available. Both economics and human taste conspired to take out of grain production land in the vicinity of the city. In some ways this land is among the richest in Attica, and we know that in the fifth century a large amount of market-gardening went on there, and that flowers, as well as vegetables, were commercially produced.[39] There is a particular reason why this land should have repaid such intensive cultivation, and that is not only the availability of casual labour for harvesting and easy facilities for marketing, but above all the availability of organic fertiliser in the form of nightsoil from the great city. Thus the intensification of land utilisation near Athens resulted in a huge increase in its productivity, consequently of its value. The resulting pattern of farming showed a tendency for farms to decrease in size as they neared the city, so that in some cases farming was gradually replaced by gardening. In the case of land further away from the markets, economic factors favoured stratification of production according to the natural situation of the land—that is, grain cropping tended mainly to be confined to the plains, vines would be found in great abundance on the lower slopes, and olives on the upper slopes.

From the point of view of feeding the maximum population, an acre of good plain land should always be more productive under grain than under olives, since it can produce more than twice the food value. When the increase in trade permitted the spread of commercial farming, i.e., specialisation in the most profitable crops according to the situation of the farm, there would be no reason to turn good plain land over to olives. The land which it would be profitable to turn over to olives would rather be that on the slopes, which was unfitted for grain production and hence carried a low yield. The trend of encroachment by olives on grain would thus naturally be downwards, until grain cropping had been driven off the slopes altogether. However, the vine country is the no-man's land between the two, since the lower slopes are admirably suited to viticulture.[40] Wine is, of course, not generally produced with an eye to its nutritive possibilities, and is more in the nature of a luxury product: the spread of viticulture is thus more dependent on a rising standard of living in the country of origin, and a sound export market. Granted these conditions, which were both fulfilled in Athens of the fifth century, wine is potentially the most valuable of the three crops, i.e., that which gives the heaviest yield per acre. The tendency then, as trade increased, would be for vines to run both into the plains and up the hills, that is to invade the traditional farming area of both grain and olives.

On plain land, grain could be expected to hold its own against vines best in areas furthest removed from the markets and ports; but the weakness of the Attic grain crop was its small proportion of wheat for breadmaking. When imported wheat became more readily available it is possible that more land, even in the hinterland, went over to vegetable production, since this is highly profitable if enough fertiliser and human labour is available, and the vegetables would improve diet by supplying the essential vitamins in which oil is deficient. Both the encroachment of vines on to the slopes, and the trend to market gardening would lead in the same direction, namely, the reduction in the size of the average farm; and both must mean that the average yield on land sown to grain must rise, because only land well suited to grain would be left producing it; the elimination of large-scale unprofitable grain cropping was one of the most important of the results of the development of Athenian trade, and a basic cause of her rural prosperity in the fifth century.

The development of trade went hand in hand with the accumulation of capital, the growth of the city of Athens, and the large-scale investment in the city services, building, and transport. The increased demand for labour in the city and ports meant that unwanted labour in the country could now be absorbed in these occupations.[41] In conditions of urban unemployment there is no easy outlet for surplus rural labour, and the labour force on farms tends to be decided more by the size of the family or household than by the requirements of farming. This presence of an unwanted labour force on the land, the Hectemors, had been a major cause of Attica's rural poverty in the sixth century, for men who had traditional ties to the land clung to them since there was no obvious alternative employment. Urban industrialisation offers the most favourable conditions for peasant farming for this reason, that it can absorb rural labour which is in excess of the economic requirements of the country. This does not necessarily mean that farms will thereby reach their optimum size in a given economic environment, because of the reluctance of rural labour to move, unless city conditions are so superior to those on the land that this is obvious to them. However, it does mean that a limit is put on the process of fragmentation, and that at any rate the worst evils of rural over-population are averted, so that the farming area has a better chance of being utilised to the best advantage.

We may sum up the preceding discussion as follows. The total volume of Attica's farm production was increased as a result of her commercial development, mainly because farmers were able to grow for the market rather than for subsistence. Agriculture became an intensive exploitation of the topsoil near the city and ports, both to feed the home market and to supply the requirements of overseas trade in wine, oil, and scent. Production was stratified in remoter areas so as to procure the yield of maximum economic value, and to improve the utilisation of the labour force available. In addition, the extension of olive production gave a status to farms on the upper slopes and increased the total farming area, that is, the rural capital on which the country could draw. At the same time as Athens was thus expanding her rural output she was energetically exploiting her mineral resources, and marketing the products of both industries through inter-state trade. The development of a free market at Athens, and the favourable conditions of trade (from Athens' point of view) ensured by her control of the Confederacy, enabled her to convert increased productivity into increased wealth.

VIII

THE SOCIAL CONSEQUENCES

THE best surviving evidence for the size of the Athenian population in the fifth century is supplied by the figures of the hoplites who were engaged or were available at any one time. The hoplite class was made up of fit males of military age, belonging to the free community and satisfying the minimum income qualification. There are serious difficulties in trying to estimate the size of the Athenian population from the size of the hoplite group, for we do not know what proportion of the free population the hoplites represent, nor do we know what percentage of the total population was free: even in the case of the hoplites our figures, in all except one case, refer to men actually committed to battle, and we have to estimate what proportion of the total field force these contingents represent.

We have the figure of the 8,000 hoplites at Plataea (479 B.C.); 13,000 at Tanagra (457 B.C.); 16,000 (including 3,000 resident aliens) in 431; and 7,000 in 424. But the most complete and reliable figures are supplied by Pericles in his statement of the city's defences in 431: his figures should be accurate, because he had access to the official list (the 'catalogue') of those qualified to serve, but his totals are different in kind from the other figures, in so far as they represent the number of men 'on the strength', not men actually sent into action at any one time. His total figure for hoplites on the mobilisation list is 29,000.[1] It is made up of two groups; the first group is of 13,000 men and represents the field force. This is the number which should be compared with those cited above. It was formed from fit male citizens aged at least twenty, and probably included men up to the age of forty-nine.[2] The second group was the reserve; it consisted of 16,000 men, and was drawn from the youngest call-up classes (18–20), and the oldest (50–60). It also included citizens of military age who for one reason or another were not available for service with the field force. The resident aliens were subject to military service just like the citizens, but they are usually mentioned separately, and it seems that they were reckoned as an extra, and were not taken into account in the sum of the field force. Thus, Thucydides mentions a figure of 16,000 men in action in 431, and this seems to be a simple addition of the citizen field force (13,000) together with 3,000 metics. Therefore, if Pericles included the metics at all in his figures, he probably reckoned them in the reserve, and this would explain why the figure for the twelve classes of the 'youngest and oldest' is actually greater than the figure for the thirty classes of men between twenty and forty-nine years of age. Many of the aliens were seafaring men and probably served with the fleet, so that the proportion which they form of the field force in 431 seems at first sight surprisingly high: the inference is that even in the upper income groups the free aliens constituted more than 25% of the population. All the battle figures must be increased by one thousand to allow for the cavalry corps; and only Pericles' figures represent the total fighting strength, for rarely would the whole army be deployed in one engagement.

The figures cited above suggest that between 480 and 430 B.C. there was a considerable increase in the number of better-off Athenian citizens; they also show quite definitely that by 430 B.C. resident aliens formed a substantial proportion of the upper class population.[3] The hoplite census itself was historically based on real income derived from farming, and at some stage the conditions had been extended to cover income based on any form of property. The inclusion of money income in the conditions of assessment meant that any change in the value of money could alter the proportion of citizens (and metics) qualifying for the hoplite class; for the minimum qualifying level remained constant, while the level of prices and personal income seems to have risen. Consequently, we cannot consider any increase in the number of hoplites as necessarily due to a population increase: the rise of hoplite figures could have been effected by the elevation of citizens formerly belonging to the lowest income group (the thetes) into the hoplite class. To estimate the size

or the growth of the citizen population as a whole we obviously
need to know what was happening to the thetic class during the
same period.

Unfortunately we possess no firm figures for the thetes class
at all during the imperial period, so we cannot hope to chart
its growth or decline. We can, however, make estimates of its
minimum numbers during this period, and these can be compared with the actual numbers for the hoplites. In 424 Athens
called up every available man, both citizen and free alien, for
an invasion of Boeotia. Apart from the corps of hoplites and
cavalry (7,000 and 1,000) the force included a mass of men
without proper equipment, *i.e.*, citizen thetes and poor metics.
Thucydides does not give their number, but he states that they
were 'many times more numerous than the enemy':[4] according
to Thucydides' preceding chapter the enemy included more
than 10,000 irregular or light-armed troops. If we can take
Thucydides seriously in this matter we must conclude that
Athens mustered over 30,000 men, from the free male population of military age and below the hoplite census, in 424 B.C.

Athens did not possess a regularly trained corps of light-
armed soldiers: those who could not furnish hoplite equipment
did their service in the fleet, and so did many of the metics.
The latter were needed, according to the *Old Oligarch*, for the
fleet; it was the common people who pushed the ships along.[5]
Now the maximum war fleet deployed by Athens was of the
order of 300 triremes,[6] each carrying a crew of about 200. When
she put out her maximum effort Athens thus needed the services
of about 60,000 seamen, apart from the merchant marine and
shore maintenance staff. These men were normally free men,
not slaves: they were recruited from both citizens and aliens,
and we know that the pool of labour in Athens was not sufficient
to meet these requirements. Athens recruited from the tributary
allies, and we do not know what proportion of the rowers
who came to Athens stayed there, and how many went home
each year after the campaign. But the organisation of the fleet
would have been very chaotic if a substantial majority of the
crews was casually recruited each year: the essence of its
efficiency was that the crews were trained and could operate as
a battle group. Athenian naval tactics were not confined simply
to boarding or setting on fire enemy ships; their success was due

to their speed and precision of manoeuvre, and this implies a high level of training together. It also assumes that the rowers were all young; few men over the age of thirty-five could stand the pace of service in a war galley.

If we assume that the front-line strength of the Athenian fleet in 430 was about 200 triremes, and that half the crew members were normally resident in Athens,[7] we are left with a minimum figure of 20,000 free men between twenty and thirty-five years of age and of less than the hoplite census. This would mean that the free male population of Athens between the ages of eighteen and sixty and below the hoplite census was not less than 33,000. If we compare this figure with the minimum estimated for those deployed in Boeotia in 424 B.C. and of the same financial and legal status, there is no obvious inconsistency. Although the evidence is so pitifully thin, it seems a reasonable conclusion that we cannot postulate a figure of less than 35,000 for the free male population below hoplite status and including resident aliens. If we add to this the figure of 30,000 for the hoplite and cavalry classes we get a total of 65,000[8] free men between eighteen and sixty years of age; and this total is by way of being a minimum. To estimate the total free population, including women and children, we should multiply this figure by four.[9] Thus the total free population of Attica about 430 B.C. would be at least a quarter of a million.

In addition to the free population there were the slaves; and we lack evidence even to form a rational estimate of their numbers. We have indeed one figure, given by Athenaeus,[10] of 400,000 slaves in Attica in the late fourth century; but as he also states that the inhospitable island of Aegina supported 470,000 slaves, the improbability of the latter figure does not inspire confidence in that given for Attica. Recent efforts have been made[11] to justify these figures, but the only plausible hypothesis offered is that they represent the turnover in the slave markets held there; in this case the figures could hardly be accepted as a valid basis for a calculation of population.

It is evident that considerable numbers of slaves were employed in the mines of Attica, for Thucydides has put it on record that more than 20,000 escaped during the occupation of Decelea (412–404 B.C.). This figure seems high, but it must be spread over eight years: it may also be compared with Xenophon's plan for a state-owned slave labour force of 10,000 for mining. To support his plan he quotes cases of men owning gangs of 1,000, 600, and 300 slaves in the mines. We cannot, however, assume a large reserve of industrial slaves apart from mining, since industrial enterprises were normally on a small scale. On the other hand the number of slaves employed as domestics may have been quite large. Xenophon assumes that a gentleman's household will include a number of slaves as a matter of course; Plato allows a retinue of 50 slaves for a rich man; an inscription from the late fifth century records the confiscated property of a resident alien at Athens as consisting of 16 slaves; even quite poor people might own several slaves; and we find a cripple appealing for public relief on the grounds that he could not even afford to keep a slave. How many slaves were employed as farm hands seems rather doubtful, but many probably doubled the roles of farm labourer and domestic; Aristotle at any rate seems to have thought that only a poor man would run a farm without slave labour: 'The ox is the poor man's slave'.[12] The Athenian government itself owned several hundred slaves who were employed on police and administrative duties. Although this evidence is too vague to form the basis of an estimate of the Athenian slave population, there can be no doubt that in the imperial period the figure was formidable.[13]

Although the available evidence relating to population is so very unsatisfactory, it is something if we can accept as a working hypothesis that the total population of Attica about 430 B.C. was at least 250,000, plus a considerable number of slaves. This conclusion may be compared with Gomme's estimate[14] of Attica's total grain consumption at about 1,600,000 medimni, or about 270,000 portions, in the fourth century, when the volume of Athenian trade (hence her capacity to import) had declined from the peak reached in the imperial period. We are probably safe in assuming that the total population of Attica in the imperial period passed the 300,000 mark at its peak.

It is generally believed that improved economic conditions in the fifth century caused a substantial rise in the citizen population of Athens during that period. As we have seen, this alleged increase cannot be proved by reference to the hoplite figures, since the increase shown there can equally well be explained by a rise in real or in money income at the time: to be certain that the number of *citizens* increased, we should need the combined figures for the thetes and the hoplites, to see whether the increase in the hoplites was at the expense of the lower class. A. H. M. Jones assumes[15] a rise in the citizen population by drawing an analogy with modern states of a similar economic pattern. He argues that there the birth rate is high, and population is kept in check only by a high death rate: when improved conditions make more food available, an immediate, and sometimes quite spectacular, increase in population is the result.

But the modern analogy may in fact be misleading when applied to classical Athens. When a peasant community in modern times responds to improved economic conditions by increasing its population, a good deal of the increase is usually attributable to improved medical services and the consequent alleviation of epidemics; a larger percentage of the population survives into the older age groups and the average age of the community rises accordingly. It is doubtful to what extent this is true of Athens in the fifth century: since food imports increased, no doubt we should expect to find a general improvement in health and an increased resistance to disease. Against this must be set the possibility of lowered hygienic standards due to rapid urbanisation and the exposure of the community to a wider range of diseases brought in by foreign ships: the obvious illustration of this is the wartime plague which carried off between one-sixth and *one-third* of the total population if the sickness figures of the hoplite class were representative.[16] Nor must we assume that improved economic conditions necessarily led to earlier marriages and consequently to larger families, as sometimes happens in modern communities: in Greece the conditions surrounding the institution of marriage were influenced more by tradition than by economics.

On the other hand an improved food supply at Athens probably meant a reduction in infant mortality due to malnutrition, and it certainly meant an increase in the rate of immigration into the country. The latter was probably the most significant factor in the population movement of Periclean Athens, and one of its results was an increase in the percentage of aliens in the community. As far as the citizens were concerned, factors operating in favour of an increase in their numbers were out-weighed by factors working in the opposite direction.

During the imperial period, Athens sent out military garrisons to keep watch on trouble centres in the empire, and in some cases members of these garrisons settled permanently in the subject territories, combining the role of guards and colonists. In other cases cleruchs and colonists were sent out for economic rather than strategic purposes. We do not know the extent of Athenian overseas colonisation during this period, and the twenty-odd settlements that are actually named in the literary or epigraphic sources can certainly not be regarded as the total number sent out.[17] In some instances a site was settled twice or even three times before a colony was firmly established. For some foundations the actual number of colonists or cleruchs is quoted, *e.g.* 1,000 in the Chersonese in 477 B.C.; 2,000 at Chalcis in 446; 1,000 at Hestiaea in 446; and 1,000 at Brea about the same time: apart from the purely Athenian settlements there were others apparently on too large a scale for Athens to handle alone, *e.g.*, those sent out to Thurii and Amphipolis (10,000 settlers), of whom a large proportion were Athenians.[18]

What proportion of the settlements actually made have found their way into the record, we cannot tell, for our list is compiled from passages where colonies are mentioned casually and some-times by way of illustration only. But even on the basis of the meagre information we possess it is apparent that the export of citizen population from Athens was on a huge scale. The num-bers we possess are for the allotments, each being intended as a family unit (although the settlers' families may not have gone out immediately with the pioneers). If therefore we should estimate as an absolute minimum a total of 10,000 allotments in the imperial period (and this may be far below the actual number), the full loss of citizen population to Athens would be in the region of 40,000.

It is only fair to mention at this point the view of A. H. M. Jones that in the case of the cleruchs, though not of the colonists, the loss of population was only theoretical; that the cleruchs never actually took up their allotments but stayed in Athens as absent landlords.[19] This was certainly not the view of Plutarch, who thought that Pericles' idea in sending out the cleruchies was to get rid of surplus population, and the theory cannot apply to the early cleruchy in Euboea, as Jones himself admits. In Plato's *Euthyphro* we have an actual example of an Athenian settler living in Naxos, whither Athens had sent a cleruchy; we should therefore have to assume that he was a member of another Athenian colony in Naxos, or that he had gone out on his own initiative and bought land there privately. This theory of Jones makes more complex the problem of estimating actual population losses through the cleruchies: on the other hand, if we believe that some cleruchs, whom we should expect to find at Naxos, were really at Athens; we must conversely allow that some Athenians, other than cleruchs, whom we expected to find at Athens, were really at Naxos, etc. In this case perhaps the estimate of the overall loss of citizen population would not be very much affected by the hypothesis.

To the losses in citizen population due to emigration must be added the losses caused by enemy action. Athens had scarcely begun to recover from the casualties she suffered during the Persian wars when she began the almost continuous series of campaigns against either the Persian empire or her own recalcitrant allies. No doubt in some seasons the operations undertaken were little more than routine sea patrols; but in others her casualties were formidable; *e.g.*, in the storming of Eion in the face of violent Persian resistance (476 B.C.); in the large-scale operations near the Eurymedon (466); and in the fiasco of Drabescus. Much heavier losses were to follow during the years of heavy fighting between 460 and 450. After her abortive expedition to Ithome, Athens seems to have tried to capitalise on the weakness of Sparta, stricken by the great earthquake and by the rising of her subject people. In the mistaken belief that the Peloponnesian League was now a spent force, Athens began a rampage of aggression upon southern Greece, seizing Naupactus, at the entrance to the Corinthian Gulf; descending upon Halieis in the Argolid peninsula; fighting the Peloponnesian fleet off Cecryphaleia; invading Aegina; and pushing an army north into Boeotia. In this series of bitterly fought campaigns Athens suffered severe losses to the hoplites, who had been the backbone not only of the rural economy but also (since the rural pattern had been the basis of the political and military organisation) of the political structure as well. It is probably with this period in mind that Aristotle wrote of Athens as suffering casualties of the order of two or three thousand on each major expedition:[20] elsewhere he attributed the shrunken numbers and influence of the upper classes to the losses they had suffered in war.

While the Athenian land force was being bled in Greece, her fleet was fighting the Persians in Egypt. Athens is said to have committed to this theatre within five years two fleets, of 200 and of 50 ships, with a complement of 50,000 men. The impression conveyed by Thucydides, our most reliable source, is that the expedition was almost a total loss, and the implications of this are so striking that some scholars have refused to believe it, in view of the fact that the Athenian war effort continued with more resilience than could be expected after such crippling casualties. It is possible that some of the Athenian forces had in fact been withdrawn before the final catastrophe, and that the terseness of Thucydides' narrative has caused him to omit mention of the recall. Even so, we can hardly estimate the losses at much less than 100 ships and 15,000 men, not all of them Athenians: it was perhaps the most costly military operation ever undertaken by a Greek state up to that time.[21]

The citizen casualties for the year 459 are documented in an inscription[22] which records the losses suffered by one of the ten Athenian tribes. The inscription reads as follows: 'These men died in action in Cyprus, Egypt, Phoenicia, Halieis, Aegina, and Megara during the same year.' The names of one hundred and seventy-seven men follow, including one priest and two generals. We cannot be sure that the losses suffered by this one tribe were typical. On the other hand we cannot assume that its losses were due to some single disastrous engagement in which the tribal regiment was cut to pieces. From the wide spread of battle areas it is clear that members of the tribe served in a number of contingents, and there seems no reason to believe that their particular losses were higher than those suffered by members of the other nine tribes. We should thus infer that in that one year alone between 1,500 and 2,000 men of the citizen community were killed in action. The casualties here recorded include some men killed in the early stages of the Egyptian campaign, but they give no indication of the scale of casualties that were to come later, when the entire operation collapsed.

Losses due to enemy action were borne entirely by men in the prime of life, as members of the expeditionary forces. Thus the losses were more far-reaching than may at first appear: not only was there an immediate loss of manpower to the community, but potential brides were left without husbands,[23] and fewer children were born. We cannot know the total casualties suffered by Athens in the imperial period, but from our knowledge of the actions in which her armed forces were engaged, and from the data on actual casualties which we possess, we cannot avoid the conclusion that her losses were of shocking proportions.

If we add the Athenian war casualties, suffered in the period 480 to 430 B.C., to the loss of citizen population she suffered through emigration, we could hardly estimate their total at less than 60,000 even on the most cautious reckoning. When this figure is compared to the previous minimum estimate for the total free population the proportion seems staggeringly high. If we assume that many of the war casualties, and all the emigrants, were citizens, it seems quite unrealistic to assume that Athens *increased* her citizen population in the imperial period: it would be almost impossible even to replace losses of this order within two or three generations.

We do not know what the Athenian birth rate was, but the sources give us a fair idea of the average number per family of children who survived past infancy. Jardé,[24] using the evidence of the fourth-century orators, pointed out that of a sample of 61 families, 20 had only one child and 19 had only two: he also indicated that the calculated average for the sample, 2·3 per family, was misleadingly high because the sample included no childless couples. Miss Mulder,[25] working with a sample of 347 families, found that of these, over 250 had only two children each: the average for the sample was 2·4 per family. Needless to say, the samples are far too small to inspire much confidence in the conclusions based upon them; but the impression they give is certainly not contradicted by other features of Athenian life which suggest that very small families were common, *e.g.*, the frequency with which families were increased by adoption, the use of childlessness as a ground for divorce, or the comic device of smuggling a foundling child into the household and passing it off as one's own. Perhaps the most one can say is that we are debarred from assuming that there was a high birth rate at Athens; if the average per family of children surviving past infancy was as low as 2·3, then there would be little chance that the adult population was replacing itself. If this is accepted, then the abnormally high losses suffered by Athens through war and emigration can be seen as practically precluding any increase in the citizen population and as indicating an absolute decrease.

Yet it is certain that the total population of Athens increased during this period. This is evident from the great increase in the volume of imported food: the vital concern on the part of Athenian politicians with the safeguarding of overseas sources of supply[26] would itself be sufficient indication that the population of Athens had outgrown its supply of home-produced food. An inscription[27] from the imperial period records work done to improve the water supply of the city of Athens, a *sine qua non* of urban development.[28] Perhaps the most significant indication of all is the military record of Athens in the imperial period, the fact that she was able to mount operations of such scope and frequency, and to survive the casualties which she thereby incurred. In the sixth century she would have been crippled by a defeat like that at Tanagra, let alone that in Egypt: it is true that in 450 even Athens apparently realised that she could not continue squandering her strength at this rate, yet within a year she was fighting again at far-away Cyprus, and within a generation she was accepting full-scale war with the most formidable military alliance in Greece. How greatly the population of Attica increased between 480 and 430 B.C. may be realised by recalling that in 480 the Athenian administration could contemplate the evacuation of almost the entire Athenian population across the sea, to be distributed among emergency billets and fed by an improvised supply system. If the population in 480 had been anything like the size of that estimated for 430, such an operation would have been quite impracticable. Even if the transport of the population could have been organised in reasonable time, there was no reception centre in southern Greece which could, at short notice, have supplied such a host with the minimum requirements of food and water.[29]

We thus reach the conclusion that the total population of Attica was increasing at the same time as the citizen population was decreasing; hence that the proportion of the population represented by the citizen component showed a very marked decline. Our most reliable figures, those based on the hoplite levies, generally give no indication of the relative proportions of citizens and metics serving. But we have one figure which refers to citizens only; in this case the citizens who received a ration of grain from a public donation in 446 B.C.:[30] the number given by Philochoros is 14,240. This number perhaps refers only to the poorer citizens living in or near the city and each recipient should represent one family. If this is so, and we allow a generous percentage for both rural, and rich urban citizens, we can hardly estimate the total citizen population at more than 120,000. This is only a half of the figure suggested as a minimum estimate for the total free population, and the calculation, crude as it is, suggests that *at least* half the free population of Athens at the time were aliens.[31]

This is entirely compatible with what we know of the economic conditions of the time, and the high rate of immigration to Athens. In the case of those foreigners who earned a living by the exchange of goods there was a very great advantage to be gained by operating from the centre, rather than from the periphery of the Athenian trading bloc. No obstacles to immigration were placed in their way by the Athenian government; a higher living standard prevailed at Athens than in many of the states from which the metics came; and their only disabilities were the liability to military service (to which they were in any case liable in their own country), and the metic tax. Apart from those who deliberately made their home in Athens for commercial reasons were those who drifted to the metropolis in search of work, having nothing to sell but their services: of the thousands who came to row in the imperial galleys no doubt many stayed to settle, and brought up their children as metics. In these circumstances it is easy to imagine that deficiency in manpower was more than outweighed by foreign immigration of free men.

As far as the slaves are concerned we can be reasonably sure that the bulk of Athens' slave population was gathered during the imperial period itself. We hear very little of slaves in Attica in the sixth century, and in its early stages it was the impoverished citizens themselves who formed the non-free element. In the edict of 480 B.C. for the evacuation of the population there was no mention of the slaves at all. On the return of the Athenians after the war all available manpower was mobilised to rebuild the city walls, even women and children being pressed into service: slaves are not mentioned by Thucydides on this occasion, though they are mentioned by the later writers Diodorus and Nepos. The only safe conclusion that can be drawn is that there was a desperate shortage of labour in Athens at the time, and no considerable reserve of slave labour. There is in fact no reason to suppose that there was any large-scale employment of slaves at Athens before the time of the Persian wars, and all the evidence which has been quoted to illustrate the use of slave labour refers to a period later than the wars. The supply of slaves must have been influenced by the large numbers of men who fell into captivity during the wars and the confederate operations which followed, *e.g.*, at Eion, Scyros, and the Eurymedon (where Diodorus states that 20,000 were enslaved): the dumping of these unfortunates upon the market should have resulted in a fall of prices, and made the domestic slave available at an economic price to a wider range of households. This increase in the supply of slaves was accompanied by an increase in the demand for labour for handicrafts and for services: the rise in real income at Athens during the imperial period enabled that demand to be satisfied.

The demand for labour at this time was apparently beyond the unaided capacity of the citizen labour force, as we should expect in a period of rapid economic development. The need for foreign labour to supplement that of the citizens is explicitly recognised by the pseudo-Xenophon: 'The city needs the metics for a mass of trades.'[32] Diodorus attributed to Themistocles a recognition of the necessity to encourage immigration to Athens for the sake of starting new industries. The building records of the Erechtheum at the end of the fifth century reveal that of 71 workers employed there only 20 were citizens.[33] Modern writers have expressed some surprise that the Athenians apparently raised no objection to the competition of foreign and slave labour, even when this labour was employed on conditions similar to those which they themselves enjoyed. This acquiescence is not so surprising if the Athenian citizens had become by 431 a minority in their own country: to maintain their existing living standards foreign labour was already a necessity.

It may, however, seem paradoxical that their minority position had been achieved by their own choice, and that the Athenians were content to see their own kin sent abroad as soldiers or colonisers while their places at home were taken by foreigners and slaves. Their approval of this process stems from the fact that those who remained behind effectively increased the privileged nature of their position in direct relation to their decrease as a proportion of the total population.

It was the aim of the Athenian radicals to make the citizens a privileged, hence an exclusive group in the Athenian community. In accordance with this aim a law was passed in 451 limiting citizenship to those born of Athenian parents on both sides. The reason given by Aristotle for the passage of the law at this time was the large number of citizens: elsewhere Aristotle[34] mentions restrictive laws of this type and connects them generally with the phenomenon of an increasing citizen population: it has therefore been assumed that he means that this was the reason for the Athenian law in question, although he does not say so. This implication, if accepted, would tell against the conclusion argued above, that the Athenian citizen population was more likely to be decreasing than increasing at this time. But the implication is not necessarily valid, nor have all scholars accepted it.[35] A law restricting the rights of citizenship to a closed group, united by blood, does not necessarily imply that this group is increasing in numbers. In so far as it has a rational (as opposed to a mystical or emotional) basis it is just as likely to reflect a desire on the part of the privileged to limit their own numbers in response to an increase in the value of their privileges. The latter were not confined to the rights of participation in cleruchies and social benefits. There was, for instance, the case of the free grain distribution of 446 B.C.: on this occasion a shipment from Egypt, a king's gift, was distributed in equal shares to all Athenian citizens who applied for it, and whose qualifications for citizenship were accepted under scrutiny. Each recipient was apparently handed about two medimni (almost three bushels), or enough grain to keep a family of four for the best part of two months, a very generous windfall indeed. The aura of privilege now acquired by the citizenship is indeed well illustrated by those occasional gestures whereby the sovereign demos graciously admitted to the exclusive group honoured outlanders such as Chaerephilus or Thrasybulus, honoured for his part in the assassination of Phrynichus.[36] Citizenship had become a prize worth seeking even at the cost of physical risk or financial sacrifice: it had become a good in itself, even to men whose native land lay elsewhere.

The material advantages of those who belonged to the citizen group were of two distinct kinds. In the first place there were those payments in money or kind, whereby the citizen body, sovereign over the state, distributed among its own members those resources which it considered to be surplus to the needs of state administration. In the second place there were the economic advantages secured by the citizens' monopoly of the country's basic industry, agriculture. The first group of benefits resulted from a conscious manipulation of public resources: the second resulted from favourable economic conditions acting upon a traditional pattern of production. The second was achieved through the establishment of a market economy: the first was achieved in spite of it.

One of the more valuable of the privileges of Athenian citizenship was the right of taking up allotments in the empire on land overseas which had been acquired by the Athenian government from the natives. In some cases the latter were removed to make room for the Athenian cleruchs; in other cases the natives remained as servants to the new settlers; in other cases again the latter were pioneers, and took with them the labour which they required. Since the cleruchs were drawn from the poorest groups in the citizen community, the general effect on the Athenian economy was to level income upwards: as artisans became proprietors overseas, their labour was lost to home production, but the average income of the citizen group remaining was raised by the reduction in the number of those members who belonged to the lowest economic strata.

A second method of relieving the burden of citizen poverty was provided by the institution of welfare payments for poor citizens (though not, of course, for non-citizens). Few aspects of Athenian administration have come in for more criticism and praise; critics have seen in them the instrument of the crudest demagogy, or the expression of a truly democratic spirit in the realm of social economics. A key passage for information about the working of the Athenian welfare state is found in Aristotle's *Athenian Constitution* (24. 3), in which he claims that in the fifth century some 20,000 Athenian citizens were supported at one time from public funds. Of this number almost 12,000 were employed in a military, and over 8,000 in a civil capacity. Army pay is not normally regarded as a welfare payment; but the employment of citizen labour in imperial defence can in this case be properly regarded as a privilege, as well as a burden, of empire, in that it enabled the Athenians to sell their services in a way that would scarcely have been possible without the financial resources of the empire. But it is upon the second group, the civilians who were supported from public funds, that our attention naturally focuses. Of these people, 500 were members of the Council, elected for one year and allowed to be re-elected only once: 700 more, according to Aristotle, served as magistrates at home, and a further 700 as magistrates abroad. (Unfortunately the text is corrupt at this point and these numbers are contradicted in a later passage of the same monograph, from which it appears that the numbers might be halved.) Although these payments were a source of temporary revenue to the recipients, they can hardly be considered as having been instituted primarily with that end in mind: the payment of office-holders is a principle highly defensible on the grounds both of efficiency and equity. The assumption of financial responsibility for war orphans is in quite a different category: morally admirable in itself, it seems inspired not by administrative convenience nor by the interests of democratic administration but by a feeling of moral responsibility on the part of the community towards its handicapped members: since its aim is to redistribute resources in the interests not primarily of efficiency but rather of moral equity, it must be considered as a welfare payment proper.

At first sight it appears that the benefits paid to orphans constitute the only item on Aristotle's list which properly deserves to be considered as a welfare payment. In that case the strictures of classical and modern critics would be unjustified: the payment for duties of a civil or military kind constituted effectively a redistribution of the community's assets in favour of the poorer members, but that distribution might properly be considered as an accidental by-product, rather than as an end, of the democratic programme, the true end being democratic efficiency. This view becomes more difficult if it can be shown that the number of people on the public payroll was obviously and seriously in excess of the numbers demanded by administrative efficiency in the interests of self-rule. Now the largest single item mentioned by Aristotle is the panel of 6,000 jurors appointed each year and paid in accordance with their attendance in court as required. Such a large number is on the face of it suspicious: it would be reasonable only if a large number of courts were operating in different parts of the country, or if the 6,000 were merely a pool from which small juries were actually empanelled. But we gather from Aristotle that, for public cases at least, 500 was a normal size for a jury, and we know that some cases in the fourth century were judged by panels of several thousands. It is difficult to believe that the ends of justice could have been served by the use of juries of this size; anyone who has been forced to address a group of unwieldy size will appreciate the difficulty of persuading such an audience to follow a complex argument, disentangle points of law, and come to a conclusion rationally based on the evidence made available. On the face of it the huge juries empanelled at Athens seem rather ludicrous as instruments of justice. They have a historic justification as the descendants of the Heliaea, or assembly of citizens operating as a 'people's court': one advantage of their size was the virtual impossibility of using bribery effectively. Perhaps such mass courts, which had operated a sort of lynch law, worked tolerably well in the days when Athens was still a small, closed community; for many of the accusations, such as those concerned with homicide, impiety, or the settlement of the vendetta, were felt to concern the whole community. The survival of such an institution into the time of imperial Athens, and its utilisation to settle complex questions of law can be defended only on the grounds that it was in the interests of democracy to draw as many citizens as possible into the actual administration of the country.[37] The Athenians were suspicious of the idea of delegating their power to tiny groups; judicial efficiency seemed less important than democratic control. But at the same time the institution of mass courts provided a very convenient channel for the distribution of welfare payments; a sceptic may be excused for questioning the motives for a policy which kept a substantial proportion of citizens on the public payroll not in the interests, but at the expense, of judicial efficiency. At any rate it is interesting to note that in the latter part of the fifth century the amount of work fed into the Athenian law courts was increased by the measures taken to compel the subject allies to bring certain classes of lawsuits to Athens. As a section of the community developed a vested interest in keeping the wheels of justice turning, the demand for legal work called into being a new service and a new profession, that of the 'sycophant', or professional informer, who kept himself busy by denouncing the rich not only among the subject peoples but also among his own fellow citizens as well.

Many critics will disagree with the suggestion that the number of jurors was kept artificially high in the interests of spreading the common resources among a wider selection of the poorer citizens. Although the number of jurors was obviously high, they were, after all, discharging, however inefficiently, a necessary duty, and deserved to be recompensed for it. But this argument can hardly apply to the theoric payments (which Plutarch ascribed to Pericles),[38] whereby citizens were paid so that they could attend the dramatic performances, organised by state-appointed officials and paid for by calls upon the richer members of the community. Unfortunately we have little information about the working of the Theoric fund, and most of the data we possess refer to the fourth century, when it became an important item of political dispute. The daily payment was small (two obols), and it was available only while the Dionysian and Panathenaean festivals were actually being celebrated, that is, for only a few days of the year.

This completes the modest list of public grants which may properly be considered as welfare payments. There were, in addition, certain grants in kind for which the citizens were eligible. We have mentioned the donation of Egyptian grain which was distributed to the citizens in 446 B.C.: this was perhaps not an isolated instance; but we have no means of estimating the frequency of such windfall distributions. Free meals were supplied as a matter of course to certain magistrates while on duty, and the meat of animals slaughtered at public sacrifices was available to those citizens who claimed it.

Finally, there is some reason to suppose that in times of stringency, food was subsidised by the releasing of grain at an artificially low price from a bulk store maintained at public expense: but this is a conjecture based on flimsy evidence.[39]

The whole system of payment for public service, and of benefits in the form of welfare grants, seemed in retrospect to ancient historians as devised solely to win popularity for democratic politicians by redistributing community resources in favour of the poorer voters. Aristotle even writes that Aristeides urged country folk to move in to town in order to seek a livelihood from the armed forces and the public service, saying that all their labour could be absorbed in this way.[40] Now it is demonstrably untrue that the whole of the Athenian labour force was ever employed in public services: it is also clear that state pay made no man rich; its effect was rather to take off the sharpest edge of citizen poverty and to ensure that no citizen need be destitute. But if the value of the individual benefits was small, the proportion of recipients seems considerable. If we can accept Aristotle's figure of 20,000 recipients, the proportion of families whose income was augmented from treasury sources would be more than half those comprising the citizen population, as we have estimated it; and this takes no account of occasional benefits such as festival payments. Even without Aristotle's testimony we know that at least 6,500 men were being paid at any one time for public service of a civilian nature; and this can hardly be less than 15% of the citizen labour force. If we add to this the number of men employed on defence and imperial administration we see that a surprisingly high proportion of citizen manpower was either employed or supported out of public funds. This number must be augmented once again by the total of those absorbed into the building industry and employed on the ambitious programme of public works undertaken by the Periclean government. Plutarch naturally couples the public works programme with the armament drive as two methods of spreading the imperial surplus throughout the citizen community:

'And it was true that his military expeditions supplied those who were in the full vigour of manhood with abundant resources from the common funds, and in his desire that the unwarlike throng of common labourers should neither have no share at all in the public receipts nor yet get fees for laziness and idleness, he boldly suggested to the people projects for great constructions and designs for works which call many arts into play and involve long periods of time, in order that the stay-at-homes, no whit less than the sailors and sentinels and soldiers, might have a pretext for getting a beneficial share of the public wealth. . . . The arts which should . . . work up these materials were those of carpenter, moulder, bronze-smith, stone-cutter, dyer, worker in gold and ivory, painter, embroiderer, embosser, to say nothing of the forwarders and furnishers of the material, such as factors, sailors and pilots . . . wagonmakers, trainers of yoked beasts, and drivers. There were also rope-makers, weavers, leather-workers, road-builders, and miners . . . for every age almost, and every capacity, the city's great abundance was distributed and scattered abroad by such demands. So then the works arose . . . towering in their grandeur . . . and yet the most wonderful thing about them was the speed with which they rose. Each one of them men thought, would require many successive generations to complete it, but all of them were fully completed in the heyday of a single administration.'[41]

The period of building activity to which Plutarch refers was in the twenty years preceding the Peloponnesian war: the most magnificent of the resulting structures were those on or near the Acropolis—the Odeon, the Propylaea, and the Parthenon, together with their sumptuous decorations. In financial terms their cost was enormous: no estimate for the Acropolis group of structures is much less than 2,000 talents, or approximately five times the estimated internal revenue of Athens.[42] At the same time she was engaged on an intensive construction programme designed to serve the ends of defence and of internal distribution. A southern wall, parallel to the existing north wall, was run from the city to the Peiraeus linking the two in a readily defensible position and converting the city area into a land peninsula. A permanent market was established at the port, with weather-proof anchorages, offices, and warehouses. Behind the quays a new built-up area arose, carefully planned, and intersected by wide, straight roads designed for the rapid and convenient movement of goods. In addition to these new projects, Athens faced the considerable task of maintaining and improving her existing structures at a time when all her facilities were strained by her increasing overall population: we cannot estimate the cost of this programme, but the expense of maintaining her city walls and the public utilities, especially roads and water supply, must have been heavy, and the number of state-employed correspondingly great. At the same time she was engaged in the construction and maintenance of a war fleet of over two hundred vessels.

From what has been said it is clear that a high proportion of the Athenian citizen population in the imperial period drew income from the public treasury: in some cases this income was in the form of welfare benefits; in others it was payment for public service; in others it was in the form of wages for employment on public construction. The first two categories of benefits were confined to citizens; the third category benefited the community as a whole, since all residents were equally eligible for employment on public works.

One important effect of this state-organised redistribution of resources was to lift the average living standards of the citizen group above the average living standards of the whole Athenian community by raising the *minimum* standards of the citizens. In Periclean Athens it was slaves and foreigners who took the place formerly occupied by citizens at the lowest economic level of society. But at the other end of the economic scale the landowning aristocrats found their position increasingly challenged by a new class whose wealth was drawn not from inheritance but from trade and industry; and such men were in many cases not citizens but resident aliens.

As the Athenian economy expanded, the income pattern changed in response to the spectacular gains which were made in the trading and industrial sectors; for those engaged on the services which fed the market profited most by its operation. Evidence for the high returns available from commerce is afforded by the level of interest charged: the rate never falls below 12% except for a personal accommodation; the commercial rate seems often to have been above 15%, and on bottomry loans 20% for one round trip was probably a minimum, lenders who could afford to take risks could command a considerably higher rate.[43] The profits of long-distance transport were shared between the actual merchant, who sailed with his ship, and the money-lenders who financed the cargo:

it was the ambition of every trader to leave the sea and join their ranks. What could be done by judicious investment is illustrated by the success story of the banker Pasion. Born a slave, he accumulated a large personal fortune, and when he died he left a network of investments, including a whole armament factory. Other wealthy metics, like Chrysippus, Heracleides, and Chaeriphilus, whose fortunes were derived from food imports, are known to us chiefly because of their public munificence.[44]

Apart from trade, mining was potentially the most lucrative field for private investment. Of those who made money quickly from mining one of the best known was a metic, Sosias of Thrace, a large-scale employer of labour.[45] But his was an exceptional case. Mining territory remained state land, and individual leases were granted to concessionaires: the grant of a lease to a foreigner was a rare privilege, and depended on the acceptance of the latter into the Athenian community as an associate-citizen for taxation purposes. In the field of secondary industry, on the other hand, foreigners were under no disabilities *vis-à-vis* the citizens, and one of the largest manufacturing establishments of which we know was owned by a metic, Cephalos, who employed 120 slaves in a shield factory. But industrial plants were usually on a much smaller scale, and the possibilities for rapid enrichment seem to have been small compared with the opportunities available in inter-state trade.

We lack the data to estimate even approximately how far the ranks of the wealthy Athenians were penetrated by aliens, and how much of Athens' real income came into their hands. One thing we can say with certainty is that whereas in the earlier period the Athenian growers had practically monopolised the upper economic strata of society, in the imperial period the ranks of the wealthy included many whose possessions did not derive from land but from commerce and industry, and many of whom were not even citizens. At the bottom of the social and economic scale were the slaves: their living conditions depended very much on their employment, and in certain sectors, especially mining, their conditions were uniformly dreadful. Slaves employed as domestics seem to have been better treated, and if hired out as workers in construction industries they earned the same rate of pay as the citizens beside whom they worked.[46]

But this tells us only that slave labour in these circumstances was officially costed as the equal of free: the wage belonged not to the slave but to his owners. There is, for what it is worth, the comment of the *Old Oligarch* that one could not tell a slave from a freeman in the streets of Athens, since both were so poorly dressed.

The preceding paragraphs have been concerned to note readjustments in the income pattern in response to state financial policy and private commercial enterprise. A question to which we should like to know the answer is whether there was an increase in average real income, and a general rise in living standards through the community. As usual we lack the material to give an unequivocal answer to the question: it is not worth while trying to estimate the total income at several points of time and dividing it by the estimated numbers of the population, since the result would be even more nebulous than the estimates. It is, however, worth pointing out that we cannot assume that the Athenian community as a whole (including the slaves) was necessarily better housed, clothed, and fed in 430 than in 490 B.C.; but it is certain that the lot of the citizen component had improved, and that certain additional benefits had been made available, some of them to the whole free community. Perhaps the question might be reframed, so as to enquire whether imperial expansion, and the economic progress achieved, did in fact bring about a reasonable standard of living in the community of Periclean Athens.

For the city of Athens itself we are dependent for our knowledge of housing conditions upon scattered literary references, and on the archaeological record. Unfortunately the latter, while shedding valuable light on the general layout, and on the details of the more impressive (hence durable) structures, tells us little about the conditions of the masses. We know from the layouts uncovered that the streets were very narrow and the houses crammed together. The use of stone for building seems to have been confined to public construction and the dwellings of the most wealthy; but wood, too, because of its scarcity, was apparently a luxury material.[47] Rammed earth or unbaked brick were the commonest building materials: a spade could be driven right through the walls, and this was the traditional ingress of the burglar: wooden doors and stone floors were a luxury; windows were mere holes in the wall. We have some revealing glimpses of housing in war-time Athens from the eye-witness accounts of Thucydides and Aristophanes;[48] but the shocking conditions there described were unusual, and brought about partly by the evacuation of the rural areas; this, however, was part of the price paid for imperial progress. The shacks and crates in which the evacuees made their homes no doubt compared poorly with the more permanent structures of the townsfolk; yet the glimpses which Aristophanes gives us of conventional housing are not encouraging. Homes are tiny and squalid; the human denizens share the accommodation with poultry, pigs, and with vermin: standards of hygiene are not high: a better-class house is said to be too crowded to relieve oneself in.[49] The houses of the wealthy, such as we hear of in the dialogues of Plato and Xenophon, were certainly more roomy and comfortable, containing enclosed courts, paved or cement floors, and wooden doors. But there is a significant comment in Demosthenes,[50] who contrasts the magnificence of the public structures with the insignificant and unpretentious homes of even the most eminent men in the land. By modern standards the internal furnishings were rather austere, and the inventory of Alcibiades' furniture makes bleak reading.[51] Furniture was normally restricted to beds, tables, seats, and boxes for storage; but mosaics, cushions, and beautiful cups or pots provided a touch of luxury in wealthier homes: much of the internal equipment mentioned by Xenophon[52] was designed for production rather than relaxation—implements for washing, grinding, cooking, spinning, and weaving. The streets of Athens, as in an African village today, were kept reasonably clean by the birds of prey which scavenged among the rubbish dumped outside.[53] It is perfectly clear, both from the literature and from the archaeological record, that the magnificent private dwellings to be found in imperial Rome (or even in Pompeii) were beyond the means of even the richest men in imperial Athens.[54]

The austerity of Athenians' housing conditions was paralleled by the simplicity of their clothing and diet. So far from implying any notable improvement in these things during his lifetime, Thucydides suggests in a famous passage[55] that better-off folk were actually worse dressed in the later than in the earlier period. 'Not long ago the elder members of the upper classes abandoned the luxury of wearing linen garments and binding their hair in a bun held together with a golden clasp.' As a matter of fact the virtual disappearance of linen clothing at Athens was caused by the decline in flax production, when improved conditions for grain growers induced them to replace flax by wheat as a cash crop. But the change from linen to wool as a material for personal wear was rightly seen by Thucydides as a move towards greater austerity in dress, for wool is not an ideal clothing material for a Greek summer. The surprising suggestion that material standards actually declined in the fifth century is supported elsewhere. Athenaeus, in more than one place, stresses how well Athenians had lived in the early period (around 490 B.C.), and with this he contrasts the wretched conditions towards the end of the century, quoting Cratinus to prove his point.[56] It is interesting that Pericles, in his eulogy of contemporary Athens and her achievements, makes no claim for improved material standards: on the contrary he makes one claim which has perplexed generations of readers: 'We combine a love of beauty with frugality [cheapness?]'. As Gomme pointed out, this certainly does not apply to the public structures erected in Periclean Athens: but it is very appropriate to the private lives of the citizens.

It would be foolish to attach much weight to remarks of this nature; the comments are too vague, and the temptation to praise the past is too well attested. But they should serve as a warning against any assumption that material standards necessarily showed a rise in the imperial period: the one conclusion which does emerge is that commercial expansion did not in fact bring about anything approaching a high material standard of living at Athens. The everyday life of ordinary folk, as portrayed by Aristophanes and Theophrastus,[57] is characterised by extreme frugality together with the meanness and avarice which are born of a miserable struggle for existence. There are no gargantuan meals, no real gourmets, even in the elegant world of Plato: bread and porridge remain the staple diet even of the wealthy, and a diet based heavily on cereals is not normally indicative of a high living standard:[58] when a feast was held, even these humble ingredients were often contributed by the guests or subscribers. One can form some idea of the gap between the living standards of the wealthy in imperial Athens and in imperial Rome by comparing the symposia described by Plato and Xenophon with the dinner of Trimalchio, or the banquets described in the letters of Seneca.

On the other hand there were at least two important respects in which living standards at Athens were improved during the period of expansion. In the first place luxury on a new scale was brought into the lives of the people by the provision of new community services of an artistic and religious nature. These were the festivals which Pericles mentions with such pride in his funeral speech; not only the elaborate processions and ceremonies, but the theatrical performances which were complementary to them. To house the musical festivals the Odeon was constructed; and as part of a programme to endow the community with enduring assets of unparalleled magnificence there were built over the years the temples which were to become the wonder of the ancient world—the Parthenon, the home of Athena in victory, the shrine of Hephaestus, the temple of Erechtheus, the great structure of the Propylaea, and the magnificent ornaments which were made for their decoration; above all, the gold and ivory statue of Athena by Pheidias. Not only was the capital city thus embellished, but other centres received their endowments; we know the temple of Poseidon overlooking the sea at Sunium, and of the temple at Eleusis.

The second important respect in which life was made easier for the free community was in the provision of cheap domestic labour. We have noted earlier the influx of slaves into Attica during the fifth century: at the beginning of our period the slave is a fallen member of the citizen group, an object of pity, as a symbol of the fate that could overtake any unfortunate member of the community. In Periclean Athens the slave is strictly alien to the citizen group, a mere chattel, and a labour-saving device. It is the reasonable expectation of every free-born family, even though their means be slender, to own at least one servant: the slave has become for his owner a symbol of status, corresponding to the modern man's motor car or T.V. It may at first sight appear curious that a people which suffered from chronic under-employment should choose to spend its resources on the purchase of extra labour. But the servant who walked behind the citizen housewife gave her self-respect, and released her from the heavy and degrading chores of the daily round. To his master he gave the pride of ownership and power, the satisfaction of knowing that however bleak may be one's own existence, there are others who would gladly change with it. Above all, the slaves gave to their owners the inestimable blessing of unenforced leisure.

Among the most characteristic features of Periclean Athens was the high value placed on leisure activities, both of a physical and intellectual kind. Prosperity, as Aristotle noted, gave the Athenians a zest for living better, in the non-material sense; it was a zest which showed itself most clearly in an undiscerning scramble after culture among the leisured classes.[59] Greek aristocratic tradition had always held up as an ideal of refined living the cultivation of body and mind, its crown of glory was the victor's wreath in the great games. When economic changes gave to a wider section of Athenians an opportunity to divert time and energy from gainful to leisure pursuits, the result was not only more idleness—more dallying in the agora, the palaestra, and the gymnasium—but also an unprecedented growth in formal education. When Pericles claimed that Athens was the school of Greece, he revealed not only the intellectual pride of his countrymen, but also the priorities of their social arrangements. The state as such provided no system of schooling, but the demand induced private enterprise to provide a network of education from the primary to the tertiary level. Nurses and tutors in the home, teachers in the schools, trained the younger males in music, literature, and gymnastics. For youths and adult males the new class of Sophists provided training in public speaking, literature, and philosophy: like a travelling circus they moved from city to city, peddling their wares of spiritual nutrition.[60] If we ask why even well-off Athenians continued to live in squalor, we may find an answer in their system of priorities, which did not attach the highest value to material progress. Theatres and sewerage systems are both important for human betterment, but when resources are limited a choice has to be made. To modern thinking a factory is more productive than a debating society: many Greeks would have found such an idea audacious and eccentric.

When one compares, however roughly, the material standards of sixth- and fifth-century Athens, one is struck by the lack of positive evidence for any real advance in creature comforts such as one cannot help noting between the standards of the early Roman republican, and early Roman imperial period. The impression given may be misleading, and due to the inadequacy of the evidence for the Athenian period. And yet it is not implausible that the heavy increase in food and materials, made available by commercial expansion, was to a large extent absorbed by the very great increase in the slave (and free alien) population. Where the slaves were employed directly in production, *e.g.*, in the mines and industry, they evidently put more into the pool of goods than they took out of it. But many of the slaves contributed little to the flow of goods, they were consumers rather than producers. We get an overall impression of Athens in the imperial period acting as a magnet to draw consumer goods from all quarters of the known Greek world. At the same time there is a movement of population, both free and unfree, from the periphery to the centre of this traffic: the goods move in, and the people follow them. Free-born aliens arrive as a result of voluntary migration, slaves as a result of commercial transactions: but the effect of both their comings is to absorb much of the increase in the supply of goods, and to keep demand in step with, or still ahead of, supply. It was surely the great increase in population at Athens in the Periclean period that kept living standards of the community at large at a low level, with the two exceptions noted above. The monumental splendour of Athens' new skyline, and the provision of cheap domestic labour were the two most notable achievements of her economic progress. Both, however, were designed directly for immediate consumer satisfaction, and neither gave much promise of increasing future production. Had the economic surplus been invested in more long-term material productive fields, Athens might conceivably have become the first European state to break permanently out of the circle of poverty: the chance, however, was lost, and did not return.

IX

SOME CONCLUSIONS

IF there is one single cause to which the economic growth of Athens can be attributed, it is the development of a market system which rivalled, and surpassed, the systems of Corinth and Miletus. The importance of the market was that it turned increased productivity in Attica into increased wealth, hence it gave incentive to further production. In this way Athens was able not only to exploit the resources of her farming and mining industries, but also to make profitable use of her manpower in administering the empire, as well as in developing the secondary industries associated with the expansion of her trading sphere. In this way Attica passed insensibly from a more or less homogeneous community of citizen subsistence farmers to a cosmopolitan community of subsistence and commercial farmers, miners, seamen, and merchants: commerce was the magic wand that turned the ore of Laureion, the flowers of the Athenian plain, and the wine of the lowlands into the grain of Russia and Egypt.

The increasing importance of trade, in its turn, led to some striking changes in the social relations of the Athenians at home, and in their activities abroad. Whereas most Athenian families had formerly depended for their food on the land where their homes stood, or on farms within walking distance, 400 miles of sea could now separate the source of their food from the place where they lived and worked. A family living entirely from the products of the plot of earth on which it dwells, forms an economic community of the simplest kind: but when the members of an economic community become geographically more remote from each other, and economically more interdependent, their interrelationship becomes more complex, and their organisation more difficult and vulnerable. A state which could put into practice the Greek ideal of autarky, or economic self-sufficiency, had this inestimable advantage that the total area which formed the source of its supply was within the area of its own administrative control. But a state which relied on sources of supply outside its own frontiers was forced to depend on the co-operation of foreign individuals or states. It was therefore led more and more to the arts of diplomacy and the practice of imperialism, in the desire to influence, or if possible to control, those peoples abroad with whom its own citizens traded, and those whose homes lay across its lines of communication. Diplomacy can be expensive; imperialism even more so: one part of the price which Athens paid for her commercial development was an increase in the proportion of her available resources which she was forced to allocate to war. The cost of the latter was bound to rise in proportion to the active opposition which Athenian policies engendered abroad, and a situation could arise in which the costs of maintaining the system actually exceeded the revenues drawn from it.

The cost of defence can be reckoned in terms of the diversion of manpower which could otherwise be productively employed; and the diversion of resources which could be otherwise devoted to consumption or investment. Athens, like other Greek states, suffered heavily from under-employment at the beginning of our period: no doubt a good deal of the slack was taken up in the development of the Peisistratid era, but in the chaos which followed the expulsion of the Tyrants, much of the economic ground which had been gained was lost. The riots which ushered in the Cleisthenic programme were symptomatic of the economic disorganisation, and this was accentuated by the Persian war period. It is therefore likely that in the early fifth century there was a pool of under-employed citizens, although there could be local and temporary shortages of labour for specific tasks. As long as available manpower exceeded the opportunities for productive employment, the diversion of men into the defence services was not a considerable drain on the resources of the community. In view of the extravagant use of citizen manpower in the administration of the country during the Periclean period, it does not seem that the citizens themselves felt their human resources were being strained. The depletion of the citizen component through war losses and emigration can hardly be regarded as a severe economic loss to the community in general, since these losses were more than replaced by the immigration of free aliens and slaves. In view of the excess manpower always available, the diversion of manpower into defence can hardly be considered as a serious economic drain. The real cost, or effect, of this diversion was the change in the racial and social pattern of the community; but this cannot be accepted as necessarily a loss in economic terms.

We can also attempt to define the cost of imperial defence in terms of the diversion of available material resources. In the case of a modern state the cost of mobilisation may be heavy, even though the men it calls up were previously adding little to production. In civilian life the food had been made available to them by the family sharing their common resources on the farm or in the home; but when the recruit is taken away, it may be a difficult task for the state authority to extract from the family the food which previously had been made available. Consequently, the cost of mobilisation is increased by the need to find extra food from other sources. This problem was less serious in the case of Athens, because she did not maintain a standing army at home, but called up men for individual campaigns; in the case of local land actions, or home defence, a man might be under arms for only a day or two: hence before Athens became a sea-power the cost of defence to the state was probably trivial. But campaigns fought overseas were a different matter. There the treasury faced the problem of financing not only the transport but also all the supplies, over and above those which could be obtained by requisitioning in the theatre of war itself. We possess some figures relating to the costs of overseas operations, and these should give an idea of the expense to Athens of maintaining her imperial position. With these figures we can compare the receipts from imperial revenue and thus form some estimate of the overall profitability of the empire to Athens.

We know that in 449 B.C. 5,000 talents of confederate money was transferred to the treasury of Athens: it seems likely that in the fifteen subsequent years 200 talents was transferred to the temple of Athena annually, and in 433 a further payment of

200 'for the other gods'. Thus, over the period of sixteen years, the temple treasuries of Athens received a total of over 8,000 talents.[1] The epigraphic evidence for these sums is confirmed by the literary evidence of Isocrates and Diodorus.[2] It was further claimed by Pericles in 431 that Athens was at that time receiving in tribute an annual income of 600 talents 'in addition to other income':[3] the evidence of the quota lists suggests that annual tribute was less than 400 talents at the time, and if Pericles' figure was correct, he must have included under the heading of tribute other moneys received from abroad, including perhaps war indemnities. Pericles also claimed (in 431) that after payment had been made for the extensive building programme, Athens still held a reserve of about 6,000 talents. Since the bulk of this reserve (5,000 talents) had been created eighteen years earlier by the transfer from the confederate treasury, it is clear that Athens had paid for all her military operations and in addition had financed her public works programme to date without running down the reserve at all; *i.e.*, imperial income had much more than covered the total defence expenditure incurred in maintaining imperial control.

It has already been noted that tribute was not the only source of revenue which Athens drew from the empire. We must also take account of the public income which Athens received as a result of her trading position, which was itself partially due to her imperial influence. Apart from the poll tax levied on resident aliens, the most important source of such revenue was the tax on imports and re-exports flowing through Athenian ports. Xenophon[4] estimated that the total public income of Athens at this time was in the vicinity of 1,000 talents annually: this, if true, would imply a receipt of 400 talents from internal taxation, and a substantial proportion of this income was directly due to Athens' imperial position.

We may set beside these impressive figures the costs of the only military operations for which we have detailed financial evidence. In 440 B.C. the island of Samos revolted and was blockaded for the best part of a year by the confederate fleet. The cost of the operation was estimated at 1,200 talents. Byzantium was also in revolt at the same time, and an inscription records what may have been the combined cost of the two operations at about 1,400 talents. The other campaign for which we possess a financial estimate is the siege of Potidaea (432–30); the sum given by Thucydides is 2,000 talents.[5]

It is quite obvious that Athens could not have afforded many operations of this type if the tribute was to be maintained at the traditional level. Even an isolated operation like that at Samos ran down the reserve; *i.e.*, Athens made a book-keeping loss on the empire in 440 B.C. But granted a stable period of peace, the empire was evidently highly profitable to Athens: unfortunately her imperial policies led her into conflict not only with her own rebellious allies, but also with the formidable power of the Peloponnesian League, and war could be fatal to the profitability of the empire. This is demonstrated by the records of loans from the temple treasure (the reserve) for war purposes during the first ten years of the Peloponnesian war: the authors of *A.T.L.* have calculated[6] that during this period the reserve fell from 6,000 to 1,450 talents (including 1,000 set aside as an 'untouchable' reserve), although, in an effort to finance the war out of current income, the tribute had at least been doubled in 425 B.C.

In peacetime the empire was apparently a profitable concern to Athens: in wartime the costs of imperial defence could, and did, outrun the receipts in terms of tribute. It also seems probable, though it cannot be demonstrated, that the cost of defence exceeded the total public income of Athens in the war years, in as much as the government was forced to the ultimate extremity of introducing capital levies upon its own citizens to pay for the war. In other words, the probability exists that (in book-keeping terms at least) the empire ran at a loss during the war, a war which was largely induced by the imperial policies themselves.

It must, however, be pointed out that even when the empire was apparently at its most profitable to Athens, the accumulation of treasure did not necessarily mean a net gain in real terms. The surplus was potentially useful as a cash reserve, for investment of a productive nature, and above all because it enabled Athens to import more goods than she exported. The treasure was not in fact used, as far as we know, to finance imports directly on behalf of the state, but was either hoarded as a war reserve or else fed into the home economy to finance public works. In the latter case it did not directly increase the supply of home-produced goods, but it did increase domestic purchasing power, and, in so far as the supply of imported goods was responsive to demand at Athens, it succeeded in raising the level of imports. To this extent the release of treasure into the economy via the public works programme was a policy which helped to raise living standards. On the other hand it produced some other results which were less desirable. In so far as the Athenian market was imperfect as a self-regulating mechanism, a rapid expansion of demand was unlikely to result automatically in a proportionate, and immediate, increase in supply. In so far as the increased purchasing power was not absorbed by an increased supply of goods (either imported or home-produced), to that extent there was bound to be a decline in the value of the currency in the home, and eventually in the overseas, market as well.

Our knowledge of the resulting inflation is unsatisfactory because of the paucity of documentary information relating to wages and prices in the pre-imperial era: but there is no doubt that prices had risen, and were still rising in the Periclean period. The traditional price for grain in the sixth century had been 1 drachma per medimnus; by the end of the fifth century the price had doubled, and early in the fourth century it stood at 3 drachmas. The daily pay of jurymen, which stood in 451 B.C. at 2 obols, in 425 was raised to 3 obols.[7] In the Solonian legislation 1 drachma is apparently regarded as a considerable sum, equal in value to about a bushel and a half of grain; by the end of the fifth century, according to the Erechtheum accounts, 1 drachma was the normal daily pay of a construction worker.[8] The inflation was not, of course, due only to the release of money from the state treasury, but also to the abnormal conditions resulting from the war. Nevertheless, part of the blame for the currency inflation must be laid at the door of the treasury action: among its effects was the reduction in the value of savings, and hence the discouragement of thrift; the partial redistribution of income to the advantage of traders and speculators and to the disadvantage of wage earners (since wages inevitably lagged behind prices), hence an economically undesirable trend towards greater inequality of income; and above all a reduction, on the international market, of the value of that silver which was one of Athens' major exports.

But there are other, and more serious, debits which would

have to be recorded in any balance-sheet of Athenian imperialism. The cost to Athens in terms of human misery and loss of
life is outside any economic reckoning, but we can consider,
though we cannot cost, the physical devastation of Athenian
property which was the direct result of the war. This entailed,
in broad terms, the sacrifice of the entire farming economy
outside the vicinity of the city walls. As a result of the annual
invasions, and the systematic destruction of the crops, Athens
temporarily forfeited most of the rural income which had,
until the development of her mining and commercial sectors,
been the sole financial support of the state. In addition, the
capital value of the land was heavily reduced by the burning
off of cover crops, the cutting down of vines and olive trees,
and the dismantling of farm buildings. In 431 the Attic farmers
are said to have objected to the evacuation of their land on the
grounds that they had only recently recovered from the effects
of the Persian occupation fifty years before. We must assume
that the physical damage inflicted on the rural stock of Attica
during the Peloponnesian war affected its farm income for at
least half a century to come.

But the farming industry was not the only one to be hit by
the war. The mining industry was dependent on a regular in-
flow of labour; and as the war progressed it was increasingly
crippled by the impossibility of holding an adequate slave
labour force. Under cover of the war, and the eventual enemy
occupation of Decelea, desertions caused a heavy reduction in
mining output, possibly the temporary abandonment of the
workings, thus reducing, or eliminating, one of the most valuable sources of Athenian revenue. It must, however, be stressed,
that the virtual abandonment of the farming, and later of the
mining industry, was a purely temporary measure, induced by
the conditions of siege in war-time Athens. It is interesting to
note that the community was prepared to accept such a policy,
and go on fighting: their acceptance is striking evidence of a
trend, increasingly noticeable in the fifth century, to regard the
soil of Attica as expendable, and the economy as dependent on
the commercial sector, itself largely in the hands of non-
Athenians.

With the neglect of rural interests we may associate the
decline in the political leadership of the farming group and the

shift of influence within the citizen body itself. Throughout the sixth, and for the first half of the fifth century, the political leaders came from the landowning class as a matter of course, and this corresponded to the dominant position which farming held in the economy. As other sectors increased in importance, the proportion of the national income commanded by the growers diminished, and with it their political influence, although with a considerable time-lag. The legal structure ensured that political power remained a monopoly of the citizen group, which was closed to alien entrepreneurs. Thus the shift of power was within the citizen group itself, and the political successors to rural aristocratic leaders, like Cimon and Pericles, are men like Nicias (whose wealth rested on mining), or Cleon and Hyperbolus, whose background was that of secondary industry and retail trade.

The relegation in importance of rural interests was a natural result of the increasing trend to urbanisation which is evident even from the time of Peisistratus. It would be easy to exaggerate this trend, with the results of the Archidamian war before us; Athens never became an industrial city, and both Thucydides and Aristophanes in their own way give warning that even after 430 B.C. a mass of Athenians still regarded themselves as country folk.[9] Even so, it is striking to what extent the interests of Athens the city, during the fifth century, come to dominate the politics of Attica the state. The latter, which in 600 B.C. had appeared as a loose federation of rural dynasties, emerged at last as a true city-state, and the transformation ushered in a political and cultural revolution.

The country folk who drifted into town during the Peisistratid era left behind them unquestioning obedience to a governing class; a tradition of urban discipline had still to be formed. The wealthy growers who were to be found in the town, found it increasingly difficult to control the newcomers: it was the first great concentration of manpower not mobilised by rural officers. There was no civilian organisation to cope with it, nor any means of preventing it coming in, and the riots of 508 showed the ugly temper of the populace once it was out of hand. The external perils which Athens faced at the beginning of the fifth century showed the aristocratic leaders at their best, and did much to mend their prestige; for more than half a century the urban masses continued to choose their leaders from the old governing class. Yet the relationship was insensibly changing. In the sixth century it was the aristocrats who used their rural following in a struggle for power: by the second half of the fifth century it was the urban populace which was using the aristocrats. Urbanisation in fact, by breaking up traditional patterns of behaviour and authority, brought in its wake political change, and Periclean democracy was the remarkable result. But if the effects of urbanisation were exciting in the sphere of politics, the achievements of the newly gathered community in the realm of art and culture were quite sensational.

Among the more remarkable of these achievements was the evolution of European drama. The crude initiation and fertility ceremonies of the Attic countryside had developed through centuries into the songs, dances, and mummery of a complex folk art. When economic development turned country people into town dwellers, they brought with them this accumulated cultural store; and eventually the ceremonies which had been performed in the improvised conditions of the countryside blossomed into new splendour in the metropolis, where ideal conditions were provided for their staging. For the first time all the necessary material conditions were available to turn peasant ceremony into sophisticated art—the theatre itself, the public, and the talent. New poets drawing upon old material rapidly developed the art form to an astonishing degree of artistic refinement—selecting, discarding, improving technique, weaving into the crude myths psychological and philosophical problems of human belief and conduct. It is interesting to note that all the Greek classical tragedies we possess were composed within the space of three generations: from the early fourth century B.C. until today European writers have followed and adapted the work of the three masters. The dramatic art of the countryside, brought to its peak in the newly formed metropolis, soon withered when cut off from its roots. Tragedy survived as an art form, but new compositions were mere echoes of the old, and eventually the form itself became stylised and dead.

At the same time as poetic drama was being produced as mass entertainment, a new prose literature was being written for the educated few. Europe saw its first literary essays in historical reconstruction, political analysis, and metaphysical speculation.

While traditional institutional arrangements were being re-shaped under economic pressure, the ideas and assumptions which underlay them were being scrutinised or discarded. The counterpart of freedom in the political sphere was scepticism and rationalism in the realm of ideas.

The striking intellectual achievements of fifth-century Athens were made possible by the formation of a new cosmopolitan community which drew on the talent, as well as the physical resources, of the whole Greek world. The development of Athens as a great imperial and trading power gave to Europe its first really cosmopolitan city, and made her, as Pericles rightly claimed, an education to all Greece. The geographical origins of some of the most famous of the Greek mathematicians and philosophers reveal that Athens was not primarily a centre of pioneer work in these fields. It was her good fortune to collect, and to build upon the intellectual inheritance of others, especially of the Ionian Greeks, who were themselves the heirs to the Asian tradition. In fact Athens was able to begin where others left off: the very works which later became the great classical models, owe their maturity to the fact that they were not the first, but the last in a series. The inheritance, and the systematic transmission of knowledge was a feature of the metropolis; the Sophists, many of them foreigners, organised the first European system of higher education. Athens was not only the first western cosmo-politan city, she was also the first European university centre.

Our evidence is unequivocal as regards the advance achieved on the artistic and intellectual front; but when we try to esti-mate the degree of material advance the position is far less certain. We cannot, on the basis of the available evidence, confidently assert that there was a substantial rise in the material living standards of the Athenian community as a whole, though it is likely that the richest members of the community (many of them aliens) were in 430 B.C. better off than the richest members in 500. However, the living conditions of the most depressed section of the rural community (the mining slaves) were in 430 as hideous as anything in the earlier period, and this was not a negligible section of the community: in addition there was certainly a great deal of acute poverty among the urban pro-letariat, even among the privileged caste of the citizens, as we know from the references in Aristophanes. What is certain is that commercial progress did not achieve for the Athenian community in general a high living standard in any sense in which we should use the term today. One reason for the somewhat disappointing material results has already been suggested: although the public income increased spectacularly, much of the increase was absorbed by population growth.

In that case the net result, as far as the Athenian economy was concerned, was an increase of her work-force; and the measure of economic progress was the extent to which the additional manpower was productively used. However, not a great deal of the imported slave labour seems to have been employed in material production. It was natural that the increased resources made available should be spent in accordance with the traditional social philosophy, and one of the most potent factors governing the circulation of wealth was the pursuit of prestige. Community standards were inherited from the old rural aristocracy, who never considered their wealth as primarily a means of amassing further wealth. The height of a gentleman's ambition had been to win the garland of victory at the games, or to become renowned for lavish hospitality to men, and noble offerings to the temples. The search for kudos reflected the reverence of the community for status in their society; and the same social attitudes which led wealthy Athenians to spend large sums on equipping a tragic chorus for the theatre, led the poorer members of the community to add to their already over-crowded households the slaves whose presence advertised the status of their owner. The resident aliens were less obviously bound by Athenian traditional attitudes, and it was they who tended to use their money for investment in trade, industry, and banking. But the primary industries were more or less closed to them, as they could not own land. Thus the rich aliens by their investment, the poor by their services, tended to concentrate on improving the chain of distribution rather than increasing the volume of production.

The additional services supplied by the new arrivals to some extent improved the lot of the citizens, and relieved them of certain duties: hence the pool of goods, as well as services, could increase if the energy thus released were used in productive employment. No doubt in some cases this did happen: in particular, the Athenian small-holder was able, as a result of the availability of cheap domestic labour, to practise more concentrated farming in the near-city areas. But in many cases the citizens who were liberated from menial tasks on the land or in the home were absorbed into the public service or the armed forces or, when they were free from official duties, they preferred to use the time in leisure activities. When Pericles decided to run his estate on a purely commercial basis, he entrusted the supervision of it to a slave steward; his sons and their families were thus free to devote themselves to any gainful employment, from making armaments to working on the docks. As far as we know they did nothing of the sort, but, according to Plutarch, they went about complaining that their father's parsimony was keeping them short of money. In fact they remained in the household and allowed their services to be replaced by those of slaves, without themselves turning to other gainful employment. The passing of the old order had taken away from them their traditional role (as farm workers) and they preferred to use their time in something more pleasant than work. One of the most striking features of fifth-century Athens, and one which most typified its civilised atmosphere, was the cult of leisure.

It is possible that the degree of capital accumulation achieved by Athens was sufficient to permit an assured rate of material progress, had the surplus been employed in the most economically efficient way; in particular, if a sufficient proportion had been invested in schemes for increasing future production. Some of the surplus was in fact employed in this way: a great deal of money was evidently spent on improving dock and harbour facilities, on roads, and on public buildings of a utilitarian nature. At the same time there was private investment in mining, shipping, and industry, especially in textiles and armaments. The money invested in mining did not bring great long-term benefits, since production was disorganised by the war. That invested in industry was on a comparatively small scale; no really large factories appeared, the manufacturing sector continued to be dominated by cottage industries, and there is never any suggestion that more than a negligible proportion of the work-force was employed full time on manufactures. Investment was most successful in merchant shipping: the network of trade built up in the imperial period survived even the collapse of the empire itself. The capital stock of shipping, the excellent dock and marketing facilities, and the trading good-will established, all were to bring in long-term dividends, and one may note that Athens has remained a centre of marine commerce ever since the Periclean period.

But a large part of the accumulated capital was spent on permanent structures which were not primarily of a utilitarian or productive nature. It is true that the temples possessed a utilitarian function, since they served the state as banks; but it is difficult to believe that the scale and cost of their construction was related to the requirements of mere safe-deposits: their grandeur and the beauty of their adornments marked them out as primarily works of art. It may seem strange that the Athenians should choose of their own will to allocate such enormous sums to works of an artistic nature when they had so many material wants left unsatisfied. It must be said, however, that the new skyline of Athens brought dividends also in terms of national pride, and to this extent acted as a status symbol itself, impressing both foreigners and Athenians with the uniqueness of the community: the citizen might live in squalid conditions, but each could feel that he had a share in the public amenities which made his city the envy of all others.

The huge sums invested in these buildings contributed little to Athenian economic progress in the short term, although they did help to establish her claim as a premier tourist centre for the Greek world: over the long term they were to draw in dividends in the form of travellers and dealers, who brought with them their goods, their skills, and their experience. The builders of Periclean Athens were unfortunate in this respect that their work on the docks and on the Acropolis was an investment the dividends of which were to be received mainly by future generations. Thus the precious resources which Athens had so dangerously collected were exhausted on projects which did not, for the most part, greatly contribute to her material progress, at any rate in the short term. Whatever were the motives which guided her choice of investment, the result was that she never in fact banished the poverty which Greeks had come to accept as a fact of life. When her imperial power was destroyed, only the busy dockyards and the magnificent buildings remained as the enduring relics of her commercial progress.

APPENDIX

The yield of grain, wine, and oil in Attica

THE theoretical figures for grain production given in the text may be compared with the statistics actually available, referring to the harvest of 329 B.C. An inscription found at Eleusis gives the amounts of the first fruits (*I G* ii² 1672). If we accept the calculation of Gomme in regard to the amount of the tithe in proportion to the harvest, the figures for the whole of Attica are 28,500 medimni of wheat and 340,350 of barley. The total area of arable land covered by the major Attic plains has been estimated at about 85,000 acres, and this figure must be increased to take account of the sown land to be found in smaller patches of the foothills. At a time of scarcity some substandard land was probably sown, and the area of fallow reduced to a minimum. In the year 329 a total area of perhaps 65,000 acres could be expected to be found under grain, and this estimate, rough as it is, may be compared with the figure for the total yield, approximately 525,500 bushels. This would give us an average yield of about 8 bushels per acre.

Any calculation of wine yield would naturally start from the figures available referring to modern times: these, however, must be treated with some caution, since they represent the harvest of stock selected for high yield, and which have been protected by spraying and fed with fertiliser. Irrigated areas of southern Greece can produce about 6 tons of grapes per acre granted all these favourable conditions; without irrigation the yield is about 3 tons. Under modern conditions about 70 to 100 gallons of wine can be expected per ton of grapes; *i.e.*, southern Greece can produce a yield of about 500 gallons of wine per acre under irrigation, or about 250 without. There can be little doubt that these yields were not approached in classical times. There were no facilities for large-scale irrigation: some of the vines were trellised, but in many cases seem to have been left on the ground, where they would grow well enough as bush vines, and would help to conserve moisture in the soil below them, but would suffer heavily from pests and diseases. In view of these considerations I have estimated the yield in classical times at less than a half that of modern times without irrigation. This may, of course, be an underestimate.

Olive oil yields would be about a tenth of this figure. This is a crude guess in view of the tremendous fluctuations which occur in olive harvests from year to year: for the striking fluctuations of recent years see *F.A.O. Commodity Studies* No. 9 of 1955.

ABBREVIATIONS USED IN THE NOTES

A.J.P.	*American Journal of Philology*
A.T.L.	*Athenian Tribute Lists* (ed. Meritt, Wade-Gery, McGregor)
Ath. Pol.	*Constitution of Athens* (attributed to Aristotle)
B.S.A.	*Journal of the British School at Athens*
C.A.H.	*Cambridge Ancient History*
C. Phil.	*Classical Philology*
C.Q.	*Classical Quarterly*
C.R.	*Classical Review*
F.G.H.	*Die Fragmente der Griechischen Historiker* (F. Jacoby)
G. & R.	*Greece and Rome*
I G²	*Inscriptiones Graecae* (editio minor)
J.H.S.	*Journal of Hellenic Studies*
P.W.	Pauly-Wissowa (*Real Encyclopädie der Classischen Altertumswissenschaft*)

BIBLIOGRAPHY AND NOTES

CHAPTER I: THE NATURAL BACKGROUND

CARY, M., *Geographic Background of Greek and Roman History*, Oxford 1949.
JUDEICH, W., *Topographie von Athen*, Munich 1931.
MYRES, SIR J. L., *Geographical History in Greek Lands*, Oxford 1953.
NEWBIGIN, M. I., *The Mediterranean Lands*, London 1924.
SEMPLE, E. C., *Geography of the Mediterranean Region*, London 1932.

[1] The importance of olive oil in human diet is apparent from a comparison, in terms of calories per pound, of oil with some other foods available to the ancient Greeks: figs 186; grapes 280; onions 104; wheat 1,630; olive oil 4,200. Man needs 2,000 to 2,500 calories per day to maintain a healthy diet.

[2] See R. M. Cook, *Greek Painted Pottery*, London 1960, Chapters II and III.

CHAPTER II: THE BREAKDOWN OF THE OLD ORDER

PRINCIPAL ANCIENT SOURCES:

ARISTOTLE, *Constitution of Athens* (referred to below as the *Ath. Pol.*) Chapters 4–14; *Politics* 1266b, 1273b–1274a, 1281b, 1296a. HERODOTUS I. 29, 59, 62. PLUTARCH, *Solon* 13–25; 29–30.

MODERN WORKS:

FINE, J. V. A., *Horoi*. Hesperia Supp. IX, 1951. FINLEY, M. I., *Studies in Land and Credit in Ancient Athens*, New Brunswick 1951. FREEMAN, K., *Work and Life of Solon*, Cardiff 1926. HIGNETT, C., *History of the Athenian Constitution*, Oxford 1958. LINFORTH, I. M., *Solon the Athenian*, Berkeley 1919. MASARACCHIA, A., *Solone*, Florence 1958. URE, P. N., *Origin of Tyranny*, Cambridge 1922. WOODHOUSE, W. J., *Solon the Liberator*, Oxford 1938.

[1] Under the conditions postulated for early Attica it would be surprising if land there had been subject to sale: when farming is almost the only gainful and acceptable family occupation, land is more or less beyond price. But the economic factor would not necessarily prevent it changing hands, *e.g.*, by ceremonial gift or dowry. We lack the evidence to show whether

land was or was not legally inalienable in early times: a test case of any taboo on alienation would arise when the owner died childless, and it may be significant that in such cases the old law of Athens apparently recognised adoption as the proper way of designating an heir: adoption into the family thus maintained the legal fiction of non-alienation. Most modern scholars seem either to reserve judgement on this question, or else, like Woodhouse, to believe that land was probably inalienable until the time of Solon: whatever provisions may have existed in the legal or traditional code, there is no doubt that land had in fact become alienated and changed hands by his time, for this was the main cause of the rural crisis. Evidence exists in Hesiod (*Works and Days* 340–1) that land in near-by Boeotia was subject to sale from the ninth century B.C.; and there is a reference in Aristotle (*Politics* 1266b 16) which implies that land in Attica was also subject to acquisition before Solon's time. Elsewhere (*Politics* 1319a 11 and 1266b 21) Aristotle lends support to the hypothesis that land in some parts of Greece remained inalienable in historic times; but on closer examination it is clear that he had in mind the settlement of colonial territories, in which legal precautions were taken to prevent the pioneers from selling the land allotted to them. Such legal arrangements cannot be considered as reliable pointers to the conditions of early Attica, and the evidence is too fragmentary to justify any firm conclusion about the alienability of land there; this view has, however, been challenged by Fine (*op. cit.*), followed by Hammond, *J.H.S.* 1961, p. 76 (Hammond's thesis was criticised in *Historia*, 1963, pp. 242–7). For a general discussion see Michell, *Canadian Journal of Economics and Political Science*, 1953, p. 245 f.

² The accounts of Aristotle and Plutarch, which must form the basis of any historical reconstruction, are meagre, vague, and schematic. Both quote Solon's poems, but the latter prove on examination to be far less helpful than might be expected. Apart from the poems, the sources on which Aristotle and Plutarch based their account date from a period not earlier than the late fifth century, *i.e.*, nearly two hundred years after the events with which they deal. During the intervening two centuries the tradition about the Solon reforms had been used and abused by political pamphleteers to support their own programmes: thus the first historians of Attica, whose work formed the basis of our own sources, inherited a tradition which was already distorted for political ends before they proceeded to edit it in the light of their own opinions and affiliations: the literary sources could be said to resemble a jigsaw puzzle of which many parts are missing, and the surviving parts of which have been trimmed by successive pairs of scissors to make them fit various patterns. Any student attempting to grapple with the problems involved in this period of history will find indispensable the book of F. Jacoby, *Atthis* (Oxford 1949), which contains a lucid analysis of the interrelationship of the sources used by the Greek historians of this period. The accounts which appear in modern history books are theoretical reconstructions based on differing interpretations of the surviving tradition. The account given in the *Cambridge Ancient History*, vol. iv, which attributes the cause of the rural crisis mainly to the spread of coined money, has been undermined by recent work of the numismatists, especially C. M. Kraay,

who date the first general use of Athenian coinage to a date long after 600 B.C., *i.e.*, later than the period to which the causes of the crisis can be assigned. For recent discussion about the causes of the agrarian crisis see: Lewis, *A.J.P.*, 1941, p. 144: French, *C.Q.*, 1956, p. 11: Lotze, *Philologus*, 1958, p. 1: Polakoff, *Economic Development and Cultural Change*, 1958, p. 99: Hammond, *J.H.S.*, 1961, p. 76.

[3] The contrast between the diet of characters in Homer and that of fifth-century Greeks has often been noted; *e.g.*, E. A. Gardner, *Companion to Greek Studies*, 2nd ed., Cambridge 1906, pp. 541–2.

[4] *Critias*, 111 a–d.

[5] In the economically more developed states of seventh-century Greece changing conditions had been reflected in a change in military organisation. The shock troops of the old Greek armies had traditionally been the aristocrats mounted on chariot or horse and followed by their retainers: from the late seventh century B.C. Greek armies were increasingly based on heavily armed foot soldiers, moving in close formation and drawn from a wider economic group than the old 'knights'. The change in military tactics was naturally connected with changes in the economic pattern of society, and in its turn it reacted upon the social order by making possible the overthrow of aristocratic rule, if social grievances should lead to open conflict (see Arist. *Politics* 1297b. Andrewes, *Greek Tyrants*, pp. 31–8). It is difficult to say how far the changes mentioned above were true of seventh-century Attica. On the one hand the impression given by our sources is one of near-feudalism, such that one hesitates to believe that aristocratic supremacy was as yet threatened by the existence of a strong middle, or hoplite, class. On the other hand the ability of the Attica militia to stand up to the hoplites of Megara implies that Athens was not militarily backward; the reforms of Solon imply the recognition of a hoplite class in being; and the willingness of the aristocrats to compromise on the issue of the reforms seems to show that they did not feel able to ignore the challenge of the Attic peasantry, *i.e.*, that it was backed by more formidable a force than our authorities seem to suggest.

[6] See F. Jacoby, *Die Fragmente der Griechischen Historiker*, 3b *Supp. vol.* I, pp. 144–6.

[7] The impression given by our sources is that a great deal of land was in question, and that some of the lost lands had been in the creditors' possession for a long time (*Ath. Pol.* 12. 4 referring to deported peasants who had forgotten their native tongue). To restore the lands would have been a formidable task indeed, and I find it hard to believe that the Athenian government in 594 had the authority to enforce all over Attica a writ likely to meet with such determined resistance as one should assume from at least some of the creditors. My own view (*C.Q.*, 1956, p. 22 f.) has not, I think, found acceptance, and I have chosen to indicate in the text what is still the more widely accepted view of scholars. The question is not crucial to the problem of long-term development, because the arrangements made by Solon were violently disturbed by the subsequent era of conflict.

[8] The comparison on grounds of nutrition is complicated by the fact that oil was also used for fuel and cleansing.

⁹ The poverty of Attic soil was proverbial; Thuc. i. 2. 5.

¹⁰ See the calculations of Jardé, *Céréales*, p. 59 f.

¹¹ *Ancient Greece at Work*, pp. 246–7.

¹² For a more detailed discussion of these figures see Appendix.

¹³ Apart from one exceptional case from the fourth century the largest Attic farm on record in the classical period is that of Alcibiades, of about 70 acres. For references see *Historia*, 1961, p. 510.

¹⁴ Kraay, C. M., *Num. Chron, XVI*, 1956, p. 65. Few historians now accept the theory of Seltman (*Athens; its History and Coinage*, p. 7), followed by the *C.A.H.*, vol. iv, pp. 40 and 129, that a coinage on the Phaedonian standard was struck in Attica before Solon's time. Kraay has convincingly demonstrated that the first Attic coinage did not much precede 570 B.C.: the date of Solon's archonship, however, is well attested to the year 594 B.C. (see Linforth, pp. 265–8; Cadoux, *J.H.S.*, 1948, p. 93 f.). We are therefore forced to choose between the conclusion that the Solonian coinage began to be issued twenty years after his archonship, or else that the tradition which attributed the coinage to him was mistaken.

It has been suggested by Hammond (*J.H.S.*, 1940, pp. 71–83) that the legislation of Solon was not in fact carried by him in the year of his archonship, but two years later, when he held extraordinary office as a conciliator. Hignett (p. 319), while rejecting the chronology of Hammond, has accepted the principle that the legislation did not necessarily fall in the year when Solon was archon, and has suggested a later date, a theory wholeheartedly accepted by Sealey (*Historia*, 1960, p. 159).

This theory, that a considerable interval of time elapsed between the archonship and the legislation, finds only flimsy support in the sources. Plutarch (*Solon* 14. 3 and 16. 3–5) implies that there was some interval between the seisachtheia and the reform of the legal code; Aristotle (*Ath. Pol.* 10) points out that the seisachtheia preceded both the legal reforms and the currency changes; but his emphasis is demonstrably not an attempt to imply that a considerable time elapsed between the reforms, but that the seisachtheia had already taken place before the new currency was issued, and that therefore the claim of Androtion, that the currency reform and the seisachtheia were basically the same thing, was entirely mistaken. The arguments in favour of separating the time of the archonship from that of the reforms are weak; whereas there are a number of references which show that the ancient historians themselves assumed that the date of the reforms coincided with the date of the Solon's archonship (*Ath. Pol.* 5; Plut. *Solon* 19. 4; Diod. Laert. 1. 62).

But while it is difficult to believe that twenty years separated the currency reforms from the archonship, the alternative, of believing that Solon was not responsible for the reforms at all, is even more disagreeable. Since the ancient historical tradition consistently attributes the currency and legal reforms to Solon, a modern historian who rejects the connexion is obviously in danger of undermining his own case. Hignett has chosen to believe that the political reforms were carried by Solon about 570 B.C.; J. G. Milne (*C.R.*, 1943, pp. 1–3) suggested that the first Attic coins were issued by Solon after his return from Egypt, and shortly before the usurpation of

Peisistratus. This reconstruction, though far from satisfactory, seems the least implausible of the alternatives available to us.

[15] To avoid misunderstanding on the part of the general reader, it should be stated that all modern explanations of the purpose of the currency decree are based on speculations, inevitably coloured by modern ideas. The ancient historians evidently did not understand the purpose of the decree at all, and, apart from Androtion, who had an axe to grind, they were apparently not much interested (the point is amusingly made by Jacoby, *F.G.H.* 3 b *Supp.*, *vol.* II, p. 467). Lacking sensible guidance from the sources, we are always in danger of attributing to Solon motives more sophisticated than he himself felt; it is possible that he (and the minters of Corinth) divided the mina into units of a hundred merely because that seemed the 'proper' number. But while recognising the danger of over-sophistication, we should, perhaps, still venture to attribute to Solon an economic motive for an economic measure.

[16] See B. L. Bailey, *J.H.S.*, 1940, p. 62: T. J. Dunbabin, *The Western Greeks*, p. 241, App. III, pp. 480–2.

[17] For the geographical setting see C. L. Seltman, *op. cit.*, p. 11.

[18] The references are: Arist. *Ath. Pol.* 13. 5: Thuc. ii. 55. The identification of the Diakria with the north-east of Attica is supported by a fragment of Sophocles, quoted by Strabo (IX. 392), and by a scholium on Aristophanes (*Lysistrata* 58). It was maintained by Ure that the Diakria comprised the mining area of south-east Attica. It is not reasonable to suppose that the terms Plain, Coast, and Hill could refer, in this connexion, to the inhabitants of level, coastal, and hilly land anywhere in Attica because (*a*) the 'plainsmen' whose faction was decisively worsted, overwhelmingly outnumbered the rest of the population put together, disposed of most of the wealth of the country, and supplied the whole militia from its numbers; (*b*) it is impossible to believe that there could have been any effective organisation of the scattered mountaineers, separated from each other by the plains, much less of the coastal dwellers, living at opposite ends of the country, even if there had been a common cause to bind them together. For a fuller discussion see French, *G. & R.*, 1959, p. 46; Sealey, *Historia*, 1960, p. 163.

[19] Apart from the references in Aristotle (*Ath. Pol.* 16. 5) and Plutarch (*Solon* 22) there is the tradition preserved by Pollux in *Onomastikon* VII. 68. But while it is true that the city gained steadily in population during the sixth and fifth centuries, caution is needed in estimating the extent of the rural depopulation. Even in 431 B.C. a majority of the Attic population still lived in the country (Thuc. ii. 14. 2).

CHAPTER III: ECONOMIC DEVELOPMENT UNDER PEISISTRATUS

SOURCES:

HERODOTUS, I. 60–4; VI. 34–9; 140. ARISTOTLE, *Ath. Pol.* 14–19. PLUTARCH, *Solon* 31–2. DIOGENES LAERTIUS, *Life of Solon.*

III: ECONOMIC DEVELOPMENT UNDER PEISISTRATUS

MODERN WORKS:

ANDREWES, A., *The Greek Tyrants*, London 1956. CORNELIUS, F., *Die Tyrannis in Athen*, Munich 1929. GRUNDY, G. B., *Thucydides and the History of his Age*, London 1911. HIGNETT, C., *op. cit.* OLIVA, P., *Raná Řecká Tyrannis*, Prague 1954. SCHACHERMEYR, F., *Peisistratos* in *P.W.*, XIX, 1938, col. 150–91. URE, P. N., *op. cit.*

[1] For the implications of this festival see Hignett, pp. 330–1.

[2] See Theognis 53 f. on conditions in Megara.

[3] Thuc. i. 13. 1.

[4] Even today it is estimated that in Greece cattle deaths through disease average 10% per year; see *Basic Data on the Economy of Greece*, U.S. Dept. of Commerce 1956.

[5] Hdt. I. 64 Τῶν δὲ ἀπὸ Στρυμόνος ποταμοῦ συνιόντων. Both gold and silver were mined in the general area to which Herodotus refers.

[6] A surviving fragment of an Archon list from the early years of Hippias' reign shows that within the space of five years representatives of two or three noble families held office with the Peisistratids; see B. D. Meritt in *Hesperia*, 1939, pp. 59–62: the co-operation of the Philaidae family is noted elsewhere.

[7] This theory has been the subject of much discussion in recent years; see, *e.g.*, Ure, who supposed that the Tyranny rested on the support of the free miners. For a straight Marxist approach see Oliva, who argues that trading and manufacturing interests were now more important in Athens than agricultural production, on which had rested the political power of the old aristocracy.

[8] Thuc. vi. 54. 5 mentions a tax of 5%.

[9] *Ath. Pol.* 16. 6 gives a picture of the newly settled farmer 'cultivating the rocks', which perhaps means the hillside with a thin layer of soil.

[10] B. L. Bailey, *J.H.S.*, 1940, p. 60. G. M. A. Richter, *B.S.A.*, vol. XI, 1904–5, p. 224.

[11] A. E. Raubitschek, *Dedications from the Athenian Acropolis*, Cambridge (Mass.), 1949, pp. 457, 465.

[12] See the comment of D. L. Page, *Sappho and Alcaeus*, pp. 152–8.

[13] For the role of the naukraries in coastal defence see Hignett, pp. 70–1. H. Bengtson, *Griechische Geschichte*, p. 111, n. 2. U. Kahrstedt, *Staatsgebiet und Staatsangehörige in Athen*, p. 266. Hommel, *P.W.*, XVI, 1935, col. 1941–3.

[14] Hdt. VI. 89.

[15] See the comment of Thuc. i. 17.

[16] Sandys, *Constitution of Athens*, pp. 65–6. We can be certain that the full tax was never collected: the possibilities of tax evasion by farmers are legion, and we know that Peisistratus used his authority to grant personal exemptions. (*Ath. Pol.* 16. 6.)

[17] Xen. *Poroi* IV. 2. See, in this connexion, Ure, pp. 36–7. R. J. Hopper, *G. & R.*, 1961, pp. 139–42.

[18] Hignett, pp. 70–1.

[19] Aristotle, *Politics* 1285a. 27–9.

[20] Assuming that the Plataean alliance should be dated to 509 B.C.: for the argument see *J.H.S.*, 1960, p. 191.

[21] Plutarch (*Solon* 31. 3) accepted the tradition which attributed this measure to Peisistratus, but suggested that it was in imitation of a law passed by Solon: the attribution to Solon is supported by a Scholiast on Aeschines I. 103. Plutarch is evidently echoing a compromise, and the implied disagreement which he found in his sources does not inspire much confidence in his own account: the tradition could have its origin merely in the reconstructions of fifth-century historians eager to father upon the early lawgivers welfare legislation familiar to them from their own time. Jacoby (*F.G.H.* 3 b *Supp. vol.* 1, p. 563) regards as an anachronism the attribution of the measure either to Peisistratus or to Solon.

[22] *Politics* 1313b. 20–5.

CHAPTER IV: THE NEW ORDER

SOURCES:

HERODOTUS, V. 62–5, 69, 90–1, 94. ARISTOTLE, *Politics* 1275b, 1319b. THUC. i. 20, vi. 53–60. PLATO, *Hipparchus*, 228–9.

MODERN WORKS:

EHRENBERG, V., *The Greek State*, Oxford 1960. HIGNETT, C., *op. cit.* ZIMMERN, A., *The Greek Commonwealth*, Oxford 1931.

[1] There is a notably aristocratic flavour in the drinking song celebrating the seizure of Leipsidrion and the exploits of the partisans (*Ath. Pol.* 19. 3), Cleisthenes' contemptuous attitude towards the masses in his early days is implied in Hdt. V. 69.

[2] In the fifth century the Solonian assessments were still officially recognised, but their money equivalents were accepted. When this acceptance began is nowhere stated in our sources, and the subject is a matter of controversy: See Hignett, pp. 225–6; Waters, *J.H.S.*, 1960, p. 183; French, *Historia*, 1961, p. 510.

CHAPTER V: THE PREPARATIONS FOR WAR

SOURCES:

HERODOTUS, V. 73–103; VI. 41, 104, 108–9; VII. 6. THUCYDIDES, iii. 68; vi. 53–60. ARISTOTLE, *Ath. Pol.* 22. 7–8. PLUTARCH, *Themistocles* 3–20.

MODERN WORKS:

ARDAILLON, E., *Les Mines de Laurion*, Paris 1897. LABARBE, J., *La Loi Navale de Thémistocle*, Paris 1957.

[1] *C.A.H.*, iv, pp. 187–8.

[2] Miltiades had held the archonship in 524: see Meritt, *Hesperia*, 1939, pp. 59–65.

V: THE PREPARATIONS FOR WAR

[3] *Klio*, IX, p. 144; E. H. Minns, *Scythians and Greeks*, p. 339. We have no reason to suppose that there was any serious interruption in Athenian trade with the west, much of which was carried in Corinthian ships: see T. J. Dunbabin, *The Western Greeks*, p. 242 f.

[4] See Chap. III, note 20.

[5] Hdt. V. 74. Herodotus does not state that Hysiae was annexed on this occasion, but his subsequent narrative makes it clear that it became Athenian territory.

[6] Herodotus (V. 77) puts the number at 4,000, Aelian (*V.H.* 6. 1) at 2,000.

[7] For the chronology see Wade-Gery, *J.H.S.*, 1951, p. 217.

[8] Ormorod (*Piracy in the Ancient World*) and Jacoby (*F.G.H.* 3b *Supp.*, vol. II, p. 322, n. 6) emphasise the difficulty of distinguishing 'illegal' piracy from patriotic privateering (see, *e.g.*, the account of Thuc. in book v., 115). For an instance of systematic piracy see the career of Polykrates (Hdt. III. 39, 47): of a similar pattern is the career of Histiaeus and the Lesbians after the battle of Lade (Hdt. VI. 5), cf. Hdt. VI. 16 for a natural assumption; see also the inscription of Teos (Tod i. 23).

[9] Kahrstedt, *op. cit.*, p. 246: see Hdt. VIII. 17 for an example of a privately owned ship fighting in the Athenian fleet at the battle of Artemisium.

[10] The design of the Greek trireme is still a matter of controversy. From the size of the crew (170 oarsmen), and the length of the ship (less than 144 feet, *i.e.*, the maximum length of the Munychia sheds), it is clear that there was not enough room for all the rowers to sit in one plane, one behind the other. Unless more than one oarsman pulled at each oar (a possibility apparently ruled out by a reference in Thucydides ii. 93), some oarsmen must evidently have rowed at a different level to others. The traditional view, in accordance with a definition of Hesychius, envisaged three banks of super-imposed oars. This explanation has been doubted because of the mechanical difficulties involved, and an alternative arrangement was suggested (by A. B. Cook and W. Richardson *C.R.*, 1905, pp. 371–7), which envisaged two levels, the oarsman at the upper level sitting between the pair below him, and using the same port aperture. A similar view was put forward by Tarn (*J.H.S.*, 1905, p. 137 f.), and supported by Brewster (*Harvard Studies in Classical Philology*, XLIV, p. 205 f.); the latter suggested that the oars passed through an outrigger, and that each group of three rowers sat side by side in a line oblique to the longitudinal axis of the ship, the inner rowers sitting nearer to the stern. The traditional view of three tiers has been defended by Köster (*Das Antike Seewesen*, p. 111 f.) and Miltner (*P.W. Supp. V*, 1931, col. 935 f.), followed by a practical seaman Rodgers (*Greek and Roman Naval Warfare*), only to be ridiculed by Tarn (*C.R.*, 1938, p. 76). A modified version of the traditional view has been put forward by J. S. Morrison (*C.Q.*, 1947, p. 122 f.). In Morrison's view a third row of oarsmen sat in an outrigger construction set not much higher than the upper tier, and was able to use oars of approximately the same length. His view was accepted without reservation by L. Casson (*Ancient Mariners*, p. 92 f.).

[11] This is the number given by Aristotle *Ath. Pol.* 22. 7: Herodotus gives the number as 200 (Hdt. VII. 144): see also Thuc. i. 14; Plut. *Them.* 4; Diod. xi. 43. 3. Labarbe (p. 42) has attempted to reconcile the two figures. Support for the higher figure has been sought in the Troezen Decree (*Hesperia*, 1960, p. 199); but as this decree is itself a late copy, its value as corroborative evidence is rather dubious. See M. Chambers, *American Historical Review*, LXVII, p. 306.

[12] Remains of such shelters at Zea and Munychia measure approximately 20 feet by 144 feet long.

[13] For a discussion on the date see Gomme *Commentary* on Thuc. i. 93. 3.

[14] Silver as the source of the nation's wealth Aesch. *Persae* 238; Alcibiades on its importance to Athens' war effort Thuc. vi. 91. 7; cf. especially Xen. *Poroi* iv. 13.

[15] *Journal of Egyptian Archaeology*, 1939, p. 177. Because of the strained relations between Athens and Persia direct trading between Athens and Egypt at this time was perhaps small. But Athenian silver found its way to Egypt as a form of international exchange; see note 9 on Chapter VII.

CHAPTER VI: ATHENS AND THE DELIAN CONFEDERACY

SOURCES:

THUCYDIDES, I. 19, 89–101; iii. 10–11; v. 18. ARISTOTLE, *Ath. Pol.* 23–4. PLUTARCH, *Aristeides*, 23–6. *Cimon*, 6, 11–15. *Themistocles*, 19–21. *Pericles*, 12. DIODORUS, XI. 39–47, 70–1.

For epigraphic evidence see M. N. Tod, *Greek Historical Inscriptions*, vol. i. nos. 30, 38, 44, 46, 50, 51, 56. Original financial documents have been preserved for posterity by the Greek custom of inscribing such records on stone: for an insight into the use and evaluation of inscriptions the general reader is referred to A. G. Woodhead, *The Study of Greek Inscriptions*, Cambridge 1959. The sources for this period were collected by G. F. Hill, *Sources for Greek History* (edited by R. Meiggs and A. Andrewes), Oxford 1951. For a valuable survey of the sources see Gomme *Commentary*: Introduction to vol. i.

MODERN WORKS:

FERGUSON, W. S., *Greek Imperialism*, Boston 1913. GOMME, A. W., *Commentary on Thucydides*, Oxford 1945–56. MERITT, B. D., *Athenian Financial Documents of the Fifth Century*, University of Michigan Studies (Humanistic Series), vol. XXVII, Ann Arbor 1932. MERITT, B. D., WADE-GERY, H. T., MCGREGOR, M. F., *The Athenian Tribute Lists*, Cambridge (Mass.) and Princeton 1939–53.

The Athenian tribute-quota lists form the most important single documentary source for this period. The quota fragments, extant assessment decrees, and other testimonia surviving through quotation in literary texts, have been edited by the three scholars named above, and sumptuously produced with a wealth of commentary in the four volumes of the Athenian

Tribute Lists (referred to below as *A.T.L.*). The lists recorded year by year the quota (one-sixtieth) handed over to the Goddess Athena from the cash tribute collected by the treasurers of the League (the Hellenotamiae) from the year 454 until the fall of the empire; the lists record each contribution separately, and the numbers of contributors, and the level of their contributions, are direct evidence of the financial organisation of the League. The records which survive to us are, though substantial, of a fragmentary nature. The lists for the first fifteen years (454–40) were inscribed on the four sides of one marble block, of which 180 fragments have been positively identified and fitted together. The records of the next eight years (439–2) were carved on a second block, of which 72 fragments have been identified. The lists are incomplete; the experts are not always in agreement about either the positioning or the interpretation of the entries; and there is a wide field for controversy about the conclusions to be drawn from them. For example, we cannot be certain that the tribute represented the whole of a city's contribution, or whether it could be supplemented or replaced by a contribution in kind; nor is it certain that in the case of all the payments made to the League by the allies a quota was given to Athena: *e.g.*, there is the case of Samos, which certainly paid money into League funds, but which was not recorded on the lists, perhaps because the money was regarded as a war indemnity; payments were also made directly to field commanders, and these were perhaps not always recorded at Athens (see Gomme, *Commentary*, ii, p. 18: *A.T.L.*, iii, p. 88).

[1] Perhaps the evacuation was not as complete as Herodotus suggests. Elsewhere (IX. 99) he mentions a batch of 500 Athenians taken prisoner in Attica and subsequently ransomed. People living in the less accessible parts of the country, especially in the hills, perhaps heard of the projected evacuation too late: such men may have driven their stock into the wilder country and thus saved them, rather than sacrifice them in a scramble for safety. The speed of the Athenian economic recovery would be more easily explicable if we could believe that in this way she saved a proportion of her grazing and draught animals.

[2] Thuc. ii. 16. 1.

[3] According to Herodotus, Gelon, the ruler of Syracuse, who apparently understood diplomacy, attached political strings to his offer of economic assistance, and the Greek states declined to meet his conditions.

[4] Plutarch (*Them.* 21. 4) in discussing this episode has preserved a non-Athenian contemporary view, reflecting the indignation of Themistocles' unfortunate hosts.

[5] One may have reservations about the historical truth of this episode: its interest lies in the light it sheds upon Themistocles' reputation in the context of his later activities.

[6] Perhaps there is some significance in the view preserved by Aristotle (*Ath. Pol.* 23. 4). 'It was Aristeides who induced the Ionians to secede from the Spartan alliance.' The allegation is rather out of character with the conventional portrait of the strait-laced Aristeides, and one would hardly expect such an allegation to be made without some good reason.

[7] Thuc. i. 96, 99: Plut. *Cimon* 11.

[8] The assumption that no general reduction of tribute occurred is supported by the fact that the phrase 'the assessment in the time of Aristeides' is used always in contexts favourable to Athenian administration and in contrast with the demands of later Athenian imperialists (see Gomme, *Commentary*, i, p. 274, note i). In 421 B.C. when the Spartans agreed to hand back to Athens certain seceded confederate cities, the interests of the latter were protected by a protocol that they should pay tribute at the level fixed in the time of Aristeides, a provision which suggests that their assessment in 421 was certainly not lower than the original figure; (Thuc. v. 18. 5).

[9] Hdt. VI. 42. Gomme, *Commentary*, i, p. 279 f. *A.T.L.*, iii, p. 234.

[10] Plut. *Aristeides* 24. τὸ κατ 'ἀξίαν ἑκάστῳ καὶ δύναμιν.

[11] *A.T.L.*, iii, p. 239 f. The view has been challenged, *e.g.*, by M. Chambers (*C. Phil.*, 1958, p. 26) who prefers to believe that Thucydides' original figure of 460 talents was an error.

[12] *Ath. Pol.* 22. 7.

[13] Gomme, *Commentary*, i, pp. 273–80.

[14] The references are: Plutarch *Per.* 11. 4; *Them.* 4. 2; Thuc. ii, 13. 8; Aristotle, *Ath. Pol.* 22. 7; Hdt. VII. 144; Diod. xi. 43.

[15] Plut., *Cimon* 12. 2.

[16] *P.W.*, xix, 1938, p. 71 f.

[17] Diod. xi. 43. 3.

[18] See Gomme's note on Thuc. i. 99. 1.

[19] Plut., *Cimon* 13. 2.

[20] Thucydides (ii. 13. 4) includes the Persian booty with the sacred treasures in the combined estimate of 500 talents.

[21] Thuc. i. 99. 3. Plut., *Cimon* 11. 2. Whereas Thucydides believed that it was the allies who were responsible for the erosion of their own position *vis-à-vis* Athens, Plutarch echoes a tradition that it was Athens, especially Cimon, who cunningly encouraged the allies to avoid service and contribute money instead. Presumably the warships hastily constructed under the threat of Persian invasion wore out and were not replaced. The building of ships at public expense was for most states merely an emergency measure which lapsed when the emergency passed.

[22] The authenticity of the so-called Peace of Callias is still in dispute. The main evidence for accepting it as historical is in Diodorus xii. 2. 1, 4. 4, 26. 1: Plut., *Cimon* 13. 4: Plato, *Menexenus* 241e: Isocrates iv. 117–18, 120; vii. 80; xii. 59: Dem. xv. 29; xix. 273–4. Doubt is cast upon its authenticity by the silence of Thucydides, and by the comments of Theopompus *frag.* 153–4; Callisthenes *frag.* 16 (Plut., *Cimon* 13. 4). For a discussion of the value of this evidence see H. T. Wade-Gery, *Harvard Studies in Classical Philology Supp. vol.* 1, 1940, p. 121 f.: Gomme, *Commentary*, i, pp. 331–5: D. Stockton, *Historia*, 1959, p. 61 f.

[23] Of course the fleet could be kept in existence for purposes other than those originally envisaged, *e.g.*, to combat piracy for the benefit of the trading states; and modern apologists for Athenian imperialism stress this useful function. But while the trading members of the Confederacy presumably approved in general terms of this aim, they would not necessarily

be any more prepared to finance anti-pirate patrols carried out by the Athenians than they had been when they were carried out by the Phoenicians.

[24] The theory was developed in *Harvard Studies in Classical Philology Supp.*, vol. 1, pp. 149–52; *A.T.L.*, iii, p. 29 f., 278, note 16. The missing year could be assigned to 449 or to 447, depending on how the pattern of the inscription is reconstructed: rather a strong case has been made out for the later date. But the inference that a break in the list means a suspension of tribute is far from certain: an alternative explanation suggested is that the whole tribute for that year, not merely the quota, was transferred to the treasury of Athena, and that the missing entry records a decree to that effect. See B. D. Meritt, *The Greek Political Experience (Studies in honour of W. K. Prentice)*, p. 53; S. Dow, *C. Phil.*, 1943, p. 20.

[25] The authority is the papyrus *Anonymus Argentinensis*, a commentary, dating from the early Christian era, on some statements of Demosthenes xxii. 13–14. For the text see *A.T.L.*, i, p. 572 (T9): ii, p. 61 (D13): (*Sources for Greek History*, p. 51). The relevant section reads as follows: '. . . after Pericles had moved a decree to earmark 5,000 talents accumulated from the tribute and standing in the public treasury'. The decree referred to is dated by *A.T.L.* to 450–49 B.C. (to 431–30 by *Sources*). The implications are discussed in *A.T.L.*, iii, pp. 281, 327–8; see also Wade-Gery in *Hesperia*, 1945, pp. 224–5; Wade-Gery and Meritt in *Hesperia*, 1957, pp. 163–88; Gomme, *Commentary*, ii, p. 28 f. Gomme tentatively accepted the dating given by *A.T.L.*, but disagreed with conclusions expressed there.

[26] Gomme, *Commentary*, ii, pp. 17–18.

[27] *A.T.L.*, ii, D.1; iii, pp. 126, 326–8, 338.

[28] *Commentary*, ii, pp. 26–33. The higher figure is supported by Isoc. xv. 234; Diod. xiii. 21. 3.

[29] Stannier (*J.H.S.*, 1953, p. 73) has estimated the total cost of the Parthenon at less than 500 talents, and the cost of the Propylaea at about a third of this amount. For a higher estimate see Cavaignac, *L'Histoire financière d'Athènes au Ve siècle*, p. 103.

[30] Michell, *Economics of Ancient Greece*, p. 378: Jones, *Athenian Democracy*, pp. 56–7, 100.

[31] *Anabasis* vii. 1. 27. Xenophon puts Athens' total revenue (including the tribute) at about 1,000 talents at the outbreak of war. For further discussion of the profitability of the empire to Athens see Chap. IX below.

CHAPTER VII: THE ECONOMIC CONDITIONS OF IMPERIAL ATHENS

The sources for this, and succeeding chapters, are too scattered to be summarised here: the general reader is referred to G. F. Hill, *op. cit.*, especially pages 340–57, 404–23.

MODERN WORKS:

BOLKESTEIN, H., *Economic Life in Greece's Golden Age*, Leiden 1958. CALHOUN, G. M., *The Business Life of Ancient Athens*, Chicago 1926. FERGUSON, W. S., *op. cit.* HASEBROEK, J., *Trade and Politics in Ancient Greece*, London 1933. KING, D. B., *Athenian Activity in the Hellespont* (unpublished dissertation— Princeton 1940). KNORRINGA, H., *Emporos*, Amsterdam 1927. ZIMMERN, A., *op. cit.*

[1] The fact that pottery is virtually indestructible has made it an object of intense interest to archaeologists, and their findings confirm the tradition of Athenian commercial penetration to the furthermost limits of the Greek world in the fifth century (see, *e.g.*, Minns, *op. cit.*, p. 340). But it is dangerous to treat the archaeological record as an index to commercial expansion, because of the technical difficulties involved; *e.g.*, the practice of itinerant potters producing in their native style abroad, the distinction between the original purchaser of the product and its last owner, the predominance in the archaeological record of the economically less important but artistically more interesting fine ware, and the fact that there is no means of measuring the proportion of trade occupied by the indestructible ceramics in comparison with that of products which disappear from the record without trace, *e.g.*, wool.

[2] See especially the work of J. Hasebroek, who protested vigorously against what he believed to be the tendency to exaggerate the importance of the trade factor in Greek history of the classical period. An opposing view was put by A. W. Gomme, *Essays in Greek History and Literature*, p. 42.

[3] Dem. xx. 32. *I G* ii² 1672.

[4] Dem. xxxiv. 37, xxxv. 20. 51. *Ath. Pol.* 51. 4.

[5] Dem. xx. 31 ἴστε γὰρ δήπου τοῦθ᾽ ὅτι πλείστῳ τῶν πάντων ἀνθρώπων ἡμεῖς ἐπεισάκτῳ σίτῳ χρώμεθα.

[6] This pamphlet was, in antiquity, already attributed to the historian Xenophon (430–354 B.C.), the author of the work *Poroi (The Revenues)*, cited elsewhere in this book. But internal evidence from the pamphlet, in particular, references to the Athenian empire as still intact, firmly date the work to the fifth century, and exclude the possibility that it was composed by the author of *Poroi*. For a summary of the discussion on the dating of the work see H. Frisch, *Constitution of the Athenians* (Copenhagen 1942), pp. 47–62: Frisch's own view is that the work was written shortly before the outbreak of the Peloponnesian war. The author of the pamphlet is critical in his attitude to the Periclean democracy, ironical in his attitude to Athenian imperial policy: the historical value of the pamphlet is enhanced once we accept the view that the author is describing a contemporary scene, but the tendentiousness of his tone invites an attitude of caution in evaluating his comments. For a full bibliography see Frisch, *op. cit.*, and for a recent evaluation see A. W. Gomme, *The Old Oligarch*, in *Harvard Studies in Classical Philology Supp. vol.* 1, 1940, p. 211. The pamphlet will be referred to below as ps.-Xen. *Resp. Ath.*

For a high estimate of the level of trade at Athens at the end of the fifth century see De Sanctis ii. p. 157.

[7] Schol. to Aristophanes *Wasps* 718. See Plut., *Pericles* 37.

[8] Sestos as the 'corn-bin of the Peiraeus' Arist., *Rhet.* 1411a. For Hellespontine states enrolled in the League see *A.T.L.*, iii, pp. 204–7. For the route

see Polybius iv. 44. 6–8. For the question of Persian influence on the south coast of the Propontis see Gomme, *Commentary*, i, pp. 289–95, 445.

[9] An analysis of hoards of Greek coins found at Egyptian sites shows that of the mainland cities Athens was the chief contributor with more than double the quantity of coins attributed to Corinth, her nearest rival. Since the majority of the Corinthian coins and a minority of the Athenian date from a period earlier than the fifth century, the preponderance of Athenian coins in the fifth century is great. Most of the imported coins seem to have been melted down for bullion by the Egyptians, consequently the surviving specimens are a fragmentary sample only and to that extent less reliable as evidence. How much trade was carried on directly between Athens and Egypt during the fifth century is obscure. Athens and Persia were officially in a state of war, at least between 490 and 449 B.C., so that by modern analogies one would expect the level of direct trading between Athens and any part of the Persian empire to be quite low. But the modern analogy may be misleading in this instance: one cannot be sure that the Persian empire was concerned to close its frontiers to visitors from 'unfriendly' states, or that it was interested in distinguishing 'friendly' from 'unfriendly' Greeks. The ancient world did not find such distinctions easy, nor was the suppression of peripheral trafficking (except in the case of siege warfare) regarded as important in the concept of grand strategy; see the Gilbertian anecdote (Hdt. VII. 147) of Xerxes' *laissez passer* to the food ships moving through the Hellespont to supply his enemies. Herodotus travelled without hindrance in Egypt, and one of his visits probably took place before 460, when Persia was still in a state of war with the Delian League (see J. E. Powell, *The History of Herodotus* [Cambridge 1939], p. 25 f.). For the numismatic evidence see C. Roebuck, *C. Phil.*, 1950, p. 236. C. H. V. Sutherland, *A.J.P.*, 1943, p. 137.

[10] See E. H. Minns, p. 339 f.

[11] It is not clear whether the Troad deposits were still being worked at this time: see M. Cary, *Mélanges G. Glotz* (Paris 1932), p. 138.

[12] Hdt. VI. 46: VII. 112. Thuc. i. 100. 3: iv. 105. 1. Plut., *Cimon* 14. 3. Schol. to Andocides *De falsa legatione* 34.

[13] Modern forces carry their own supply organisation, backed by national credit: ancient forces were forced to rely on supplies of ready cash. It is this that enables an ancient historian to estimate the exact cost of a military operation, *e.g.*, Thucydides' estimate of the cost of the siege of Potidaea. Few historians would try to assess the cost of an isolated operation in modern war. For references see *Ath. Pol.* 23. 1. Thuc. vi. 31. 5; 44. 1. Xen., *Cyrop.* vi. ii. 38; and the comments of Polanyi, *Trade and Market in the early Empires*, pp. 84–6. For a glimpse of naval supply operations at work see Aristotle, *Econ.* ii. 1350a–b.

[14] For the convoying of merchant ships in the fourth century see Dem. xviii. 73.

[15] There is evidence that piracy was a serious threat to trade at the time: for references see Chapter V, note 8.

[16] Thuc. i. 11. 1.

[17] For an estimate of the proportion of foreigners resident in Athens see

the following chapter; contemporary references leave no doubt that they represented a considerable section of the population. An analysis of tomb inscriptions from Attica was used by M. Clerc, *Métèques Athéniens* (Paris 1893), p. 381 to point out the widely based geographical origins of the metics: the number of Levantine residents was noted by Xenophon, *Poroi* ii. 3. For an evaluation of the evidence see H. Hommel, *Metoikoi*, in *P.W.* xv, 1932, col. 1413–57.

[18] Isocrates iv. 42. 'Athens provided in the midst of Greece the Peiraeus market containing such a surplus of commodities that it was easily able to supply things difficult of access for individual states.' Xenophon, *Poroi* i. 6. 'One might regard Athens as the centre of Greece and the civilised world: for . . . whoever wishes to travel from one end of Greece to the other goes through, or by, Athens as the mid-point of a circle . . . every wind brings in what she needs and conveys out whatever she wishes, for she lies between two seas.'

[19] *I G* i² 57. Tod i. 61. *A.T.L.* i. D 3–6.

[20] *I G* i² 71, dated to about 436 B.C. by the authors of *A.T.L.* (iii, pp. 313–14, note 61). Evidence relating to the fourth century is supplied by *I G* ii² 212 (Tod ii., p. 194, l. 14–17), and by Dem. xx. 31. 33.

[21] ps.-Xen., *Resp. Ath.* 2. 11–12. We know of no other cases in which Athens used her power to exclude the trade of competitors from the harbours of her empire: the Megarian Decree was quite exceptional, and seemed shocking even to some Athenians. Its aim was not commercial gain but economic pressure, and the operation might be regarded as an act of war.

[22] Tod i. 67. See E. S. G. Robinson, *Hesperia Supp. vol.* viii, 1949, p. 339. H. Mattingly has recently argued for a later dating which would make the measure a war-time decree; *Historia*, 1961, p. 148.

[23] Xen., *Poroi* iii. 2.

[24] Xen., *Poroi* iv. 14 and 24.

[25] Arist., *Econ.* ii. 1346a.

[26] The references are: Andocides i. 133; Dem. xxxiv. 7; ps.-Xen., *Resp. Ath.* i. 17; Aristoph., *Wasps* 658; Pollux 9. 30. See the comments of Busolt i. p. 614: ii. p. 1228; Michell, p. 256; Andreades, p. 296.

[27] Arist., *Econ.* ii. 1350a; Polybius xxx. 31. 12. During the Peloponnesian war Athens replaced the tribute by a 5% customs duty on the traffic passing through the harbours of the empire (Thuc. vii. 28. 4). The aim of the measure was to raise income from the League, hence the level of income from the impost was expected to be at least 1,000 talents, *i.e.*, representing a turnover of 20,000 talents, or 120,000,000 drachmae. See the comments of De Sanctis ii. p. 157.

[28] Busolt ii. p. 1222.

[29] Xen., *Poroi* iii. 5.

[30] Knorringa, p. 92.

[31] ps.-Xen., *Resp. Ath.* i. 16; Thuc. i. 77. 1: see the discussion of this passage in Gomme, *Commentary*. Alcibiades suggested that the loss of court revenues would be a serious thing for the Athenian economy (Thuc. vi. 91.7).

[32] ps.-Xen., *Resp. Ath.* 1. 17.

[33] *Ath. Pol.* 24.

[34] Tod i. 47; Wade-Gery in *Num. Chron.*, 1930, p. 16; Busolt i. p. 197. The effects of inflation in Athens were certainly reduced by the hoarding which kept so much money out of circulation.

[35] *Frag. adesp.* 1320; Dem. xlii. 20, 31; Busolt i. p. 198: Beloch vol. iii. pp. 339–40 (2nd ed.).

[36] Plut., *Per.* 16. 4.

[37] Aristoph., *Eccl.* 817 f.

[38] Aristoph., *Ach.* 33–6 for a picture of the 'ideal' self-sufficient community in pre-war Attica.

[39] Old Comedy abounds in references to the trade in the products of local market-gardening: Aristoph., *Peace* 575–81; *Clouds* 234; *Frogs* 840, etc. Expressions taken from gardening passed into the language as proverbial sayings; Aristoph., *Wasps* 480; *Clouds* 327. In part of the agora only flowers were sold; Aristoph., *Thesm.* 448. Bee-keeping and poultry-keeping were also extensively practised in Attica. For a valuable discussion see V. Ehrenberg, *People of Aristophanes*, pp. 59–61.

[40] The chorus in Aristophanes' *Acharnians* hail from the lower slopes of Mt. Parnes: they produce charcoal, wine, figs, and olives; l. 995–1,000.

[41] Xenophon commented on the tendency for rural labour to be absorbed in city services, and associated it with low returns for farm produce (*Poroi* 4. 6). He is referring to cash crops, and the dependence of the commercial farmer on reigning prices. If Xenophon is right in his diagnosis, it is one of the few recorded instances from Greek history of the classical period, showing how the market mechanism functioned to drive out of business the 'inefficient' farmer; *i.e.*, the farmer whose costs of production did not allow him to compete successfully with his rivals, both domestic and foreign.

CHAPTER VIII: THE SOCIAL CONSEQUENCES

MODERN WORKS:

BOLKESTEIN, H., *op. cit.* EHRENBERG, V., *The People of Aristophanes*, Oxford 1943. GOMME, A. W., *Population of Athens in the Fifth and Fourth Centuries*, Glasgow 1933. HILL, G. F., *op. cit.* JONES, A. H. M., *Athenian Democracy*, Oxford, 1960. ZIMMERN, A., *op. cit.*

[1] The references are (Plataea) Hdt. IX. 28; (Tanagra) Thuc. i. 107. 5; (431) Thuc. ii. 31. 2; (424) Thuc. iv. 94. 1; (Pericles' 'state of the nation' report) Thuc. ii. 13. 6. The figure of 13,000 at Tanagra includes allied contingents of unknown size; the apparent rise in the figures between 479 and 457 is therefore not as spectacular as at first appears.

[2] Since Socrates had apparently turned forty-five when he fought at Delium, it is assumed that the field force included men up to the age of forty-nine. For a discussion on the age groups see Gomme, *Commentary*, ii, p. 37.

[3] The presence of so many resident aliens is perhaps not solely due to a high level of immigration. It is possible to argue that owing to a redefinition

of the qualifications for citizenship certain people who would have qualified in the earlier period fell into the category of aliens in the latter (see n. 35 below).

⁴ Thuc. iv. 94. Athens also had a fleet of 40 ships operating at this time; Thuc. iv. 77. 1: 89.1: 101. 3.

⁵ ps.-Xen., *Resp. Ath.* 1. 2.

⁶ Thuc. ii. 13. 8: iii. 17.

⁷ There is no doubt that many of the men who rowed the Athenian war fleets were aliens; there is a suggestion (Thuc. i. 121. 3) that Athens would have been crippled if enough of her hired seamen were tempted away by higher pay; and Pericles (Thuc. i. 143) implies that he was aware of this danger. But the question here is not the proportion of alien to native seamen, but that of non-resident to resident. Even if 75% of the seamen were aliens (rather an extreme estimate) surely many of the latter would have chosen domicile in Athens rather than commute each year. After the plague, of course, the situation was different.

⁸ Perhaps it is worth recalling the conventional figure of 30,000 adult male citizens, quoted by Herodotus (V. 97) as applicable to the early fifth century; and by Aristophanes (*Eccl.* 1132) referring to the early fourth. This is the round figure which the Athenians traditionally used to describe the size of the voting population, and it would be odd if it were grotesquely wrong *as a round number*. The estimated minimum of 65,000, suggested in the text, represents all adult free males, including aliens.

⁹ See Gomme, *Population of Athens*, p. 75. For more recent figures see *The Demographic Yearbook of the U.N.*, 1959, p. 161. These figures show that in modern Greece males in the 18–60 age groups account for about 28% of the population. We may assume that in classical times there would be a lower percentage of people surviving into the later age groups.

¹⁰ Athenaeus vi. 272 C.

¹¹ *Proceedings of the Camb. Phil. Soc.*, 1935, p. 1. G. Thompson, *Oresteia*, i. p. 70, n. 1; ii. pp. 357–9. *J.H.S.*, 1946, p. 127.

¹² The references are: Thuc. vii. 27. 5: Xen., *Poroi* iv. 24: *Oec.* vii. 41, ix. 5: Plato, *Rep.* 578 d: *I G* i² 329 (Tod. i. 79): Aristoph., *Plutus* 26, 228: *Wasps* 606 f.: Lysias 24. 6: Aristotle *Politics* 1252b.

¹³ See W. L. Westermann, *Athenaeus and the Slaves of Athens: Harvard Studies in Class. Phil. Supp.* i, 1940, p. 451 f. (reprinted in *Slavery in Classical Antiquity*, Cambridge 1960).

¹⁴ Gomme, *Population of Athens*, pp. 28–33.

¹⁵ Jones, *Athenian Democracy*, pp. 177–8.

¹⁶ Plague carried off 4,400 hoplites 'from the regiments' (Thuc. iii. 87. 3). It is not clear whether the latter phrase refers to the field force (13,000), or to the total mobilisation strength (29,000). The former belief was maintained by Gomme (*Commentary*, on this passage); the latter by Jones (p. 165). Thucydides also states that 300 cavalrymen died by plague (from a total of 1,000), and if we are to take the hoplite losses as a proportion of the higher figure (*i.e.*, about 15%), the proportion of losses suffered by the cavalry (30%) seems to be at startling variance with it. Needless to say, the statistics are too fragmentary to form the basis of any firm conclusion.

[17] Gomme, *Commentary*, i. p. 373 f.: *A.T.L.*, iii. pp. 284–97: Jones, pp. 168–77.

[18] Thuc. i. 100. 3.

[19] Jones, p. 174 f. Among the evidence to support this view is a passage in Thucydides (iii. 50. 2) referring to the cleruchy established on Lesbos in 427. From this it is clear that it was the natives who went on cultivating the land, as before, only now they were to pay a rent to their new masters: theoretically therefore the latter could have drawn their rents without leaving Athens. Thucydides, however, states that the Athenians 'sent out' cleruchs (κληρούχους τοὺς λαχόντας ἀπέπεμψαν) and one would need some evidence that the term was used in only a metaphorical sense.

[20] *Ath. Pol.* 26. 1.

[21] Thuc. i. 110. 1. ὀλίγοι ἀπὸ πολλῶν . . . ἐσώθησαν, οἱ δὲ πλεῖστοι ἀπώλοντο. Ctesias (*Persica* 32, 34) speaks of 40 allied ships and says that rather more than 6,000 men surrendered (but this does not include an Athenian reinforcement squadron of 50 ships which was subsequently lost). Isocrates (viii. 86) says that 200 ships in all were lost. The account of Thucydides must of course be considered our best source; but this is in fact a summary only, and he would not necessarily be concerned to give details of an earlier withdrawal of forces.

[22] *I G* i² 929. Tod i. 26.

[23] Some writers have argued from the opposite point of view, claiming that the practice of infanticide caused an unbalance of the sexes in favour of the males. But the theory of wide-spread infanticide rests on shaky evidence (see Gomme, *Population*, p. 79 f.). There is no sign of a shortage of Athenian brides, we know only of a shortage of husbands: see Aristoph., *Lys.* 593 f.

[24] Jardé, *Céréales*, p. 138.

[25] *Quaestiones nonnullae ad Atheniensium matrimonia vitamque coniugalem pertinentes*, Utrecht 1920.

[26] In his quizzing of Glaucon (Xen., *Mem.* iii. 6. 13) Socrates assumes as a matter of course that the securing of grain supplies was one of the first questions on which a politician should inform himself. In the fourth century the same question formed a routine item on the agenda of the popular assembly (*Ath. Pol.* 43. 4).

[27] *I G* i² 54. *A.T.L.*, ii. D.19.

[28] It may be argued that an increase in the supply of food and drink is indicative of rising living standards rather than population increase. But the latter seems a preferable inference in this case, in view of the fact that the great increase is in basic, not luxury food; mainly, in fact, in bread and water.

[29] There is no suggestion that the increase in population between 480 and 430 explains the difference in the strategy advocated by Themistocles and Pericles respectively. In 431 Athens had no need to evacuate, even had it been practicable, because she felt fully protected behind the cover of her fleet and her land fortifications.

[30] Schol. to Aristoph., *Wasps* 718 (Philochoros *frag.* 90; no. 119 in Jacoby): Plut., *Per.* 37. 4. See note 35 below.

[31] Arist., *Politics* 1278a for the assumption that the majority of working people would be either foreigners or slaves.

[32] ps.-Xen., *Resp. Ath.* 1. 12.

[33] *I G* i² 374.

[34] Arist., *Politics* 1278a. See also *Ath. Pol.* 26. 4.

[35] Busolt-Swoboda, ii, p. 900, n. 4. Hignett, p. 343. The statistical implications of this law are complicated by the possibility that it was retroactive in effect: in that case the numerical relationship between citizens and metics would be affected by legal redefinition as well as by natural increase and immigration. In applying the law, the question would also arise how far back the enquiry was to be carried: *e.g.*, if a citizen were found to possess a maternal grandmother of foreign blood, would he thereby forfeit his citizenship, and (since only citizens could own land in Attica) his inheritance as well? One hesitates to believe that the effect of the law was retroactive, because of the administrative difficulties in applying it in the absence of a comprehensive register of births, and also because of the legal and economic complications which would have resulted from its strict application. But the most serious reason for doubt arises from the fact that prominent Athenians of mixed descent are found holding high office at Athens subsequent to the passage of the law (see the comments of Gomme, *J.H.S.*, 1930, pp. 106–7).

Those who argue that the law had retrospective force find apparent support in the anecdote of the free grain distribution of 446 (see p. 148 and note 30 above). According to these accounts, about a quarter of those who applied to receive the grain were rejected, because, under the recent citizenship law, they were ineligible for citizenship, and hence ineligible for the gift (Plutarch adds the picturesque but improbable detail that the rejects were sold into slavery; a mistake arising apparently from his misunderstanding of the procedure described in Aristotle *Ath. Pol.* 42. 1). Philochoros (*frag.* 90) quotes exact numbers for those who received the dole (14,240), and those who were rejected (4,760), making a total of 19,000 in all. These figures, if correct, would certainly suggest that the effect of the law was to redistribute a high percentage of the populace from the citizen to the noncitizen sector. On the other hand, if the legal redefinition had been going on for six years, it seems strange that in 446 the lists were still so corrupt that a quarter of the entries were wrong, and almost incredible that this sweeping scrutiny could have been carried through in the interval of time between the arrival of the grain ship and the distribution of its cargo, more particularly since the question of deprivation of citizen rights should have been settled only by the rejection of a legal appeal. The round total of 19,000 is rather suspicious, and it was a convincing suggestion of Beloch (*Die Bevölkerung der Griechisch-Römischen Welt*, p. 77) that the number of rejects was obtained simply by subtracting the number of recipients (probably based on documentary evidence) from what Philochoros believed to be the total (adult male) citizen body below the highest economic level. Why he should postulate a total of 19,000 is not clear: perhaps he adapted, according to some formula, the census of his own day (21,000); or perhaps he assumed for the fifth century a round figure of two myriads, and subtracted the richest group (the cavalry corps), believing that they would not have taken part in the distribution. In any case, the high number of rejected applicants, as given by Philochoros and echoed by Plutarch, does not seem, on closer examination, to lend convincing support to the theory that the citizen law was retroactive in effect. For the fullest discussion of this question see Jacoby, *F.G.H.* 3b *Supp. vol.* 1, pp. 471–82.

[36] Athenaeus iii. 119 f. *I G* i² 110. Tod i. 86, 96.

[37] Direct control of the courts by the people was considered by Aristotle (*Ath. Pol.* 9. 1) to be fundamental to the democratic system: κύριος γὰρ ὢν ὁ δῆμος τῆς ψήφου κύριος γίγνεται τῆς πολιτείας. For a discussion of the principle involved see J. W. Headlam, *Election by lot at Athens* (ed. D. C. MacGregor: Cambridge 1933), pp. 7, 150–3.

[38] Plut., *Per. 9.* The reference gives no clear indication when the theoric payment was introduced: it must be placed within the span of Pericles' active political life at Athens, and at a time when Athenian public revenues made the measure financially practicable, perhaps not earlier than 450 B.C. The *theorikon* is often confused with the *diobelia*, or two-obol dole, which was introduced during the Peloponnesian war (*Ath. Pol.* 28. 3). For the chronology see Schwahn in *P.W.* (2nd series), vol. V, 1934, col. 2233–5; Busolt-Swoboda, p. 899, n. 5; Wade-Gery, *A.J.P.*, 1938, p. 132; Jacoby, *F.G.H.*, 3b *Supp. vol.* 1, p. 319.

[39] Thuc. viii. 90. 5. Jardé, *Céréales*, p. 177, n. 6.

[40] *Ath. Pol.* 24. 1.

[41] Plut., *Per.* 12.5–13.1 (translation by B. Perrin).

[42] Thuc. ii. 13. 3: Diod. xii. 40. 2: Gomme, *Commentary*, ii, p. 21 f.: *A.T.L.*, iii, p. 124: R. S. Stannier, *J.H.S.*, 1953, p. 68 f.

[43] Knorringa, p. 95. Michell, p. 348. High interest rates imply not only high profits but also high risks and a shortage of ready capital for investment. Considerable caution is needed, however, in drawing conclusions about the conditions of trading from the rate of interest. We can never assume for the ancient world the kind of self-regulating economic conditions to which we are accustomed in the modern. In Greece interest rates, like prices, probably were influenced as much by tradition as by the conditions of supply and demand: a certain level of return on capital was held to be somehow 'right'. It is worth noting that the commercial rate of approximately one-sixth, received on trading loans in the fifth century, is the same as that received on rural loans in Solon's day, although the conditions surrounding the two types of loan were completely different.

[44] Dem. xxxiv. 38. Athenaeus iii. p. 119 f.

[45] Xen., *Poroi* iv. 14.

[46] *I G* i² 372–4.

[47] Dem. xlix. 29. In 431 B.C. the Athenian evacuees from the country stripped off the woodwork from their farms and carried it with them to Athens (Thuc. ii. 14).

[48] Thuc. ii. 17. 1–3: 52. 2. Aristoph., *Knights*, 792–3.

[49] For references see Ehrenberg, *People of Aristophanes*, p. 149 f.

[50] Dem. iii. 25.

[51] *I G* i² 330. Tod i. 80.

[52] Xen., *Oec.* 9. 6–7.

[53] Thuc. ii. 50. 1.

[54] See the remarks of Gomme, *Commentary*, ii, p. 116. R. E. Wycherley, *How the Greeks built cities*, pp. 177, 186.

[55] Thuc. i. 6. 3.

[56] Athenaeus vi. 267e: xii. 512 b–c., 553e. See also Thuc. i. 6. 4 and Gomme, *Commentary*, i, pp. 104–6.

[57] For references see Zimmern, p. 216 f. Ehrenberg, p. 169 f.

[58] For some interesting comments see N. Jasny, *Osiris*, vol. 9, p. 244. 'One has to reconcile oneself to the idea that the glorious era of Pericles, Demosthenes, Aristotle, and Plato was based on "bread" which now . . . would be considered good enough only for swine.'

[59] Arist., *Politics* 1341a. σχολαστικώτεροι γὰρ γιγνόμενοι διὰ τὰς εὐπορίας καὶ μεγαλοψυχότεροι πρὸς τὴν ἀρετήν . . . πάσης ἥπτοντο μαθήσεως οὐδὲν διακρίνοντες ἀλλ' ἐπιζητοῦντες.

[60] Plato, *Protagoras* 313c–d.

CHAPTER IX: SOME CONCLUSIONS

[1] *A.T.L.*, ii, D. 13. Hill, G. F., *op. cit.*, p. 51. *I G* i² 91–2. Tod. i. 51. *A.T.L.*, ii, D. 1–2. The interpretation of the decrees is discussed in *A.T.L.*, iii, p. 326 f.

[2] Isoc. viii. 126. Diod. xii. 38. 2.

[3] Thuc. ii. 13. 3.

[4] Xen., *Anab.* vii. 1. 27.

[5] Isoc. xv. 111. Diod. xii. 28. 3. *I G* i² 293. Tod. i. 50. Thuc. ii. 70. 2.

[6] *A.T.L.*, iii, p. 342 f. Gomme, *Commentary*, ii, p. 432 (doubling of the tribute). Plut., *Aristeides* 24. 3–5. *I G* i² 63. Tod. i. 66. Gomme, *Commentary*, iii, p. 500.

[7] Busolt-Swoboda ii. p. 898, n. 4.

[8] *I G* i² 372–4.

[9] Thuc. ii. 14. 2 (see note 19 on Chapter II).

SHORT GENERAL BIBLIOGRAPHY

(additional to titles listed under Bibliography and Notes)

ANDREADES, A. M. (trans. by C. N. BROWN), *History of Greek Public Finance*, Cambridge (Mass.) 1933.

BEAZLEY, J. D., *Attic Black-Figure Vase Painters*, Oxford 1942.

BELOCH, K. J., *Griechische Geschichte*, Berlin-Leipzig 1913–23.

BENGTSON, H., *Griechische Geschichte*, Munich 1950.

BOECKH, A. (trans. by G. C. LEWIS), *The Public Economy of Athens*, London 1842.

BURN, A. R., *The Lyric Age of Greece*, London 1960.

BURNS, A. R., *Money and Monetary Policy in Early Times*, London 1927.

BURY, J. B. (3rd ed. revised by R. MEIGGS), *History of Greece*, London 1951.

BUSOLT, G. and SWOBODA, H., *Griechische Staatskunde*, Munich 1926.

CAMBRIDGE ANCIENT HISTORY, vols. IV and V, Cambridge 1953–8.

CAVAIGNAC, E., *L'Économie grecque*, Paris 1951.

CAVAIGNAC, E., *Population et Capital dans le monde méditerranéen antique*, Strasbourg 1923.

DAY, G. and CHAMBERS, M., *Aristotle's History of Athenian Democracy*, Berkeley and Los Angeles 1962.

DE SANCTIS, G., *Storia dei Greci*, Florence 1940.

EHRENBERG, V., *Aspects of the Ancient World*, Oxford 1946.

FINLEY, M. I. (ed.), *Slavery in Classical Antiquity*, Cambridge 1960.

FORBES, R. J., *Studies in Ancient Technology*, Leiden 1955–6.

FRANCOTTE, H., *L'Industrie dans la Grèce ancienne*, Brussels 1900–1.

FRISCH, H., *Constitution of the Athenians*, Copenhagen 1942.

GERNET, L., *L'Approvisionnement d'Athènes en blé au Vᵉ et IVᵉ siècles*, Paris 1909.

GLOTZ, G. (trans. by M. R. DOBIE), *Ancient Greece at Work*, London 1926.

GLOTZ, G. (trans. by N. MALLINSON), *The Greek City*, London 1929.

GOMME, A. W., *Essays in Greek History and Literature*, Oxford 1937.

HAMMOND, N. G. L., *History of Greece*, Oxford 1959.

HEICHELHEIM, F. M., *Wirtschaftsgeschichte des Altertums*, Leiden 1938.

HEICHELHEIM, F. M., *An Ancient Economic History*, Leiden 1958.

HEITLAND, W. E., *Agricola*, Cambridge 1921.

HICKS, E. L. and HILL, G. F., *Manual of Greek Historical Inscriptions*, Oxford 1901.

SHORT GENERAL BIBLIOGRAPHY

JACOBY, F., *Fragmente der Griechischen Historiker*, Part 3b Supplementary vols. I and II, Leiden 1954.

JACOBY, F., *Atthis: The local chronicles of ancient Athens*, Oxford 1949.

JARDÉ, A., *Les Céréales dans l'Antiquité Grecque*, Paris 1925.

JARDÉ, A., *La Formation du Peuple Grecque*, Paris 1922.

KAHRSTEDT, U., *Studien zum öffentlichen Recht Athens*, Stuttgart-Berlin 1934–6.

LAISTNER, M. L. W., *Greek Economics*, London 1923.

LAUFFER, S., *Die Bergwerkssklaven von Laureion*, Wiesbaden 1955–6.

MACAN, R. W., *Herodotus*, London 1895–1908.

MICHELL, H., *Economics of Ancient Greece*, Cambridge 1957.

MINNS, E. H., *Scythians and Greeks*, Cambridge 1913.

NEURATH, O., *Antike Wirtschaftsgeschichte*, Leipzig 1909.

ORMOROD, H. A., *Piracy in the Ancient World*, Liverpool 1924.

PAULY-WISSOWA, *Real-Encyclopädie der classischen Altertumswissenschaft*, Stuttgart 1894– .

POLANYI, K., ARENSBERG, C. M., and PEARSON, H. W., *Trade and Market in the Early Empires*, Illinois 1957.

ROSE, J. H., *The Mediterranean in the Ancient World*, Cambridge 1934.

ROSTOVTSEFF, M., *History of the Ancient World*, vol. I, Oxford 1926.

ROSTOVTSEFF, M., *Iranians and Greeks in South Russia*, Oxford 1922.

SANDYS, J. E., *Aristotle's Constitution of Athens*, London 1912.

SARGENT, R. L., *Size of the Slave Population at Athens in the 5th and 4th Centuries B.C.*, Illinois 1924.

SELTMAN, C. T., *Athens, its History and Coinage before the Persian Invasion*, Cambridge 1924.

SELTMAN, C. T., *Greek Coins*, London 1933.

SIEGFRIED, A., *The Mediterranean*, London 1948.

TOD, M. N., *Selection of Greek Historical Inscriptions*, Oxford 1933 and 1948.

TOUTAIN, J. F. (trans. by M. R. DOBIE), *Economic Life of the Ancient World*, London 1930.

VICKERY, K. F., *Food in Early Greece*, Illinois 1936.

WADE-GERY, H. T., *Essays in Greek History*, Oxford 1958.

WYCHERLEY, R. E., *How the Greeks built Cities*, London 1962.

INDEX

INDEX

Mercenary troops, 34, 36–9, 53, 60, 63, 71
Merchants, *see* Traders
Mesogeia, 6
Messenia, 3
Metals, *see* Minerals
Methone, 119
Metics, 52, 126, 128, 136–7, 139, 146, 148, 155–6, 162, 165–6, 172–3, 175
Miletus, 49, 75, 85, 111–12, 121–3, 163
Militia, citizen, 19, 53, 60, 69, 74, 135–7
Milk, 10
Miltiades, 47–8, 71–3, 75
Mina, 23
Minerals, 5, 9, 51–2, 77–9, 120
Mining, 9, 35–6, 50–2, 77–9, 84, 128, 162–3, 169; investment in, 57, 156, 174; working conditions in, 122–3, 172; numbers employed in, 138–9
Mohair, 8
Money, changes in the value of, 80, 95–6, 114, 129, 136, 140, 168. *See also* Coins
Money-lenders, 155
Monopolies, 113, 119–20
Mycenae, 4
Mykale, 85–6
Mytilene, 46–7

Naucraries, 52
Naukratis, 79, 113
Naupactus, 142
Naxos, 34, 48, 112, 116, 142
Nepos, Cornelius, 147
Nicias, 123, 170
Nymphaeum, 120

Odeon, 154, 160
Oil, *see* Olive
Olbia, 111
Oligarch, the *Old*, 108, 120, 137, 157
Olive oil: economic importance of, 1, 5; nutritive value of, 19–20, 133; yield of, 20–1; price of, 129;

trade in, 17, 79, 83, 113, 123–4, 127, 131; assessment in terms of, 19. *See also* Olives
Olives, 1, 5, 7, 22, 43–4, 54, 82, 109, 113, 129, 131–2
Oropus, 74
Oxen, 7, 109, 139

Panathenaic festival, 31, 56, 58, 152
Pangaeus, 34–5, 51, 113
Panticapaeum, 111, 113
Papyrus decree, 103
Paraloi, 26
Paros, 75–6, 84, 122
Parthenon, 154, 160
Pasion, 156
Pasture, 1, 6–7, 10–11, 43
Pausanias, 88
Pediakoi, 26
Peiraeus, 77, 79, 95, 104, 113–14, 117–18, 120–1, 125–7, 130–1, 154
Peisistratus, 26–60, 63, 71, 77, 122, 124, 164, 170
Peloponnese, 34, 84, 108
Peloponnesian league, 86, 142, 167
Peloponnesian war, 94, 109, 119, 145, 154, 167, 169–70
Peloponnesians, 85, 87–8, 111
Pentakosiomedimni, 19
Pentekonters, 76
Pentelicus, 6, 122
People's courts, 151
Pericles, 39, 94, 101–2, 105, 108–9, 117, 120, 125, 127–8, 130, 135–6, 141, 152–3, 155, 157, 159–62, 164, 166, 170–2, 174–5
Persia, 36, 71–6, 78, 80–91, 95, 99–102, 109–12, 142–3, 147, 164, 169
Phaleron, 25–6, 76
Phaselis, 99
Phasis, 111
Pheidias, 160
Pheidonian standard, 24
Philaidae, 48
Philochoros, 146
Phocaea, 113
Phoenicians, 72, 75, 84–5, 87, 112, 143

205